Marriage Mindset

A HOLISTIC APPROACH TO FAMILY LIFE

WRITTEN BY DR. NABI RAZA MIR (ABIDI)
ASSISTANT WRITER: DR. TAYMAZ TABRIZI

Marriage Mindset: A Holistic Approach to Family Life
Written by Moulana Nabi R. Mir (Abidi)
Assistant Writer: Dr. Taymaz Tabrizi

ISBN: 978-1-68312-355-2

Disclaimer: Religious texts have **not** been translated verbatim so as to meet the developmental and comprehension needs of the audience.

Library of Congress Control Number: 2023910416

For permission requests, please write to the publisher at the address below.

Kisa Publications
4415 Fortran Court
San Jose, CA 95134
www.alkisafoundation.org
admin@alkisafoundation.org

Marḥūmīn Dedication

Please recite a Sūrah al-Fātiḥah for the marḥūmīn of the Hudda, Manji-Daya, and Bhimji families; and Marḥūm Amanullah Sajanlal, Shabber Ali Khan, and Marḥūmah Mazhar Sultana

Dedication

This book is dedicated to the beloved Imām of our time ﷺ. May Allah ﷻ hasten his reappearance and help us to become his true companions.

Acknowledgments

Prophet Muḥammad ﷺ said:

يـوزن يـوم القيامـة مـداد العلمـآء ودمـآء الشـهدآء فيرجـح مـداد العلمـآء علـى دمـآء الشـهدآء.

"On the Day of Resurrection, the ink of the scholars will be weighed up against the blood of the martyrs, and the ink of the scholars will be heavier than the blood of the martyrs."[1]

True rewards are with Allah ﷻ, but we would like to sincerely thank:

Shaykh Ehsan Ahmadi, Shaykh Saleem Bhimji, Brothers Abbas Raza, Eiyad Alkutubi; and Sisters Sabika Mithani, Abeda Khimji, Laila Khan, Arifa Hudda, Sakeena Ahsan Kalyan, Masooma Hydary Kalyan, Ziba Hashmy, Syeda Aimen Fatima, Samya Zitouni, Fatima Hussain, and Rumina Hashmani.

May Allah ﷻ bless them in this world and the next.

---

[1] Pāyānade, *Nahj al-Faṣāhah*, Saying #3222.

Table of Contents

Transliteration Table iii
Symbol Usage v
About the Author vii

Introduction 9
Marriage and its Purpose 9
The Purpose of Marriage: An Islamic Perspective 12
The Crisis of Marriage in Muslim Communities 13
How to Perceive Marriage 14
An Important Word on the Contents of this Book 16

1

Strengthening Your Marriage 19
Rekindling Romance 21
- Respect Your Spouse's Dreams 21
- Keep Some Time Apart 23
- Give Compliments to Your Spouse Regularly and Naturally 23
- Good Memories Should Outnumber the Bad 24
- Date Regularly ... Without the Kids 25
- Sit with Your Spouse in Loving Silence 26
- Remembering the Early Phase of Your Relationship 26
- Express More Love after Children 27
- Watch What You Eat 29
- Write to Your Spouse 29
- Beautify Yourself Inside the Home, Not Outside 31
- Share Your Future Plans 32
- Find a Babysitter 33
- Prevent Emotional Unfaithfulness 34
- Sharing Passwords 35

Be Mindful of Your Spouse's Sensitivities 36
Have Constructive Conversations 37
Fake It Till You Make It 38
Inspire Love When You Don't See Love 40
Marriage Counseling 40
A Precautionary Note 40
Help Couples Find their Needs, Not Wants 41
Wants are Independent, but Needs are Interdependent 43
Conflicts are in the Now 43
Be a Good Investigator of Emotions 44
Empathy Precedes Understanding 45
Counselors Should Learn Human Needs 45
When Counselors Need to Interrupt 46
Conclusion 47
A Concluding Remark: Humble Advice for Counselors 47

2

Improving Your Marriage 49
Improving Marriage by Working on Yourself 51
Marriage's Goal: Not Just Happiness 51
Give Your Best Self to Your Spouse 52
Identify with God Rather than the "Self" 53
The Importance of Small Gestures 54
Improve Marriage to Prevent Marital Deterioration 55
Go Back in Time: Fix Your Marriage 55
Forgiveness is a Gift to Yourself 56
The Power of Humor 58
Seven Things which Harm Communication 59

Give Your Spouse Gifts 61
Improving Marriage Before and After Conflicts 62
"Saving" Your Marriage can Make it Worse 62
Mental Distance Prevents Marital Improvement 63
Do Not Text Important Conversations 64
Do Not Poke a Sleeping Bear 65
Improving Marriage When You are Together 66
Washing Dishes the Right Way 66
Reciting Daily Prayers Together 66
Presence versus Being Present: Healthy Family Activities 68
Feed Your Spouse with Admiration and Compliments 69
Start Your Conversations with Praise 69
Improving Your Marriage When You are Apart 70
Answer When Your Spouse Calls 70
Be With People who Support Your Marriage 71
General Recommendations 72
5 Tips on How to Forgive Someone 72
Relationship Maps 73
The Limits of an Outsider's Marital Advice 74
Six Things to Avoid in a Conversation 75
When Honesty is Lacking in a Marriage 76
Making Promises that You Cannot Fulfill 77

3

Marriage as a Process of Transformation 79
Make Excuses for Your Spouse 83
Marriage: A Blessing or a Burden? 84
A Person who Loves God will Welcome Criticism 84

Making Good Deeds a Harmonious Flow 85
When Criticized for Doing Something Right 86
Be Grateful for Your Spouse's Criticisms 87
Success With God is Success With Marriage 88
Changing the Paradigm of Marriage 89
Pray for Your Spouse Even When They Hurt You 89
Transformation is a Long and Slow Process 90
Peace Comes with Letting Go of Grudges 91
The End Result of Marriage 92
Change Yourself, Change Your Spouse 92
Bear Your Sufferings with Patience 93
Your Spouse's Problems can be Spiritual Medicine 93
Emotions Do Not Care about the Facts 94
Marriage is There to Help You Grow 95
Do Not Love Codependently, Love Completely 96

4

Family and Raising Children 99
Our Personal Histories and the Self 100
Philosophy and Mindset of Raising Children 102
Introduction 102
Families are Founded on Marriages - Not Children 102
Do Not Always be Serious with Children 104
Abuse is More than Just Hitting 105
Fear-based Upbringing Corrupts Morality 106
The Downstairs Brain vs. The Upstairs Brain 107
Pick up Crying Children from Their Bed 110
Reality of Upbringing Children 111

Our Children will Inherit Our Emotions 112
Give Space for Growth and Rejuvenation 113
Children Follow the Religion of Their Friends 114
Stepparents: Prioritize Marriage over Kids 115
Speak Gently with Your Daughters 117
Avoid Lecturing 118
Your Children will Make Mistakes 119
Giving Orders is Not a Conversation 120
Tone of Voice can Matter More than Words 121
Some Advice for Husbands and Fathers 122
Families should Exercise Together 123
Learning vs. Regretting Consequences 123
Misusing Time-Outs and Encouraging Time-Ins 124
Teaching Your Child Self-Regulation 126
Avoid Reacting Negatively to a Child's Dysregulation 127
Bring Yourself to Your Child's Eye-Level 129
Connect with Your Child's Feelings 129
Challenges and Opportunities for Raising Children 131
Introduction 131
Parenthood is Not Pausing Marriage 132
Dividing Parental Duties "50/50" Does Not Work 133
Children Who have Lost a Parent 134
Relaying Consequences in a Nurturing Manner 136
Limit Violent Video Games and Social Media 137
Teach Your Children Humility 138
Partner with Your Child for Behavior Solutions 140
Learning from the Experience of Others 140
Introduction 140

Anxieties Should Not Make Us Forget Our Families 141
The Importance of Regularly Playing with Children................. 142
Preserve Your Child's Unconditional Love For You................... 143
Listening to What is Not Being Said 144
A Healthy Family is One who Forgives.. 145
Be an Authoritative Parent, Not Authoritarian........................... 146
Your Child's Lash-out is Not Rudeness.. 148
Giving Orders is Not Talking and Connecting 149
Your Family Associations and Spiritual Growth 150
Takeaways 151
Teaching Our Kids to Avoid Sins is Not the End-Goal 152
The Consequences of a Child Living in Fear 153
Your Spouse has Priority Over Your Family 154
Responsibilities Toward Parents vs. Spouse 155
The 7-7-7 Prophetic Principle in Raising Children..................... 158

5

A Realistic Mindset in Marriage..159
Changing Your Spouse will be Slow.. 159
Where do Unrealistic Expectations Come From?....................... 160
Realism vs. Fantasy 162
Compassion vs. Perfection in a Spouse.. 162
Your Spouse's Perceived Flaws Can Save You............................ 163
Discomfort with People and Eternal Reward 164
Unexpressed Gratitude can Feel Like Ingratitude 165
Useful Tips 166
Heart Over Logic: Spouse Perspective 166
Your Spouse's Faults are the Price You Pay for Their Virtues 167

Compassion Resolves Emotional Needs, Not Logic 168
Show Appreciation Without Expectation 168

6

Conflict Resolution 171
Psycho-social Well-being 172
Pessimism and Learning to be Positive 172
Forgetting to Pray for Your Spouse 173
Egotistical Feedback and Learning Humility 174
Paradigms of Conflict Resolution 175
How Fear and Shame Block Healthy Communication 175
Healthy Couples Fight as Much as Unhealthy Ones 177
Do Not Hide from Arguments 178
Criticizing vs. Non-judgmental Notices 180
Dangers of Jokes and Sarcasm 180
Your Home is Not a Courtroom 181
Some Thoughts on Conflict Prevention 182
Do Not Bottle Things Up 182
Avoid Lectures if Your Spouse Makes a Mistake 183
The Origin of Anger 184
Looking at Marital Conflict through Awareness, Not Pride 184
Choice in Jobs and Legitimate (Ḥalāl) Income 185
Creating a Culture of Conversation for Conflict Resolution 186
What can Cloud our Judgments 187
Who to Seek Counseling From 188
Be Soft in Speech 189
Actionable Puzzles During Conflict 190
Formulating Criticisms the Right Way 190

Avoid Arguing When in a State of Anger 192
Bite Your Tongue and Do Not Say that Mean Thing 193
Wait Before Giving Your Side of the Story 194
Just Because it is True, Does Not Mean You have to Say it 195
Know When to Stop 196
The Importance of being Heard during Conflicts 197
Always Maintain Respect 197
Do Not Censure during Moments of Animosity 198
Post-Conflict Thoughts 199
Being Right the Wrong Way is Wrong 199
Criticize the Action, Not the Person 200
Being Right vs. Having a Relationship 201
Kindness vs. Shaming and Blaming 202
Understanding Criticisms as Unmet Needs 203
The Importance of Honesty 204
Do Not Deny Your Mistakes 204
General Advice on Conflict Resolution 205
Be Aware of the False Wisdom of Your Anger 205
Five Quick Rules for Marital Conflict 206

7

Dealing with a Difficult Spouse 207
Do Not Try to 'Fix' Your Spouse's Emotions 210
When Your Spouse is Angry, Speak through Kindness 212
Do Not Withhold Praise 212
The Blessings of Having a Difficult Spouse 213
Origins of Some Forms of Negativity 213
Do Not Force Your Will on Your Spouse 214

How You Talk to Your Spouse is How You Talk to God 215
Be Thankful for a Difficult Spouse 215
Hidden Blessing when Your Spouse is Unjust 217
Connect and then Correct 218
If Your Spouse is Upset, Listen 218
Your Spouse is Not Responsible for Your Reaction 219
Trying to Fix Your Marriage can Backfire 220
Criticism Should be Followed with Three Positive Actions 221
How to Enjoy Life with a Difficult Spouse 222
Respond to Your Spouse's Bad Mood with Empathy 222
Being Calm when Your Spouse is Moody 224
Do Not Speak Ill of Your Spouse to Others 224

8

Reality of Marriage and Divorce 227
What to Expect When You Get Married 227
What to Expect after Marriage 228
The Causes and Consequences of Divorce 231
Your Spouse is Not Responsible for Your Happiness 231
Reminder: There are Two People in a Relationship 232
Put that Smartphone or Gadget Away 233
Your Spouse Cannot Read Your Mind 233
Winning an Argument at the Cost of Your Marriage 235
Rights vs. Responsibilities in Marriage, Which Comes First? 236
The Opposite of Love is Not Always Hatred, But Fear 237
Financial Success can Sometimes Lead to Divorce 238
Be Consistent in Your Acts of Goodness, Avoid Randomness 239
Throwing Money at Marriage Problems 240

Dreams vs. Reality in a Marriage 241
A Good Marriage is Something You Struggle to Make 241
Dating Standards are Not for Marriage 242
Loving Someone Does Not Mean You will Love Life Together 244
What True Commitment in Marriage Really Is 244
Your Wife's Work at Home is Priceless 245
Falling In and Out of Love Many Times During Marriage 247
Letting Go of Destructive False Hopes 249
Unfaithfulness Can be Symptom of a Troubled Marriage 249
The Purpose of Marriage is Not Only Happiness 250
Your Real Full-Time Job is Your Family 252
Treat Your Marriage Better than Your Career 252
Going Over the Pros and Cons of Staying Together 253

9

Changing Your Spouse 255
Alignment of Heart, Mind, and the Reality of Marital Life 255
The Heart Takes Longer to Change than the Mind 255
Be a Comedian in Your Home 257
Give Advice with Love, and Avoid Criticism 258
Have Good Akhlāq for God, Not for Worldly Fear 259
A Person Cannot Connect with One's Spouse in Fear 260
Change Yourself to See Changes in the Future 262
Find the Truth in What Your Spouse is Saying 262
Healthy Self-Esteem and Defensiveness in Marriage 264
Experiential Gifts vs. Physical Gifts 266
Solving Marriage Problems is Not Always the Solution 267
Let Go and Let God Deal with It 268

High Price of Emotional Decisions........ 270
Never Use Your Spouse's Past Flaws Against Them........ 270
Deep Down Inside, Your Spouse Knows Their Flaws........ 272
Do Not Compete on Who had the Worst Day........ 273
Avoid Suspecting Your Spouse........ 274

Conclusion........ 277
Where the Problem Truly Comes From........ 277
The Paradigm Shift........ 279
Glossary........ 281

Transliteration Table

The method of transliteration of Islamic terminology from the Arabic and Farsi language has been carried out according to the standard transliteration table mentioned below.

ء	'	ر	r	ف	f
ا	a	ز	z	ق	q
ب	b	س	s	ك	k
ت	t	ش	sh	ل	l
ث	th	ص	ṣ	م	m
ج	j	ض	ḍ	ن	n
ح	ḥ	ط	ṭ	و	w
خ	kh	ظ	ḍ	ه	h
د	d	ع	ʿ	ي	y
ذ	dh	غ	gh		

Vowels

ا	ā	ي	ī	و	ū

Vowels

ـَ	a	ـِ	i	ـُ	u

Farsi Letters	پ	p	چ	ch
	ژ	jh	گ	g

Symbol Usage

Throughout this work, when taking the name of any of the revered personalities in Islamic history, including Allah سبحانه وتعالى, Prophet Muḥammad ﷺ, his select family members, and religious scholars, we have employed the following Arabic symbols to show the reverence to each of them. As a part of Islamic culture, readers are requested to send the salutations upon these personalities when they read this work.

سبحانه وتعالى

All glory belongs to God, the Glorified and Exalted
Used exclusively for God - Allah سبحانه وتعالى

ﷺ

Blessings of Allah be upon him and his Immaculate Progeny
Used exclusively for Prophet Muḥammad ﷺ

عليه السلام

Peace be upon him
Used for one honored male

عليهما السلام

Peace be upon them both
Used for two honored men or women or a combination

عليهم السلام

Peace be upon all of them
Used for three or more honored men or women or a combination

عليها السلام

Peace be upon her
Used for one honored female

عجل الله تعالى فرجه الشريف

May Allah, the Most High, hasten his noble return
Used exclusively for Imam al-Mahdī عجل الله تعالى فرجه الشريف

About the Author

Moulana Nabi R. Mir (Abidi) was born in Alipur, India, and raised in a religious *Sayyid* family.

After completing his early education, he moved to Iran at the age of 14 to pursue Islamic studies. He spent the first two years in Najafabad learning Farsi, basic Arabic grammar, and Islamic rulings (*Aḥkām*).

Following this, he spent the next 14 years in Qum where he studied at different Islamic Seminaries (*Ḥawzas*) namely Ḥujjatiyyah, Fayḍiyyah, and the Institute of Imām Jaʿfar aṣ-Ṣādiq under Āyatullāh Jaʿfar Subḥānī. Concurrently, he earned a PhD in Theology and Philosophy from the University of Tehran.

After completing his preliminary and secondary level of Islamic studies, he participated in *Baḥth al-Khārij* (the highest level of Islamic studies in the field of Jurisprudence) under reputable scholars such as the late Āyatullāh Fāḍil Lankarānī, Āyatullāh Jaʿfar Subḥānī, Āyatullāh Nāṣir Makārim Shirāzī, and many others.

Moulana Abidi spent 4 years answering questions in the office of the late Āyatullāh Fāḍil Lankarānī, and another 5 years conducting research in theology and philosophy under Āyatullāh Jaʿfar Subḥānī, where he also helped write and publish books on various topics.

For the next 5 years, he taught *Usūl*, *Fiqh*, Philosophy, and *Tafsīr* in several Islamic Seminaries namely: Ḥujjatiyyah, Fayḍiyyah, and Jāmiʿatuz Zahrā.

In 2002, Moulana Abidi moved to San Jose, California to serve as the Resident Scholar (*ʿĀlim*) of SABA Islamic Center. Under his guidance, SABA has expanded tremendously and incorporated many successful undertakings, including a full-time school by the name of RISE Academy. Additionally, he has helped to establish and overlook many *masājid.*

He is also the founder of Al-Kisa Foundation and its subsidiaries, including Kisa Kids.

Moulana Abidi serves on various school boards, provides guidance to several full-time and weekend Islamic schools around the world, as well as provides guidance to SABA Sunday School and RISE Education System.

He continues to further his studies in Islamic Gnosticism (*ʿIrfān*), Philosophy, and *Baḥth al-Khārij* with renowned scholars.

Introduction

Marriage and its Purpose

There is no relationship which exists between human beings that is more important than marriage. The journey of humankind began when God created Prophet Ādam (Adam) ﷺ from non-existence. He was then given a lofty position, and all of the angels were commanded to prostrate (do sajdah) to him; but when God asked Ādam ﷺ how he felt, the Prophet replied: "I am grateful for Your blessings, and how You created me from non-existence; however, I am in this high position but I do not feel any peace or tranquility." Then God created Ḥawwā' (Eve), and married Ādam ﷺ to Ḥawwā', and after that He asked Ādam ﷺ: "How do you feel now?" Ādam ﷺ replied that now he feels as if he has a goal and purpose in life, and through his offspring, generations can continue to inhabit the Earth. So God then told Ādam ﷺ to go with his wife and have some rest. Therefore the first relationship ever with another human being was that of marriage. This was the beginning of the journey of life.[1]

Marriage between a man and a woman who become husband and wife is the nucleus of a family, as it is the first and foremost relationship. It is therefore the most sacred and loved relationship by God Almighty. After marriage comes parenthood, and with parenthood comes children, siblings, grandparents, aunts, and uncles. This is why Prophet Muḥammad ﷺ said: *"There is no foundation more beloved to God, the Exalted and Majestic, than marriage"* [2] If people have a strong foundation of marriage, then they will be able to achieve all of the bounties, blessings, and mercy of the Creator.

---

[1] For the context of this story, see ʿAllāmah Majlisī, *Biḥār al-Anwār al-Jāmiʿah li-Durar Akhbār al-A'immah al-Aṭhār*, 110 Vols., Ed. by a committee of researchers (Beirut: Dār Iḥyā' al-Turāth al-ʿArabī, 1403/1982), Vol. 11, Pp. 220-221.

[2] Ibid., Vol. 100, P. 222.

Followers of the Ahlul Bayt ﷺ especially must be true ambassadors of the Qur'ān and Islam, and be role models for the communities.

In order to strengthen one's marriage, a person has to remember the five foundational pillars of a successful relationship which are: trust, honesty, love, communication, and forgiveness. We will elaborate more on these topics in the next few chapters. This book was written to emphasize how important the concept of marriage is; but unfortunately due to external influences or internal factors, the concept of marriage is slowly becoming destroyed, and there is an increase in suspicion and cynicism toward marriage. Therefore, we wanted to present a different perspective and mindset in regards to this sacred union - between a man and a woman - referred to as marriage.

A substantial number of people believe that marriage leads to unhappiness. Unfortunately, there are many misconceptions that exist today which imply that there is no value or benefit in getting married. For example, there are misconceptions that marriage provides a net benefit for women, but is a net loss for men because the husband has to provide financially for his wife. This is because the bigger picture of marriage - which is that it is a means to find peace, take care of one's physical needs, and be able to focus on the true purpose of life which is getting closer to God - has been lost. Attaining proximity to God can only be done through the path that God, the Creator, has outlined for humanity. It is through the roles and responsibilities that the All-Knowing God - who knows what is best for everyone - has defined for human beings to follow. It is not a matter of **how much** one does in this world, but rather **what one does** and **who** it is done for. Losing sight of the bigger picture will cause a person to get stuck in the smaller details; but when one has the bigger picture as the goal, then one will be able to sacrifice more and be more flexible in life.

There is a lot of research that shows why marriage between a man and woman is more beneficial rather than remaining single. For example, there are psychological and emotional reasons why married couples fare better financially. Marriage gives a better sense of self-discipline for both partners in the relationship. It provides them a way to deal with setbacks, tragedies, illnesses, and other difficulties. The emotional stability that marriage provides gives the mental and emotional fortitude for people to deal with life's challenges. Single adults are more likely to spend and indulge themselves, whereas married couples are more likely to save and invest their resources. Similarly, children born and raised in a married household are significantly more likely to perform better academically and earn more later on in adult life.[3] The effects of marriage are generational. Overall, married people are generally happier, live longer than single people,[4] and are more likely to survive cancer compared to single people who have a higher cancer death risk.[5] This includes both prostate and breast cancer, the two most common forms of cancer for men and women respectively.

Beyond this, Islam shows us that life is a race to do good deeds. The mindset of marriage can be a chance for individuals to see how much they can do for their families, and how much they can thrive in their roles and responsibilities for the sake of God. It is a chance to get closer to the Almighty Creator. Marriage is not there to stop growth, contrary to some people's belief, but rather it is there to facilitate growth, because through marriage a person can receive peace and tranquility, and will be able to fulfill one's needs so that they can focus on different ways to serve others and carry out their

---

[3] "The Marriage Effect: Money or Parenting?" Brookings, last modified September 4, 2014, https://www.brookings.edu/research/the-marriage-effect-money-or-parenting/.

[4] "Marriage Tied to Longer Life Span, New Data Shows," Web MD, last modified October 10, 2019, https://www.webmd.com/a-to-z-guides/news/20191010/marriage-tied-to-longer-life-span-new-data-shows#1.

[5] "Married People More Likely to Survive Cancer," Web MD, last modified October 14, 2011, https://www.webmd.com/cancer/news/20111014/married-people-more-likely-survive-cancer.

necessary responsibilities. Of course both parties need to be on the same page, have good communication, display love, be flexible, and be willing to sacrifice in order to reach their shared goal of nearness to God.

The Purpose of Marriage: An Islamic Perspective

Marriage brings about worldly success and happiness to people more than singlehood. However, for people of faith, marriage means a lot more than just worldly gains.

From an Islamic perspective, marriage has multiple purposes. It gives a person focus and vision in life, stability and enjoyment, the creation of offspring, peace, blessings, love, and enjoyment in life. But the primary purpose of marriage is to help an individual find salvation by inviting God's grace in this world and the next. It is there to help purify one's heart and reduce sins in a person's life. This means that although happiness can be an important factor in a marriage, it is not its ultimate aim. Marriage in the Islamic viewpoint is there to help transform a person mentally, emotionally, socially, and spiritually.

People grow through learning patience and forgiveness with their spouses, having compassion with one another, being selfless, and learning to be responsible and mature servants of God. In order to reach this fulfillment, pain and sacrifice are needed, just like with all good and beautiful things in life. Pain and sacrifice are required for completing our studies, having a successful career, maintaining a good job, and raising healthy children - nothing is exempt from this. Through this experience of sacrifice, pain, and the beauty and wonder that come out of this toil, human beings are able to fulfill their purpose in this world, and enter into the transforming love of God, and have a pleasant life in the eternal world to come.

The Crisis of Marriage in Muslim Communities

Despite the worldly and spiritual benefits of marriage, marital relationships and families today are in crisis among Muslim communities all over the world, especially those living in the West. Some youth are being put off completely by marriage because of the anti-marriage myths they have come to believe. Marital dissatisfaction and divorce rates among Muslims in America, and other parts around the globe are on the rise. In my own experience, I used to see divorces largely among younger couples only, but now more and more, I am having elderly couples come into my office seeking divorce.

In my two plus decades of marital counseling, only a small number of cases have had to do with abuse and addiction. The majority of the cases of marital discord, dissatisfaction, and divorce that I have dealt with have been primarily caused by inaccurate perceptions and high expectations. Some individuals see trouble in other people's marriages, get discouraged, and fear marriage to begin with, thus they avoid getting married themselves.

Oftentimes, people enter marriages confusing lust with love. They believe that bliss and joy are supposed to be permanent and continuous features of their relationships. They hold their marriages and spouses responsible for their happiness. They ignore the frailty and fallibility of the human being and expect impossible standards from their spouses. They are disappointed when they cannot realize the idealized love that they always fantasized about.

Another reason why some people wanting to get married end up remaining single is because they expect an extensive list of characteristics in a spouse, and they feel as if they will be "selling themselves short" if they marry someone below those standards. This attitude results in people delaying marriage. The delay brings a risk of falling into a danger zone that often has age-related complications that make the prospects of a marriage and family life even more difficult, or they simply get to a point where they do not get married and end up remaining alone. As these attitudes are growing, it is not surprising to see that there is an epidemic of loneliness in the United States. This in turn has serious repercussions on the physical and mental health of Americans,[6] ranging from depression and anxiety, to cancer and autoimmune diseases.

The above attitudes and perceptions also lead people to end their marriages because their spouses do not meet their current expectations. These groups of people leave their spouses with the belief that they can easily find another spouse who can better meet their expectations. I have seen too many cases of this happening, and they end up getting disappointed because everyone has flaws.

How to Perceive Marriage

There is no such thing as love at first sight: there is only lust at first sight. There is no such thing as 'the one' meaning that there is no one in this world who will ever be able to fulfill even most of a person's expectations in a spouse, let alone being nearly perfect. This is not just because some people's expectations are not realistic, but also because expectations are rarely static, they change and shift over the years and few people can ever play catch up with those expectations. When a person's expectations do get met, their mind will simply produce new ones.

Everyone has certain flaws in some way or another, and no one is perfect. All individuals are just one person existing in different versions and forms throughout their lives and in every breath that is taken. Stories and selves change, sometimes on a daily basis. The true selves of human beings as God made them are wrapped in thousands of veils as a consequence of human history, and people's

[6] "The Loneliness Epidemic Has Very Real Consequences," Web MD, last modified November 29, 2018, https://www.webmd.com/balance/features/loneliness-epidemic-consequences.

own direct experiences and choices in this world. It is with clashes, difficulties, pains, sufferings, and ultimately God's guidance and providence that these layers are unveiled and revealed. It is through these experiences that human beings grow, change, and find the inner treasures of their spirit (*dafāʾin al-ʿuqūl*); and it is through them that they transform and are 'reborn' into what they were created by God to be.

In one tradition attributed to the Prophet ʿĪsā (Jesus) ﷺ, he says:

لن يلج ملكوت السموات من لم يولد مرّتين

"A person who is not born twice will not be able to enter the Kingdom of Heaven."[7]

But just as human beings vary in different versions and forms of life, they are also veiled in layers, and change and transform 'interdependently' not independently. This means that they do not suffer and transform in isolation. They suffer and face difficulties, change, and transform as they interact, love, and clash with the world and other people. As the layers peel off in this 'interdependent process,' one is reborn when a person acts responsibly with the ups and downs in life. The real deep pain that a person experiences in marriage, and not just in its moments of joy, are important components of transformation, self-reformation, and ultimately salvation. The story of transformation is never complete, and it continues on until the end of one's life, and far into the hereafter.

This brings us to the subject of love. We said earlier that there is no such thing as love at first sight. True love in marriage is born through this process of unveiling. It is the product of a long-term relationship; it is a phenomenon that does not just grow through moments of joy, but is unwittingly nourished through struggles, fights, and resentments. This kind of love takes years, and often

---

[7] Al-Shīrāzī, Ṣadr ad-Dīn (Mullāh Ṣadrā), *Sharḥ Uṣūl al-Kāfī*, 4 Vols., Ed. Muḥammad Kwājavī (Tehran: Muʾassasah-yi Muṭāliʿāt va Taḥqīqāt-i Farhangī, 1383 H.Sh/2004-05), Vol. 1, P. 361.

even two to three decades to mature. I have seen cases where fully blossomed love took over thirty-five years to be fully realized after many moments and years of struggle. The years of struggle were not wasted years, they were years of human learning and flourishing which made the couple appreciate a life well lived.

Think of the Chinese bamboo tree. After its seeds have been planted, it takes about five years of regular watering. It is only after five years that it finally breaks through the soil and grows over 90 feet in just five weeks. In the struggles of marriage, people often feel that the years that they put in made no difference, and that their relationships stayed the same or maybe even got worse. However, this is often an illusion and is not correct. Under that dark soil, there are immense changes that are happening that people are not aware and conscious of. But if they are patient and bear with the burden of transformations over the years, then they will most likely see the rapid growth spurt of love, wholeness, and equanimity in a short amount of time. I have seen couples who after many years of struggle - in a matter of days - radically changed in their love for each other and overall happiness in life.

An Important Word on the Contents of this Book

In this book, we offer many 'techniques' on how to better a person's marriage. But techniques are just that - techniques. They will only get one so far. In order for a person to see real and meaningful reciprocal changes in one's marriage, one needs to change how one spouse **feels** about the other spouse and vice versa. It is not about what one's spouse **thinks** about what to **do** necessarily, but how they **feel** about the other spouse as a **person**. This kind of change is difficult to achieve because it begins with how we feel inside about ourselves. How other people feel about us depends on the auras we emit, and that cannot be achieved through outward actions and techniques alone.

In order for this change to happen, we must change how we feel about ourselves first in a positive way. This begins with how we relate to God and ourselves. It is through an arduous and long process of interior self-reformation that we will be able to transform ourselves, then our relationships, and finally how we relate to the world. Techniques are therefore useful as long as they are accompanied by a greater effort of spiritual transformation in God. Respect and healing must start with one's relationship with the self, then a person's relationship with others will fall in line once the first step has been taken care of.

This book is therefore a mix between techniques to help a person's marriage in the short-run; but more importantly, it contains points on guiding principles for spiritual transformation in the long-run.

It is also understood that marriages do not exist in a vacuum, nor are they only between a husband and a wife, but rather this institution affects other people as well, especially children. Therefore, although this is a book primarily for married couples, we have also included some guidance on how to raise children because how people upbring and relate to their children is intricately tied to the success of their marriages.

God willing, we hope that this book will be of benefit to all families who are either struggling in their marriages, or wish to further strengthen their relationships.

Nabi R. Mir (Abidi)

1

Strengthening Your Marriage

"We are the sum of our actions, and therefore our habits make all the difference." - Aristotle

Just as our personalities are the sum of our actions and habits, so are our relationships. The state of our marriages is also the sum of the actions and habits that we choose and enact in the course of our relationships.

There is not a single married person who wishes to have a bad marriage. Every married person wants to have the kind of marriage that will bring them happiness. Setting for yourself the goal of strengthening your marriage is a good thing, but it will only take you so far. There needs to be something more. As James Clear pointed out in his book *Atomic Habits:* "You do not rise to the level of your goals. You fall to the level of your systems." [1]

Goals are directions, but systems are the strategic habits you put into place in order to attain real progress. For example, a goal is wanting to lose ten pounds, but a system would be to establish the habit of going to the gym four days a week, along with adhering to a healthy diet. The actions and habits you take between your goal

[1] Clear, James, *Atomic Habits: An Easy and Proven Way to Build Good Habits & Break Bad Ones,* (New York: Penguin Random House, 2018), P. 28.

and its ultimate outcome is what makes the difference.

People who have good and bad marriages share the same goal: to have a happy marriage. What makes one happy, and the other not so happy comes back to the systems which are adopted during the relationship.

Simply wishing or fantasizing about a stronger marriage will lead a person nowhere. Concrete steps need to be taken, and these steps need to become part of a system of habits. To borrow from James Clear again (but slightly change its wording): Every action you take in your relationship is a vote to the kind of marriage you wish to have.[2]

In this chapter, we will cover a series of actions and habits that a person can undertake in a relationship in order to rekindle romance, and progress toward strengthening one's marriage.

A critical component for progressing toward this goal is also to seek marital counseling. In this chapter, we will outline a number of important qualities that couples should look for in a marriage counselor or advisor. These qualities are also pointers for counselors and advisors themselves who may read this book.

Before you begin implementing these suggestions, bear the following in mind: these actions and habits cannot be sustained in the long-term until you begin to love the process itself, and see it as more important than attaining the goal of a romantic and happy marriage.

Once you love the process and take delight in your daily personal transformation, you will enjoy the building of your system more than the end product you seek. Ultimately, do not seek the goal but a day well lived; and what you will discover in the process will be infinitely greater and more meaningful than what you first set out to achieve.

---

[2] Clear states: "Every action you take is a vote for the type of person you wish to become. No single instance will transform your beliefs, but as the votes build up, so does the evidence of your new identity." P. 38.

Rekindling Romance

Respect Your Spouse's Dreams

لا غنـى بالـزوج عـن ثلاثـة اشـياء فيمـا بينـه و بيـن زوجتـه و هـي الموافقـة ليجتلـب بهـا موافقتهـا و محبتهـا و هواهـا و حسـن خلقـه معهـا و اسـتمالة قلبهـا بالهيئـة الحسـنة فـي عينهـا و توسـعته عليهـا. و لا غنـى بالزوجـة فيمـا بينهـا و بيـن زوجهـا الموافـق لهـا عـن ثـلاث خصـال و هّـنَ: صيانـة نفسـها عـن كل دنـس حتـى يطمئـنّ قلبـه الـى الثقـة بهـا فـي حـال المحبـوب والمكـروه. و حياطتهـا ليكـون ذلـک عاطفـا عليهـا عنـد زلّـة تكـون منهـا. وإظهـار العشـق لـه بالخلابـة والهيئـة الحسـنة لهـا فـي عينـه.

Imām aṣ-Ṣādiq ﷺ said: *"A husband should uphold three things between him and his wife [in order to nourish his relationship with her]:*

1) Be easy going (pleasant) with her so it encourages her to be amicable, loving, and compassionate to him;
2) Be virtuous (respectful) toward her; and attract her heart by being in good appearance;
3) Be generous toward her;

Similarly, a wife should maintain three characters between her and her husband [in order to nourish her relationship with him]:

1) She should keep herself away from anything that could contaminate her soul, so that he can trust her in good and bad situations;
2) Be cautious so that he will be forgiving when she makes a mistake;
3) Express affection for him through loving (words), and be in an

appealing and beautiful appearance that he likes."[3]

We all have dreams and hopes in life. They give us a sense of direction and grounding in this world. They form our values, and our values in turn form them. When someone respects them, they respect a deep part of us.

Note, however, not all dreams, hopes, and wishes are practical, realistic, or even healthy. Some may even be destructive. But one must select the appropriate way in approaching a spouse's dreams and hopes. You can approach your spouse's dreams and hopes in three types of ways:

1. Give compliments, listen, and give the person false hope. By doing so you may damage and hurt your spouse.

2. Dismiss your spouse's dreams outright and demoralize them. This can have a negative impact on your marriage, and/or the emotional well-being of your spouse.

3. Respect, listen, and kindly guide your spouse to more practical approaches and solutions if there are any. If not, then you can at least encourage hope, but not encourage destructive behavior.

By taking the third option, a better mutual understanding and empathy will grow in your relationship. You will strengthen your marriage and see good outcomes for both sides.

Remember that for the most part, people's dreams and hopes fall within the range of possibility so take advantage of this. One of the best means to revivify your spouse's love for you is to find out what their dreams are and work hard to respect them. Sometimes it may be a hobby, and other times it is simply being a good parent to your children. Try this out and see how your spouse's view of you changes, and how it may spark a new era of romance in your life.

---

[3] ʿAllāmah Majlisī, *Biḥār al-Anwār al-Jāmiʿah li-Durar Akhbār al-A'immah al-Aṭhār*, 110 Vols., Ed. by a committee of researchers, (Beirut: Dār Iḥyā' al-Turāth al-ʿArabī, 1403/1982), Vol. 75, P. 75.

Keep Some Time Apart

المؤمن سِيرته القصد.

Imām ʿAlī said: *"A believer is moderate in all of one's affairs."* [4]

Some people believe that a sign of a healthy marriage is that couples spend all of their time together. The other extreme is to purposefully stay away from each other for long periods of time in order to rekindle love, however that is also a mistake.

It is almost impossible to find someone in this world with whom you can spend every minute of your life without getting tired of them. Everyone needs a break and some space. These breaks help us find ourselves and rekindle positive emotions.

So here is the secret to a good marriage and rekindling romance: Do not spend all of your time together. A healthy amount of distance from time to time can make the heart grow fonder and give you more things to talk about.

It is natural for people who are in close proximity all of the time to have conflicts and become "tired" or "frustrated" with one another. Some distance can give a sense of renewal, and an ability to reconnect at a deeper level. However, be careful not to take this to an extreme because regular and consistent distance can sometimes have the opposite effect, and it can often pull couples apart.

Give Compliments to Your Spouse Regularly and Naturally

لَئِنْ شَكَرْتُمْ لَأَزِيدَنَّكُمْ

"If you are grateful, then I will surely enhance you with more [blessings]." [5]

---

[4] Al-Āmidī, ʿAbdul Wāḥid al-Tamīmī, *Ghurar al-Ḥikam wa Durar al-Kalim*, Ed. Mahdī Rajāʾī, (Qum: Dār al-Kitāb al-Islāmī, 1410/1989-1990), P. 80.

[5] Noble Qurʾān, Sūrah Ibrāhīm (14), Verse 7.

Feed your spouse's mind with admiration and compliments. Take a piece of paper, or write it in a journal - all of the things which you admire about your spouse, and all of the compliments that you can give to them. Then on a daily basis, give out these compliments bit by bit.

This may feel weird at first, especially if you are not in the habit of giving out compliments, but it will become natural over time. After a while, take a step back and think about how much of a difference this made in your marriage, and how much better you yourself feel.

Remember that consistency is the key. Consistency will slowly but surely form a positive outlook of your spouse in your heart where you will eventually come to believe in this positivity yourself. That is the beauty of repetition. Even if initially your spouse thinks that you are not serious, over time your spouse will be convinced of your sincerity as you will also become more sincere about it through the positivity that you display.

Be mindful of the following: Do not give too many compliments all in one shot as it will look insincere. Start slowly and build up gradually. The naturalness of your approach will add greater blessings to your marriage.

Good Memories Should Outnumber the Bad

خیر اخوانک من نسی ذنبک و ذکر احسانک الیه.

Imām al-ʿAskarī ﷺ said: *"The best of your friends are those who forget your bad deeds and keep your good ones in mind."*[6]

What saves marriages from crises and rekindles romance are good memories that outweigh the bad ones.

Make sure to invest in your marriage by creating as many good memories as you can so that when bad times come, remembering

[6] *Biḥār al-Anwār*, Vol. 75, P. 52.

all of the good times will keep you from doing something you may regret later on. It may also help prevent your spouse from doing things that he or she will feel remorseful about afterward.

Good memories mitigate and reduce the intensity of bad times. On the opposite side, too many bad memories lessen the sweetness of good memories. The quality of your marriage, and by extension, the level of romance in your relationship is largely determined by the ratio of good memories to bad ones.

Even if you do not have too many good memories, as long as you are both alive, there is always a chance to create good memories. The more you make, the stronger and sweeter they will become; and eventually they will overtake the bad ones and transform your marriage.

Do not give up, and do not put all of your energy into putting out fires. Take a step back, put the tension aside, and focus your energies on being creative.

Here is an important point: Do not wait for your spouse to start or establish good memories. Make yourself responsible for being creative, and over time your spouse will also change through what you started and maintained. You will reap the fruits of your labor even if it is one sided.

Date Regularly ... Without the Kids

كلما ازداد العبد ايمانا ازداد حبا للنسآء.

Prophet Muḥammad ﷺ said: *"The more a servant's faith increases, the more his care for women will increase."* [7]

A good place to start in making great memories is to go out on dates together ... without the kids. It is normal for couples to fight on their first few dates, especially if they have not been on one for a long time.

[7] *Biḥār al-Anwār*, Vol. 100, P. 228.

It does not matter if you have a good day or bad day on your date. It also does not matter whether you are in a good or bad mood. Make it a routine to go out on dates regularly, and make it a culture in your marriage. If your spouse reacts in a way that you may not like, try not to respond negatively.

See the bigger and long-term picture of the mission that you have undertaken. Instill positivity in your outings, and your spouse will eventually be influenced by your mood.

Sit with Your Spouse in Loving Silence

جلوس المرء عند عياله احب الى الله تعالى من اعتكاف فى مسجدى هذا.

Prophet Muḥammad (ṣ) said: *"A man who sits with his family is more beloved to God, the Exalted, than a person who secludes himself in my mosque (masjid) to worship."* [8]

When you are sitting with your spouse, it is not necessary to always be talking. From time to time, just go and sit beside them; and if asked what you want, simply reply: "I just want to sit next to you."

It may be that your spouse will start talking to you in a relaxed manner because the conversation is not forced. If he or she does not respond much, just relax and enjoy the moment. Not all communication is verbal, your loving energy will be communicated in silence.

Remembering the Early Phase of Your Relationship

تفكر ساعة خير من عبادة سنة.

Imām aṣ-Ṣādiq ﷺ said: *"An hour of contemplation is better than a year of worship."* [9]

[8] Qarā'atī, Muḥsin, *Tafsīre Nūr,* 10 Vols, (Tehran: Markaz-i Farhangī Dars-Hāyi az Qur'ān, 1383/2004), Vol. 10, P. 97.

[9] Shaykh Kulaynī, *Al-Kāfī,* 15 Vols., Ed. Dār al-Ḥadīth/Mūsā Shubayrī Zanjānī, (Qum: Dār al-Ḥadīth, 1429/2008), Vol. 3, P. 141.

Many married couples complain that they have lost the initial romance which they had when they first got married. Remember that although people go into a comfort level later on in marriage and lose the initial emotional intensity that was there in the beginning, they can still hold on to romance.

Try this: Remember what you did during the initial phase of your marriage - do you think that your relationship would be better if you started doing some of the things that kept the spark alive earlier on?

Although we grow in wisdom as we get older, there are lost gems that we can find in our youth that may be even more useful for us now. Think about it, how much time did you both spend communicating with each other? How much time did you spend alone walking outside? These were not benign actions - they were critical in building and sustaining the romance that you had initially in your marriage.

The majority of the decisions we make are based on partial facts, prejudices, prejudgments, or conclusions that we make out of anger. Contemplation and remembering the good days of your marriage will give you a better and more holistic frame of thought in order to make better decisions about your relationship. Based on experience, most people later on regret their emotionally triggered decisions, when they look back in hindsight.

Express More Love after Children

وَالَّذِينَ يَقُولُونَ رَبَّنَا هَبْ لَنَا مِنْ أَزْوَاجِنَا وَذُرِّيَّاتِنَا قُرَّةَ أَعْيُنٍ وَاجْعَلْنَا
لِلْمُتَّقِينَ إِمَامًا

"And [they are] those who say: 'Our Lord, make our spouses and our children the delight of our eyes.'" [10]

It is highly important for a man to express love toward his wife, and

---

[10] Noble Qur'ān, Sūrah al-Furqān (25), Verse 74.

even more so after having children. Husbands should pay attention to their spouses and make them the most important concern in their lives. Most problems concerning intimacy happen when there is a lack of balance - either the expression of attention is too little, too much, or not done properly.

As a husband, he may have tried and seen what works and what does not work. Now speak to the wife, and get her honest opinion.

On a similar level, wives must also not forget their husbands after having children. It is natural for women to divide their attention and begin focusing more on their children, especially when they are young. However, unfortunately many times husbands barely get any attention after they have children.

Mothers need to remember that this can be very damaging to the children, and can alienate the father from the family. It can sometimes create hidden resentment in husbands which manifest themselves in indirect ways (working long hours, getting angry at irrelevant and small things, etc.) but because many men have pride, they will seldom express the real source of their frustration and resentment for fear of shame and embarrassment.

If there is one thing that is more important for the psychological, emotional, social, and spiritual well-being of a child than a good parent-child relationship, it is the relationship between their mother and father. It is the strong and close, intimate relationship between their mother and father that is the primary source of a child's sense of security and stability in life that will sustain their emotional and psychological well-being.

If this marital bond is weak or compromised, then the child will grow up greatly damaged even if the parent-child relationship was perfect. Do not trick yourself into thinking that you will work on your marriage "later," the damage done early on will have a long-term impact on not only the marriage, but on the child as well. Young children need a strong marriage between their parents in order to grow up as healthy adults. What happens in childhood will greatly affect what transpires in adulthood.

Prevention is better than cure, both for the marriage and for the children.

Watch What You Eat

كُلُوْا مِنْ طَيِّبَاتِ مَا رَزَقْنَاكُمْ وَاشْكُرُوْا لِلّٰهِ

"Eat of the good (lawful and wholesome) things which We have provided for you, and be grateful to God." [11]

One of the major areas that contributes to the lack of sexual intimacy is an unhealthy diet. Specialists say that fast foods, sugars, processed foods, and other unhealthy foods directly affect your mental and physical well-being. Often coupled with a lack of exercise, they create a number of psychological and physical issues that are directly related to arousal problems that affect intimacy between couples.

If you want to increase intimacy in your marriage, then you must eat healthy, and exercise. Not only will it change your physical appearance and make you more attractive to your spouse, but it will also affect you mentally and how you behave, thus making you more energized and romantic.

The Imāms from Prophet Muḥammad's Noble Household recommended us to make nuts, fruits, beans, vegetables, and seeds as the core source of our nutrition.

Write to Your Spouse

القلب يتكل على الكتابة.

Imām aṣ-Ṣādiq said: *"The heart trusts that what is written."* [12]

It has been narrated that a companion of Imām Jaʿfar aṣ-Ṣādiq, by

---
[11] Noble Qurʾān, Sūrah al-Baqarah (2), Verse 172.
[12] *Al-Kāfī*, Vol. 1, P. 129.

the name of Abū Baṣīr, found that his relationship with his wife had deteriorated, so the Imām ﷺ recommended him to write a letter to her. The companion did not know how to read and write, so the Imām ﷺ instructed him to learn so that he could then write her a letter.

Writing is a powerful tool. When we speak, a lot of our thoughts are disorganized and may be jumbled up. Writing forces our mind to ponder our thoughts more deeply. It helps us structure our thoughts in a more organized and better processed way. It reduces the chaos of our thoughts and grounds them in a more solid fashion. This is why some psychologists have noted that journaling can oftentimes be more effective than one-on-one therapy in processing heavy emotions.

When you write to your spouse, you will be surprised at the words that flow out from your hands. You will begin to acquaint yourself with thoughts and emotions that you were not aware of, but were hidden and behind your behavior all along. You will be able to express them more clearly, and the effort you put into what you wrote may touch your spouse more deeply than speaking.

Although speaking with our spouse is good, writing things down gives us an opportunity to express ourselves to our spouses in a clearer, more thoughtful, and coherent manner that is less likely to exacerbate tensions in a conflict when calm communication is needed the most, but may be difficult to adhere to. Furthermore, a spoken word is often forgotten, but written words, if saved, is something we can always come back to. As well, we can re-read our letter over a few times before we give it to our spouse to make sure there is nothing detrimental in it; but when we speak, sometimes we may say something that we did not think through completely and this could make the situation worse, and we may will regret it later on.

In today's day and age, even though we have text messaging or whatsapp, we advise couples to avoid using those except for small messages. A serious message would be better off hand-written. The science of neurology has shown that your mind processes words at a deeper level when they are hand-written (and your spouse will appreciate it more, especially if you take the time to write your letter with good penmanship). If that is not possible, then your next best option would be to write your letter to your spouse in email form.

Written letters–either by hand or email–can do wonders for rekindling romance.

Word of caution: just as writing can be a powerful positive tool, it can also be a powerful negative tool. If you write negative things, they will have a much more negative impact than if you were to verbally speak those things. Think back and reflect, and make sure that you choose positive words, as well as a good platform to write with. This means that serious writings should **not** be in the form of text messaging.

Some people often save bad text messages to use against their spouses for years to come. Spoken words can sometimes be forgotten, but written messages can linger on for your entire life.

Beautify Yourself Inside the Home, Not Outside

ان من خير نسائكم المتبرجة لزوجها، الحصان عن غيره.

Prophet Muḥammad ﷺ said: *"Among the best of your women are those who beautify themselves for their husband, but protect [cover] themselves from other men."*[13]

When the Prophet ﷺ used to come home, he would perfume himself, wear nice clothes, comb his hair and beard, and brush his teeth before speaking to his wives.

Many people beautify themselves when they leave the home, but when they are at home, they slack off and do not show their best

[13] Borujerdī, Ḥusayn, *Jāmiʿ Aḥādīth ash-Shīʿah*, 31 Vols. (Tehran: Intishārāt-i Farhang-i Sabz, 1386 H.Sh/2007), Vol. 25, P. 492.

selves. This can be damaging to a marriage. Why should a spouse beautify themselves for strangers outside, but not do anything nice while at home? Who should they be attracting - strangers or their spouses?

We are not saying that people should be dressed inside of the home as if they are going to a wedding, but people should be mindful to look sharp and attractive for their spouses at home. They need to maintain their physical, hygienic, and clothing standards at home. This will keep the attraction between couples high, and show your spouse that you truly care about them, and it will instill more closeness and deeper intimacy between you both.

Share Your Future Plans

أيما امرأة أعانت زوجها على الحج والجهاد أو طلب العلم
أعطاها الله من الثواب ما يعطي امرأة أيوب.

Prophet Muḥammad ﷺ said: *"Any woman who helps her husband in performing the Pilgrimage (Ḥajj), struggle (in the way of God - jihād), and acquiring knowledge, God will give her the same reward as He gave to the wife of Prophet Ayyūb [Job]."* [14]

Intimacy goes down in a marriage when trust goes down. One of the most important elements to our identity as human beings are the future plans that we make. Spouses should share their future plans with each other, and they should never put one another down because of them. Sharing these plans increases trust, and thereby closeness and intimacy.

We often share our plans with our friends, coworkers, siblings, and even strangers. However, we sometimes refrain from doing so with our spouses because we fear that they will not listen to us or that they will make fun of us. In other words, we fear sharing our

[14] Aṭ-Ṭabrisī, *Makārim al-Akhlāq*, (Qum: ash-Sharīf ar-Rāḍī, 1412/1991-1992), P. 201.

plans because of a lack of trust. Both spouses need to make sure that enough trust exists so that they can share with each other what they would share with their friends.

At the end of the day, the person who has the greatest say or 'skin in the game' of your future plans is your spouse, not your friends or anyone else.

Find a Babysitter

سافروا تصحوا وتغنموا.

Prophet Muḥammad ﷺ said: *"Travel so that you gain health and wealth."* [15]

Sometimes parents have a hard time communicating and being intimate with one another because work and children have tired them out. When they want to communicate, children can often interrupt and prevent meaningful conversation.

This is why couples need some alone time every so often. It is a good idea for couples to go out of town with each other for some time **without the children**. Long travels may not be possible, but sometimes it can be doable to find a babysitter for a couple of hours during the day. You can leave in the morning and come back at night, and go somewhere that you have never gone before such as another city.

Traveling out of town takes people outside of what is familiar and puts them somewhere that is less familiar. When couples travel, they tend to grow closer to one another as they create new experiences together. These endeavors will have a deeper impact on positive memories than familiar ones, and the new memories will create more positive emotions thus improving intimacy.

The recommendation is that couples should travel together at least once every six months. If that is not possible, then at least

[15] *Biḥār al-Anwār*, Vol. 59, P. 267.

once a year. If they can go somewhere far, then it is recommended that they go on *ziyārah* trips where they can also benefit spiritually. Cultural trips to other countries are other options.

Prevent Emotional Unfaithfulness

إذا نظـر أحدكـم إلـى المـرأة الحسـناء فليـأت أهلـه فـإن الـذى معهـا مثـل الـذى مـع تلـک.

Prophet Muḥammad ﷺ said: *"If one of you looks at a beautiful woman, then let him come back (home) to his family, for that which she (the beautiful woman) has [as a woman], your wife also has."* [16]

It is part of our spiritual nature (*fiṭrah*) to want to connect and be close to other people. Everyone wants to love and be loved, and care and be cared for. Sometimes, it may happen that couples deny each other this kind of intimate affection. Although it does not always lead to adultery, there are times when people will flirt or have inappropriate conversations, interactions, and connections with others because it is lacking in their marital lives.

Unfortunately, these may get out of hand and turn into emotional unfaithfulness. Even though emotional unfaithfulness, or emotional adultery, or any type of adultery can never be justified, remember that the coldness in your home can often be a stimulus (not a cause, as the cause is one's own choice) for unfaithfulness. Even if you do not feel like it, you must make an effort to pay quality and positive attention to your spouse - just like you do with your children even when you do not really feel like it. This will have a long-term impact on the quality of your marriage, and overall happiness in your life.

[16] *Al-Kāfī*, Vol. 11, P. 129.

Sharing Passwords

يَا أَيُّهَا الَّذِينَ آمَنُوا اجْتَنِبُوا كَثِيرًا مِنَ الظَّنِّ إِنَّ بَعْضَ الظَّنِّ إِثْمٌ ۖ وَلَا تَجَسَّسُوا

"O you who have faith! Avoid much suspicion, indeed some suspicion is a sin, and do not spy (on one another)." [17]

God created us and gave us certain rights. One of these rights is the right to privacy and personal boundaries. A person should not enter another person's boundaries without their permission.

Although husbands and wives are one unit, they still have the right to their privacy, and that should be honored and respected.

The best and healthiest couples are those who trust each other. They are those who do not transgress against the commands of God, and do not transgress against each other.

The moment you want to "spy" on your spouse (e.g., by putting a chip in the phone, or wanting their password), then you have a bigger problem than just wanting a password. In our society, emails and phones are considered our private belongings and these boundaries must be respected. If a person shares their personal passwords, or does not mind if you check their personal things, then this is a different situation, otherwise it is a grave sin to do this without their permission.

If you are worried that your spouse may be cheating on you with someone else, then know that they can find some other way to hide it from you. It is best to resolve your issues at their roots, rather than opting for unhealthy surveillance options.

You should not do anything that could compromise the trust between you and your spouse. You should not be obliged to share the passwords to your emails, phones, etc. You may think that this is showing trust, but it can have the opposite effect. The very fact

[17] Noble Qur'ān, Sūrah al-Ḥujurāt (49), Verse 12.

that a spouse wants these passwords signals that there is a trust problem. This can have a negative impact on the closeness of your relationship.

If there are trust issues related to emails and texts, then you can share the passwords for a small duration of time until the trust is once again established and the problem is solved, but this should not be a permanent or long-term feature of your relationship.

Healthy couples are those who work with one another, share the same mission and vision in life, and find common grounds. Each person in the marriage has to understand that regardless of the intention or action of the other person, one has to start by working internally to bring peace and tranquility, thus setting the stage for rekindling trust. One should not wait for the other person to initiate, or even expect them to necessarily cooperate.

Be Mindful of Your Spouse's Sensitivities

أحسن إلى جميع الناس كما تحب أن يحسن إليك.

Imām ʿAlī ﷺ said: *"Be good to all people as you like others to be good to you."*[18]

We all have sensitivities to different things in life. Sometimes these sensitivities may not make sense to others, but they make a lot of sense to us in light of our upbringing, values, and experiences in life. Understanding this is one of the roots of empathy and compassion. When people respect our sensitivities, then we are more likely to respect theirs. We are also more likely to be in a deeper, trusting, and secure relationship with them.

For example, a big point of sensitivity is when a spouse speaks to a particular person (especially of the opposite gender) that the other spouse does not like. If this is the case, then do not insist

---

[18] Shaykh Ṣadūq, *Man lā Yaḥḍuruhu al-Faqīh*, 4 Vols., Ed. ʿAlī Akbar Ghaffārī, (Qum: Daftar-i Intishārāt-i Islāmī, 1413/1993), Vol. 4, P. 387.

on speaking to this person as your life will not end if you stop talking to them. Keep your distance from them out of respect for your spouse's concerns, and if you are obliged to speak to them (for example, at work), then keep the conversation to a minimum, be formal, and professional.

If your spouse is sensitive about something, do not argue or fight with them in regard to that. Respect the sensitivity, and honor your spouse's values. You will eventually gain trust, and have some of your own sensitivities respected as well. Even if your spouse does not reciprocate in honoring your sensitivities, do not stop or take revenge. Honor their sensitivities for the sake of pleasing God and your marriage and life will improve in different and better ways. The trust in your marriage will grow, and your intimacy will likely improve as well.

A word of caution: we must make sure not to fall into extremes and that we act within **reasonable limits.** You must avoid scenarios where couples follow every single sensitivity in some imagined attempt at perfection, otherwise this will affect your life negatively and upend your mental and emotional well-being. On the other hand, there are other couples who have no structure in their relationship, and do not want to try to improve their marriages or honor their spouses. We must have a proper balance in everything.

Have Constructive Conversations

اجملوا في الخِطاب تسمعوا جميل الجواب.

Imām ʿAlī ﷷ said: *"Beautify your speech so that you hear a beautiful answer [in return]."* [19]

There is a lot of importance that must be given in regards to communication between spouses. Communication can have a negative impact in a marriage if it is not done in the right way.

[19] *Ghurar al-Ḥikam*, P. 158.

For example, if a couple spends their time together gossiping and backbiting about others, then this will negatively impact their relationship. Sometimes a political conversation can also be bad if spouses share different political leanings, so these conversations are often best to avoid.

Positive frames of discussions can include:

1) your shared life-interests and values like your children, your future, life in general, etc.
2) shared leisure interests, or sources of entertainment
3) shared religious and spiritual values
4) social and cultural discussions or endeavors

You can also choose a book that you mutually like and create a mini-book club for yourselves where once a week you sit down and discuss the contents of the book.

There are many ways you can have positive and constructive conversations with your spouse that do not involve speaking negatively about other people.

Finally, when discussing things, look at the sources of information that you are using. Instead of assumptions, refer to experts and authorities that you hold in high esteem.

Fake It Till You Make It

قول الرجل للمراة انى احبک لا یذهب من قلبها ابد.

Prophet Muḥammad ﷺ said: *"When a man says to his wife: 'I love you' it will never leave her heart."*[20]

There is a false notion in our community that you must feel a certain way before you act, otherwise you are just being hypocritical. That is not how virtue works according to Islam.

It is correct that character affects our behavior, but our behavior also affects our character. That is why, for example, the Qur'ān

[20] *Al-Kāfī*, Vol. 11, P. 316.

teaches us that the action of prayer can change our character into more self-controlled and conscientious people:

اُتْلُ مَا أُوحِيَ إِلَيْكَ مِنَ الْكِتَابِ وَأَقِمِ الصَّلَاةَ ۖ إِنَّ الصَّلَاةَ تَنْهَىٰ عَنِ الْفَحْشَاءِ وَالْمُنكَرِ ۗ وَلَذِكْرُ اللَّهِ أَكْبَرُ ۗ وَاللَّهُ يَعْلَمُ مَا تَصْنَعُونَ

"Recite what has been revealed to you of the Book, and establish the prayer. Verily prayer prevents indecency and abomination, and the remembrance of God is surely greater. And God knows whatever you do." [21]

There is an erroneous belief that we need to feel loving and romantic in order to behave lovingly and romantically with our spouses. This belief also holds that we need to feel attracted to our spouses in order to behave like we are attracted to them. This approach insists that if what we feel and think inside does not match with our behavior outside, then somehow we are hypocrites.

This is incorrect and can be dangerous and could even weaken our marriage bonds. Just like our character shapes our behavior and virtuousness, our outward behavior through repetition will slowly but surely change our inner feelings, character, and virtuousness.

You will become what you repeatedly do.

From an Islamic perspective, it is recommended for you to repeat good actions that are pleasing to God despite your inner feelings to the contrary. Eventually the actions will change your heart. In this sense, it is good to: *"fake it till you make it."*

This process works the other way as well. The more you avoid acting romantically and lovingly, and instead waiting for something to change inside of you spontaneously before you show some affection, I can almost guarantee that things will become even worse in your marriage. You will become less loving and less romantic over time. Therefore, do not wait - start pretending; and behave as if you have love and romance already in your heart.

[21] Noble Qur'ān, Sūrah al-ʿAnkabūt (29), Verse 45.

Inspire Love When You Don't See Love

فدارها على كل حال واحسن الصحبة لها فيصفو عيشک.

Imām ʿAlī ﷺ said: *"Always be tolerant and patient with your spouse, live with her in kindness and goodness so that your life may become serene and felicitous."*[22]

You cannot make someone love you, but you can create the conditions for it to arise. This happens by being less judgmental, more open, warmer, and kinder. We can create the conditions for love to arise - not by trying to make it happen, not by trying to hold on to it - but by creating the space for love to be present.

Love cannot be imposed on the self or on others; but true love can be established through unconditional kindness.

Marriage Counseling

A Precautionary Note

Premarital and post marital counseling are both equally important. Most people seek counseling when their marriage runs into trouble. However, counseling should not only be used to help marital problems, but also to strengthen the marriage, and prevent difficult situations before problems occur.

A high-ranking religious scholar and counselor said that he himself would seek counseling between him and his wife at least once a year. He did not do this because they had serious marital problems (they did not), but he sought counseling to gain a deeper insight into his relationship in order to strengthen it. We all need to get counseling even in good times.

However, this counseling can sometimes be dangerous. If you find a counselor who does not understand the cultural, spiritual,

[22] *Jāmiʿ Aḥadīth ash-Shīʿah*, Vol. 25, P. 540.

religious, emotional, and contemporary needs of the couple, or if the counselor is only secular and does not believe in spiritual and religious values, then that counselor may end up destroying a marriage rather than help it.

Counselors who are good in one area may not be good in another. A secular counselor may be good in one area but clueless in another. The same applies to religious counselors.

A good counselor must therefore be holistically trained. If the counselor is not right, and people who come to them are fragile, then this can sometimes open the doors to dangerous situations. The counselor should be able to distinguish between religious, spiritual, physical, or psychological problems.

Help Couples Find their Needs, Not Wants

لـو أن لابـن آدم واديـاً مـن ذهـب أحـب أن يكـون لـه واديـان،
ولـن يمـلأ فـاه إلا التـراب، ويتـوب اللـه علـى مـن تـاب.

Prophet Muḥammad ﷺ said: *"If a child of Ādam (Adam) had a valley full of gold, they will want to have two valleys. Nothing fills their mouth but the dirt of the grave, but God will show mercy to whoever repents to Him."* [23]

There is a fundamental difference between needs and wants. "Needs" are universal to all human beings. They include physical needs, the need for connection, peace, and meaning in life. In other words, they are elements without which people cannot function properly in life.

"Wants" are things that people desire in life, but they may not necessarily need in order to function. If one does not get what they want strictly speaking, then nothing bad should happen. But if we

[23] Al-Iṣfahānī, Abī Naʿīm, *Al-Musnad al-Mustakhraj 'alá Ṣaḥīḥ al-Imām Muslim,* 4 Vols., Ed. Muḥammad Ḥasan al-Shāfiʿī, (Beirut: Dār al-Kutub al-ʿIlmiyah, 1996), Vol. 3, P. 114.

do not get what we need, then life may become very complicated.

For example, you may need transportation to get to work with a regular car, but you want a brand-new car. You may not be able to function without a means of transportation to work, but you can still function without a brand-new car.

It is often the case that in marital conflict, wants and needs become conflated. Couples get stuck in trying to meet the other spouse's wants, but by doing so they never seem to get any closer to resolving their marital problems. This is because couples get distracted by the wants without addressing the real needs that are the source of the problem.

When spouses learn what their needs are and are able to express them, and when those 'doable needs' are met and addressed, then conflicts begin to resolve.

The wants of human beings are infinite, and it is almost impossible to address all of them. A person may want one thing on a particular day, but he or she will want something else another day. However, this does not mean that we should dismiss all wants because wants can often be an expression of an unmet need which has been the conclusion of Marshall B. Rosenberg's lifelong research which supports our own Islamic observations.[24] In my own experience working with couples as a resident scholar (ʿālim), once a need is met, I have frequently seen the wants disappear or become less significant in the relationship.

So, what is the role of a counselor in marital counseling? The primary responsibility of a marital counselor is not to make one party comply with the wishes of the other, but rather, to facilitate mutual understanding of the needs of each party. When both parties grasp these needs, they can then engage in a dialogue about addressing them, creating an opportunity for potential reconciliation.

---

[24] Rosenberg, Marshall B., See the culmination of his thought in his book, *Nonviolent Communication: A Language of Life*, 3rd Ed., (Encinitas: PuddleDancer Press, 2015).

Wants are Independent, but Needs are Interdependent

لا يؤمن أحدكم حتى يحب لأخيه ما يحب لنفسه.

Prophet Muḥammad ﷺ said: *"No one (from) among you truly believes until they love for their brother (or sister) that which they love for themselves."* [25]

It is not always easy to get people to serve and help one another. This is because people look at themselves in terms of their wants which are often independent. An experienced counselor will foster quality concern and respect between a couple by highlighting the interdependence of their needs with one another.

When couples realize that their needs are interdependent, they are more likely to act and strategize to meet those needs, and thus reconcile and strengthen their marriage. This is because interdependence not only fosters compassion and decreases hostility, but it also appeals to a person's self-interest which most people will address once they realize what their own interests are. [26] As a result, they are more willing to sacrifice their wants for greater needs.

Conflicts are in the Now

ألا أخبركم بأفضل من درجة الصيام والصلاة والصدقة قالوا بلى قال صلاح ذات البين فإن فساد ذات البين هي الحالقة.

Prophet Muḥammad ﷺ said: *"Shall I tell you what is more excellent than fasting, prayer, and charity?"* The people replied: *"Yes."* He continued: *"It is fixing the relationships (between*

[25] Pāyāndeh, Abūl Qāsim, *Nahj al-Faṣāḥah*, Tehran: Dunyā-yi Dānish, [2003-2004], P. 678.

[26] *Nonviolent Communication: A Language of Life*, P. 162.

people), for the corruption of relationships will destroy them." [27]

The most fundamental conflicts in marriage are always about what is going on in the present. For example, if there was a case of unfaithfulness in the past, the current conflict may be more about the crisis of trust in the present moment, rather than because of a past incident that cannot be changed anymore.

A counselor must help a couple identify what their present needs are. Once those present needs are identified, then couples can take the steps to have them addressed. Many conflicts about the past or future may be resolved.

Be a Good Investigator of Emotions

مـن كظـم غيظـا وهـو يقـدر علـى إمضائـه حشـا اللّـه قلبـه أمنـا وإيمانـا يـوم القيامـة.

Imām al-Bāqir ﷺ said: *"A person who suppresses one's rage while they are capable of unleashing it, God will fill their heart with peace and faith on the Day of Judgment."* [28]

When couples fight, they may say or do many hurtful things. They may insult, make hurtful assumptions and judgments, or simply give the silent treatment. However, a spouse needs to learn to discover and investigate what need is really behind the reaction of the other spouse. Sometimes one may find it difficult to figure this out, thus an experienced counselor can help facilitate this investigation by asking the right questions and setting the grounds for honest and introspective conversation.

At times some forms of counseling may reveal hidden traumas that are the source of such behaviors, and the healing of these traumas may help the relationship with one's self and with others.

---

[27] *Nahj al-Faṣāḥah*, P. 240.

[28] *Al-Kāfī*, Vol. 3, P. 275.

Empathy Precedes Understanding

مـن أراد أن ينصـف النـاس مـن نفسـه فليحـب لهـم مـا يحـب لنفسـه.

Imām ʿAlī ﷺ said: *"A person who desires to be fair with people, should love for them whatever they love for themselves."* [29]

When people become emotional, they seldom hear what the other person is saying. Furthermore, when a person feels that their emotions and feelings are being disregarded, they generally are not willing to try to understand the opposite side's feelings.

If someone wants to have their spouse understand them, then they must demonstrate that they empathize with the other person's feelings as well. A good way to do this is to attentively listen to what is being said without interrupting the other person, except in a case where the listener wants some clarification. Once the feeling and need is understood, then the listener should repeat a summary of what was said to show that they were carefully listening and have understood the situation.

When this happens, the person listening will feel empathy, and the other individual who spoke will feel understood. That is when hostility and defensiveness will decrease, and the foundations for healing and strengthening the marriage will set in.

Counselors Should Learn Human Needs

المشـورة لا تكـون الا بحدودهـا [فمـن عرفهـا بحدودهـا] والا كانـت مضرتهـا علـى المستشـير اكثـر مـن منفعتهـا.

Imām aṣ-Ṣādiq ﷺ said: *"Advice should not be given except within its limits; [so whoever knows its limits will give beneficial*

[29] Bāslūm, Majdī, *Mawsūʿah Āl Bayt an-Nabī*, 2 Vols., Beirut: Dār al-Kutub al-ʿIlmiyyah, 2010, Vol. 2, P. 90.

advice], otherwise its harms will outweigh its benefits." [30]

People often think they know themselves, but in reality they do not. They are aware that they are frustrated, angry, anxious, and above all - in pain. They make the mistake of rooting their pain in superficial wants and desires that they have in life, and in doing so, they partly or fully blame their spouses because they are unable or unwilling to meet them. Even when they do meet them, these wants, like a chameleon, end up shifting thus creating a whole new chain of wants that the spouse must now fulfill. When the spouse is no longer able to meet those sets of wants, new conflicts arise.

Superficial wants are manifestations of deeper universal needs in humans as we discussed before. Counselors should be well versed about the needs of human beings, and learn to identify them through the confusing fog of the infinite array of wants that individuals in a marriage may express.

This requires counselors to have deep introspection into themselves, then use that as a springboard to identify the reality of other people's states. It is most often the case that dysfunctional marriages are not the result of irreconcilable differences, but people's inability to truly know themselves and their needs.

When Counselors Need to Interrupt

شاور فی امورک مما یقتضی الدین فیه خمس خصال: عقل و علم و تجربة و نصح و تقوی فان لم تجد فاستعمل الخمسة و اعظم و توکل علی الله فان ذلک یؤدیک الی الصواب.

Imām aṣ-Ṣādiq ﷺ said: *"Consult regarding your affairs with those whom the religion requires to have five characteristics: intellect, knowledge, experience, sound advice, and God-consciousness. If you do not find such a person, then use those*

[30] *Biḥār al-Anwār*, Vol. 62, P. 102.

five characters and try your best [to resolve your issue], and rely on God as that will lead you to the right decision." [31]

One of the most difficult parts about counseling married couples is the continuous tendency for spouses to interrupt each other, change the subject, go off on tangents, or make personal attacks. In such moments, counselors may have to be firm and intervene as much as is needed in order to redirect the conversation, and restore it to addressing the needs of the present moment. In other words, here the purpose of interrupting is to restore the process of mediation.

Conclusion

A Concluding Remark: Humble Advice for Counselors

Counseling and guiding couples is a noble cause that will be immensely rewarded by God. It is a Divine duty for our communities to produce good counselors.

We have many types of counselors:

Licensed marriage therapists. They have good experience and a proper education, but their training may not be entirely holistic, especially when it comes to understanding the spiritual and religious ways of being in this world.

Religious and spiritual advisors. They may have a lot of knowledge about religion and the culture of the couples they are counseling, but may lack training in psychology and the proper modes of therapy.

Wise elders and trusted family members. They may have good experience and intentions, but they probably lack the scientific expertise and often do not have religious training, even though they may more or less give good advice.

Not everyone is perfect, but a good counselor and advisor is someone

[31] *Biḥār al-Anwār*, Vol. 62, P. 102.

who knows one's own limitations. By being aware of knowledge gaps, a counselor or advisor can seek the cooperation of others in maximizing positive guidance for couples.

Counselors must also avoid conflicts of interest. If they feel that they will be biased toward one side, then it is best that they step back and let someone else do the counseling and advising. A counselor must also be aware that it is easy to take the side of one person, or give emotional advice, because many counselors often come from a background of codependency in their own lives (which is one of the reasons why they may have become counselors in the first place!), and end up transferring this codependency in their counseling relations.

Again, what this means is that some of the most important qualities for a counselor are humility and being impartial. If a counselor or advisor feels that their involvement may be counterproductive, or that they may be 'allowing' the counselee to continue a negative behavior, then this person should be honest and let someone who is more competent and/or less biased do the counseling.

2

Improving Your Marriage

Almost any married person wants to improve his or her marriage. Although people's intentions and their hearts are generally in the right place, their judgments on how to improve their marriages, and by extension, how not to let their marriages deteriorate further can be faulty and misguided.

If there is an underlying theme that repeats itself in all of the chapters of this book, it is the idea of not making your spouse responsible for your happiness. This simple, but essential attitude toward marriage is one of the primary reasons why marriages improve or they **do not** improve.

As human beings, we all have a range of physical, spiritual, emotional, and psychological needs. Although marriage can and should help address some of our needs, our partners should not be held responsible for meeting them holistically. In other words, although they can play a role in influencing the improvement of such needs, we should not hold our spouses responsible for fulfilling them at the core level. That responsibility lies entirely with us and our relationship with our Almighty Creator.

Marriages fail to improve and often even deteriorate because we make our spouses responsible for fixing our insecurities, our low self-esteem, and other types of neuroses. We see them as a means of fulfilling our various unhealthy addictions in life. We think that our spouses should be like our parents who usually make us feel better about ourselves, rather than an equal partner in life. We make them responsible for our feelings, and for meeting all of our unmet needs and unresolved traumas.

This often results in a constant need to control, whether we do it directly by managing everything they do, or indirectly by unconsciously trying to groom them to be a certain way. In almost all marriage cases I have counseled, this approach has either led to extreme discouragement because control was impossible, or if control was somewhat possible, then it led to extreme resentment and other unintended consequences from the controlled spouse. In both scenarios, it backfired.

According to Islam, the tool to address your psychological, spiritual, and emotional needs at a *fundamental* level is your relationship with God and the spiritual practices that follow. Your job is to allow God to improve yourself and make that your primary focus.

In order to achieve this goal of your own improvement, your focus needs to be on yourself and should involve digging into your own spiritual resources - be it through following the precepts of your spiritual practices, or finding suitable spiritual mentors that can help you along this path.

Your goal in marriage is to share a vision of self-improvement with your spouse, and encourage closeness to God. Your goal should be to take ownership of your own faults, find your spiritual self, and come out of your neuroses by exercising patience, self-restraint, self-contemplation, and practicing altruism.

Your goal should be to find out how you can be of value and service to your spouse, and not the other way around. Your goal is working toward the best outcome for your spouse, not yourself. Paradoxically, by transcending your ego and working for the best outcome for your spouse, you will end up creating the best outcome for yourself. Service to others is ultimately service to the self; and it is a kind of charity which will find itself at the root of your happiness. Focusing primarily on servicing yourself and your needs is the root of depression and unhappiness.

By improving yourself with the help of God, you will end up improving your marriage. We live in a world of cause and effect, and reciprocity. The world will react to you depending on how you conduct yourself in it. By transforming yourself, you will transform your marriage, and thereby your spouse.

Improving Marriage by Working on Yourself

Marriage's Goal: Not Just Happiness

من أحب أن يلقى الله طاهرا مطهرا فليلقه بزوجة.

Prophet Muḥammad ﷺ said: *"Whoever wants to meet God (while in a state of being) pure and immaculate should meet Him accompanied by a spouse."* [1]

There is a big misconception among people in which they believe that marriage is either for lust and/or happiness. This goes against the teachings of Islam which sees marriage as a means of pleasing God and building a relationship of patience that supports our quest for transformation and closeness to our Lord.

There is a problem with seeing "happiness" as the primary goal of a marriage. By making it an overarching goal, you will make your spouse responsible for your happiness, and by extension your misery. It will put you in a position where most of what you expect out of marriage is what "you" can get out of it - like a grocery store where you pick what you want and leave behind what you do not want. This approach will ultimately lead to misery because like other

[1] *Biḥār al-Anwār*, Vol. 100, P. 220.

people, you do not have any control over your spouse (their flaws, moods, mistakes, etc.), and it will inevitably lead to disappointment, anger, and resentment.

What your goal should be is **your** own growth, and how you can better **yourself** in order to better your relationship with God and your spouse.

Here are a few tips to help with this:

1. Have a proper mentor who you can look up to. Someone who is a good example for you to follow.
2. Have a good set of friends who will respectfully point out your flaws, rather than just encourage your sanctimoniousness and your sense of victimhood.

If you can have a good grounding in managing your marriage, then this skill will allow you to create harmony in your other relationships as well. By doing so, you will grow as a human being and a Muslim, and find a greater sense of purpose and meaning in your life. This is what will bring happiness to your life.

Happiness is therefore a byproduct of the kind of life you live, not something you look for outside of yourself in other people or things.

Reflect: Who do you aspire to be like, and who can be your mentor? What are some goals you can set for your own growth?

Give Your Best Self to Your Spouse

لَنْ تَنَالُوا الْبِرَّ حَتَّىٰ تُنْفِقُوا مِمَّا تُحِبُّونَ ۚ وَمَا تُنْفِقُوا مِنْ شَيْءٍ فَإِنَّ اللَّهَ بِهِ عَلِيْمٌ

"You will never attain righteousness until you spend out of what you love, and whatever you spend, surely God knows it." [2]

When you give a gift to someone, you should give them something

---
[2] Noble Qur'ān, Sūrah Āl 'Imrān (3), Verse 92.

that they would like and want, not what you necessarily want. A gift that you give is meant to make the other person happy first and foremost. As such, it is about prioritizing the other person over yourself.

A person should make sure to give one's best self to your spouse. Do not leave the crumbs for them after you have given your best to everyone else; and yes that "everyone else" includes your parents, friends, bosses, and children.

We are very good at watching what we say and do in front of other people. We understand that despite some of our difficult emotions inside, it is often counterproductive to unleash ourselves on others.

Yet many of us forget that our spouses also have the right to our good and best selves. They are human beings who deserve good comportment, respectful behavior, and proper communication from us as well. Your spouse should be the most important person in your life, and as such deserves the best side of you. This is the best gift that anyone can give to one's spouse.

Identify with God Rather than the "Self"

من تزوج فقد أحرز شطر دينه فليتق الله في الباقي.

Prophet Muḥammad ﷺ said: *"When a person gets married, they have fortified half of their religion, so they should have God-consciousness in the rest (other half)."* [3]

One of the greatest obstacles and threats in a marriage is selfishness. This is why when it comes to marriage, our task is to get married and live a married life for the pleasure of God. Doing so will take our focus off of ourselves and repurpose our actions with a moral and compassionate objective. Acting in accordance to the Will of God through following His rulings (*Aḥkām*) will play a special role

[3] Shaykh Ṭūsī, *Al-Amālī*, P. 518.

in our happiness - both in this world and the next.

Whenever you are in a conflict, observe how much of your inner "self" is involved and how much God is present. The more you identify with the "I" and "me" - the stronger the chance that your mind will have less focus on compassion. The end result will be that you see things less clearly, and will have to suffer and struggle more in resolving your conflicts and disagreements.

When you identify with God's perspective as taught to us in the Qur'ān and by the Ahlul Bayt 🕮, we are forced to acknowledge that we ourselves are sinners, and that others have rights upon us and deserve compassion when they make mistakes. If God is All Compassionate and All-Forgiving toward us, then do other human beings - especially our spouses - not deserve the same from us?

The Importance of Small Gestures

ما استجلبت المحبّة بمثل [بامثل من] السّخا و الرّفق و حسن الخلق.

Imām ʿAlī 🕮 said: *"Nothing will bring forth love better than generosity, gentleness, and good character."* [4]

In marriage, small gestures can go a very long way in improving one's relationship. Think of a number of small things that your spouse would like and make a list of them. Try to do some of them every day to increase the love between you.

For example, you can make them some tea or give them a cold drink, or drop everything you are doing to greet them at the door when they come home. Then try to make a list of the excuses you may have for not doing them and give them up.

Small gestures are important because they continuously remind your spouse that you love, value, care, and support them in their life. It is very easy to feel alone and isolated in this modern world,

---

[4] *Ghurar al-Ḥikam wa Durar al-Kalim*, P. 289.

so even small gestures will make your spouse feel that they are not alone, but they are loved, seen, heard, and appreciated. Try making a list of what some things your spouse likes and see how you can incorporate these small gestures into your day.

Commit yourself to doing these small things every day, and it is highly likely that your relationship will begin to get its spark back.

Improve Marriage to Prevent Marital Deterioration

Go Back in Time: Fix Your Marriage

وَ أَنْ لَيْسَ لِلْإِنْسَانِ إِلَّا مَا سَعٰى

"And there is nothing for a person except that for which one strives."[5]

One of the major dysfunctions of marriages today is that people stay in the past, however this not only ruins their present, but it will also ruin their future as well.

Yes, you can go back in time to some extent, and fix your marriage and other relationships - figuratively speaking; but what is important is not to stay there.

One may ask: "How can we go to the past and fix it?" Our past is not a concrete and objective set of events, at least insofar as our minds process it.

Our minds are in a perpetual state of reinventing, reinterpreting, and reshaping what we think about the past - based on our current state of awareness, knowledge, and emotions. Countless couples complain about how horrible or mediocre their spouses have been in the years of their marriage even though things were not really that bad. Oftentimes it happens that after a person shares one's painful experiences and gets some advice, they realize upon reflection that

[5] Noble Qur'ān, Sūrah an-Najm (53), Verse 39.

their situation is not as bad and pessimistic as they thought it was.

Alternatively, there are many couples who say the opposite - how positive their marriages have been over the decades despite some of the greatest difficulties and rocky relationships they have had to face in the past.

For this reason, the past in everyone's mind is fluid. Based on one's current emotional state: some things are remembered, other things are forgotten and dismissed, some things are exaggerated, and others are justified.

If your marriage or any other relationship is facing difficulties and the past is being brought up, do not lose hope. Be understanding and compassionate about the feelings of the past that are being discussed, and acknowledge and show that you understand the other person's frustrations, then follow it with a loving action. Although the event happened in the past, the emotions are still very raw in the present. By addressing these current feelings, you can also help heal the past. By healing the emotions, positive behaviors will also follow. This exercise in compassion for others is a critical tool in fixing and healing yourself, your hurts, and your resentments.

So begin with improving yourself, not your spouse; and as you grow, so will your spouse. Trying to change your spouse will most likely backfire.

It may take some time, but work on building positivity in your present state. Slowly, but surely, you will see that both you and your spouse will begin to see the past in a more positive light. Instead of seeing it as a dark episode in your life, you will look back on it with a sense of triumph and pride which will further strengthen your present and future marriage.

Forgiveness is a Gift to Yourself

وَجَزَٰٓؤُا۟ سَيِّئَةٍ سَيِّئَةٌ مِّثْلُهَا ۖ فَمَنْ عَفَا وَأَصْلَحَ فَأَجْرُهُۥ عَلَى ٱللَّهِ ۚ
إِنَّهُۥ لَا يُحِبُّ ٱلظَّـٰلِمِينَ

"And the requital of evil is an evil like it. But whoever forgives and reconciles, their reward will be with God. Indeed, He does not love the evildoers." [6]

Usually when we forgive people, we think that we are doing them a favor. We may even feel that it is a form of charity. But this is the opposite from reality.

There is a Taoist story about a sage who gave his disciple an empty sack and a basket full of potatoes. The sage asked his disciple to think of all the people whom he had not forgiven in his life, and then for each person he was to carve out his or her name on a potato and put it in the sack. After he had finished the task, the sage asked his disciple to carry the bag with him for a week everywhere he went.

After a week, the disciple came back. The sage asked him how the week went by. He responded that initially it was very easy to carry the bag, but after some time it began to feel heavy and burdened him. After a few more days, the potatoes started to rot and they began to emit a foul smell that irritated him and made him feel very sick.

The sage then responded that not forgiving others is a similar comparison. At first we do not feel anything, but after a while it takes a toll on us and begins emitting a stench in our lives that makes us feel sick. It is therefore very important that we learn to forgive others - not for their sake, but for our own sake.

Forgiveness is a gift that we give to ourselves. It helps us to grow and attain humility. It is the best favor which we can give to ourselves.

Not forgiving others will only end up tormenting us in the future.

Holding on to anger and hatred is like holding on to a hot iron with our bare hands expecting to throw it at the person who offended us, but we will end up hurting ourselves the most.

What does this mean? Resentment is a difficult emotion to hold

---

[6] Noble Qurʾān, Sūrah ash-Shūrā (42), Verse 40.

on to. It makes us angry, agitated, and can bring upon despair. The one who holds onto the resentment is often inflicted with more mental and emotional pain than the one whom the resentment is directed toward. It will leave a stench in our lives everywhere we go - just like the rotten potatoes in the story above.

Forgiving does not mean that you forget; rather it is letting go of resentment. By doing so you free yourself from a prison of negative emotions, and allow yourself to gain a better perspective; then ultimately, it helps you relate to your spouse in a wiser way that will not only help your spouse, but will improve the future of your marriage as well.

How does this happen? You reach some kind of resolution in your mind with your spouse regardless of the outcome, then you consciously disconnect their future mistakes with the past resentments that you may be holding onto - keeping in mind that this is how you would like to be treated if you were in their position. This entails a lot of conscious effort, but with practice it can lead to success.

The Power of Humor

أحب الأعمال إلى الله إدخال السرور على قلب المؤمن.

Imām al-Bāqir ﷺ said: *"The most beloved of actions to God is to bring joy to a believer's heart."*[7]

Marriage is filled with emotions and passion. Judging one another based on cold facts will not get you anywhere. Marriage is not a business where things can be resolved and managed in all seriousness.

One of the best tools for fostering a good marriage is humor. Sometimes it may not work because one is using it at the wrong

[7] Al-Barqī, Aḥmad ibn Muḥammad ibn Khālid, *Kitāb al-Maḥāsin*, 2 Vols., Ed. Jalāl al-Dīn Muḥaddith, (Qum: Dār al-Kutub al-Islāmīyah, 1371/1953), Vol. 2, P. 388.

time, or it may be interpreted as sarcasm, so a person must be mindful and cautious about when and how to use it. Aggressive humor, such as when you make fun of your spouse, or when you are trying to distract them from anxiety or serious problems, can make things worse.

Humor can be very helpful though if you are simply trying to create a more relaxed atmosphere in order to help facilitate reconciliation. This is usually beneficial after tense situations have calmed down, or if the argument was over something minor and benign.

Couples who laugh together (but not at each other) are naturally happier and more intimate with one another.

Prophet Muḥammad ﷺ always used humor with his family and friends. One day the Messenger ﷺ and Imām ʿAlī ؑ were eating dates next to each other. As the Prophet ﷺ ate his dates, he would discretely place the seeds from them next to the seeds of Imām ʿAlī ؑ. Once they both finished eating, all of the seeds were piled in front of Imām ʿAlī ؑ. At this moment, the Prophet ﷺ [jokingly] said to the Imām ؑ: *"O ʿAlī! You ate way too much!"* Imām ʿAlī ؑ [jokingly] responded back: *"The one who ate them all with their seeds even is the [actual] one who ate too much!"* [8]

Try discussing with your spouse what humor means to them, and what they like to laugh at, versus what they feel offended or sad about; and then discuss what you like and what offends you.

Seven Things which Harm Communication

أوصيكما ... بتقوى الله ، و نظم أمركم.

Imām ʿAlī ؑ said: *"I advise you... to have God-consciousness, and to organize your affairs."* [9]

---

[8] Narāqī, Mullāh Ahmad (narrated from 1001 stories from the life of Imām ʿAlī ؑ), *Al-Khazāin*, (Muhammad Redha Ramzī Owhadi, Saʿid Novin Publication).

[9] *Nahj al-Balāghah*, Ed. Ṣubḥī Ṣāliḥ, (Qum: Hijrat, 1414/1993), P. 421.

If we lack discipline and organization in how we communicate with our loved ones, then our lives may fall into great difficulty. The following are seven points that can harm us from having good communication in our relationships:

1. **Not having a proper schedule.** For example, not being at home at consistent times (if one can help it), or not having enough time or a good schedule to connect with our family members.
2. **Being addicted to social media.** This means that a person spends way too much time on one's smartphone or other gadgets in the presence of one's spouse. Even though one may physically be there, they are mentally and emotionally not present.
3. **Excessive family social events.** Couples need to have their own private time. Although it is important to have extended family social gatherings, family time together does not mean that the extended family has to be there for all occasions.
4. **Grudges and animosity.** When a person holds onto grudges, they are like a ticking time bomb that can blow up at any time, even when one thinks they are having a good time. Practice forgiveness, and letting go of resentments (as was detailed in our previous section on forgiving one's spouse).
5. **Shyness.** Excessive shyness can prevent a person from being able to express one's feelings, needs, and expectations. With shyness, humor also becomes rare. As an individual's feelings get bottled up, sooner or later one will blow up as well.
6. **Fearing that the other person will get angry.** If one spouse is hot-tempered such that the other spouse

cannot even talk to them, then this will prevent one from communicating with them, and in the long term this will lead to one emotionally bottling things up.

7. **Not having personal time to talk.** Personal scheduled time is vital, otherwise healthy communication will break down, and as the days go by and family and work life increase, communication will further deteriorate. Lack of communication will lead to keeping issues unresolved and bottle up resentments.

Give Your Spouse Gifts

تهادوا تحابوا، فإن الهدية تذهب بالضغائن.

Imām aṣ-Ṣādiq ﷺ said: *"Exchange gifts and love, because gifts eliminate grudges."*[10]

Giving gifts is a way to express to your spouse how much you care and understand them. Gifts also activate reward mechanisms and positive feeling systems in the brain that help decrease tension and feelings of resentment.

You do not have to get expensive gifts all of the time. What is important is that they are considerate and thoughtful.

When giving gifts, keep this in mind: Your goal is to make your spouse happy, not yourself. Give your spouse a gift that they would like and want, otherwise the giving of gifts may backfire.

Think about what your spouse likes and what will make them happy, and create a list to help you know what type of gifts you can give them. If you cannot think of anything, then ask your spouse about their interests.

[10] *Al-Kāfī*, Vol. 9, P. 746.

Improving Marriage Before and After Conflicts

"Saving" Your Marriage can Make it Worse

العاقل من تجرع الغصة حتى ينال الفرصة.

Imām al-Kāẓim relates [that Prophet Muḥammad once said]: *"Surely an intelligent person is one who holds oneself back until they get the opportunity for something good."* [11]

Avoid using quick fixes all of the time for everything. Quick fixes are like Tylenol, they may be useful for the time being, but they are not real solutions. For example, buying flowers for someone after a fight. Flowers are thoughtful and nice, but they will not resolve the root of the issue.

Quick fixes seem easy, but they can sometimes even be dishonest and will not tackle the root of the problems you may be facing. They may give you short term satisfaction, but in the long term they can be counterproductive.

Sometimes trying to "save" your marriage could end up having the opposite effect. This is because your mind goes into survival mode. Anyone familiar with being in survival mode will know that it makes people very tense. Being tense leads people to hypersensitivity, anger, and eventual resentment. You can imagine that being in such an emotional state will not get you far, and it can make matters worse, thus hastening the deterioration of your marriage.

Another approach is to let go of this survival mode. Try being grateful instead. When you are grateful, you think more clearly and become more creative. More importantly, your emotional and spiritual states will end up changing: you will become more compassionate, less tense, less angry, more genuine, less fake, and

---

[11] *Biḥār al-Anwār*, Vol 6, P. 52.

more real. Even if you are criticized or insulted, you will be more patient and take it less personally.

Your aura (*haybah*) will also end up changing, and it will inevitably affect your spouse. Real positive energy is contagious. Remember our previous recommendation: You cannot change your spouse through sheer will, you can only change them by changing yourself.

Here is a good activity to perform: Take a piece of paper and write down a number of things that you are grateful for that are present in your spouse (it can be 5, 10, or more things). Under each point, elaborate what you mean by it. It is not enough to just list some things, the emotional effects of elaboration are much more effective.

Another activity could be to buy yourself a daily planner, and use it every day to write one positive thing about your spouse. It can be something that they did or did not do, or just some general feeling. Keep it a secret, and after one year give it to your spouse and see their reaction.

These exercises in gratitude will do wonders for your relationship and your state of mind.

Mental Distance Prevents Marital Improvement

هُنَّ لِبَاسٌ لَكُمْ وَأَنْتُمْ لِبَاسٌ لَهُنَّ

"Your spouses are garments for you,
and you are garments for them." [12]

Humans are complex beings and cannot be simplistically limited to one or two things. We are holistic beings, thus need to be understood on multiple levels in order to be healthy and have healthy relationships. Our complex needs range from physical, mental, emotional, and spiritual plains. Only focusing on one aspect

[12] Noble Qur'ān, Sūrah al-Baqarah (2), Verse 187.

can lead to the destruction of oneself and one's relationships.

A common problem in our community is mental distance between couples. Mental distance often leads to parallel lives in a marriage. Some couples believe that just because they are physically present with each other, all is well in their marriages. Mental and emotional distance can sometimes be worse than physical distance. This means that although the couple is in the same house or even in the same room, they barely interact with one another, or when they do it is just superficial and cold.

In order to close the gap on emotional distance, try doing a fun couple's activity at least once a week so as to preserve and grow the integrity of your connection. Make sure that these activities allow for some conversation. For example, going to the movies is sometimes not the best idea as that is not an ideal place for improving communication.

Make a list with your spouse of some different activities that you want to do together, then cut each idea and put it in a jar, every week you can pick one paper and do that activity.

Do Not Text Important Conversations

نٓ ۚ وَالْقَلَمِ وَمَا يَسْطُرُونَ

"Nūn. (I swear) By the Pen and what they write." [13]

Texting is a useful tool for small and quick messages. But for important conversations, texting can be a disaster. True emotions and tones can be misinterpreted, contexts can be missed, and important clarifications can be omitted. This can lead to difficult and damaging misunderstandings.

Save your important conversations when you are with your spouse in person. Seeing their face, tone, and the facility of expressing oneself can save couples from many regrets later on.

[13] Noble Qur'ān, Sūrah al-Qalam (68), Verse 1.

Do Not Poke a Sleeping Bear

وإذا اسيئ إليكم فاعفوا واصفحوا كما تحبون أن يعفى عنكم.

Imām ʿAlī ﷺ said: *"If someone wrongs you [or does something bad to you], then forgive them and turn a blind eye to it just as you would like others to be forgiving toward you."*[14]

العفو عند القدرة من سنن المرسلين و المتقين.

Imām aṣ-Ṣādiq ﷺ said: *"Forgiving people while being in a state of power is the practice the Prophets and the pious ones."*[15]

Bringing up bitter past and hurtful events and weaknesses is like poking a sleeping bear. It will wake up and attack you. So avoid the following at all costs:

1. Do not talk about or repeat known weaknesses. This will not help them resolve their mistakes, it will just generate resentment.
2. Do not talk about sensitive topics. For example, the parent of your spouse may have committed an immoral act and they do not want to talk about it. If you keep bringing up that issue it may lead to a fight and make your spouse feel emotionally unsafe with you. Pay attention to what subjects your spouse is sensitive about and do not address those. If you insist on bringing up sensitive subjects, then it will create animosity which can lead to emotional divorce between couples.

---

[14] Al-Ḥarrānī, Ḥasan ibn ʿAlī, *Tuḥaf al-ʿUqūl*, Ed. ʿAlī Akbar Ghaffārī (Qum: Jāmiʿ-yi Mudarrisīn, 1404/1983), P. 151.

[15] *Biḥār al-Anwār*, Vol 68, P. 423.

Improving Marriage When You are Together

Washing Dishes the Right Way

أكمل المؤمنين إيماناً، احسنهم خلقاً، و خيارکم خيارکم لنسائه.

Prophet Muḥammad ﷺ said: *"The most perfect in faith are those who have the best manners, and the best among you are those who are the best with their wives."* [16]

One of the best ways to bond with one another is to do household chores together. This can be cleaning, doing laundry, or whatever else you have to do around the house. Doing these activities together can bring more blessings of God into your home.

Washing the dishes is an excellent way to help out your spouse, but what would make them happier and your marriage even better is if you dried the dishes, put them back in their proper spots, and cleaned the counter as well! People do not like having to put away a mountain of dishes!

Oftentimes, people want to do good deeds, but sometimes those good deeds are incomplete or end up creating more work for our spouses. Let us be considerate and complete the job! They will surely be appreciated by our spouses.

Remember what was mentioned earlier: Small gestures are important because they continuously remind your spouse that you love, value, care, and support them in your marriage. It is very easy to feel alone and isolated in this modern world, but small gestures will help make your spouse feel that they are not alone, rather they are loved, seen, heard, and appreciated.

Reciting Daily Prayers Together

وَأْمُرْ أَهْلَكَ بِالصَّلَاةِ وَاصْطَبِرْ عَلَيْهَا ۖ لَا نَسْأَلُكَ رِزْقًا ۖ

[16] *Al-Kāfī,* Vol. 3, P. 256.

نَّحْنُ نَرْزُقُكَ ۗ وَالْعَاقِبَةُ لِلتَّقْوَىٰ

"And enjoin prayer upon your family, and be steadfast in maintaining it. We do not ask for sustenance from you, it is We who sustain you, and the [best] outcome will be for the God-conscious ones." [17]

Spending quality time with someone is not only about physical interaction. There needs to be emotional, mental, social, and spiritual bonds as well. One of the best ways to build spiritual bonds is by performing religious activities together.

These can include reciting the Qur'ān together, having a good religious discussion, or reciting congregational prayers (*Ṣalātul Jamāʿah*) with one another. These activities have a great impact on the heart, and can align people's missions and visions to be in harmony for the future.

Many couples 'think' that they are spending time together, but in actuality they are not. They may be watching TV side by side, or silently browsing their smartphones, however these things are not really quality times spent together, on the contrary they may even deteriorate a marriage by cutting off time for healthy activities that couples could be doing together instead.

An under-appreciated activity for the good health of a marriage and family is praying *Ṣalātul Jamāʿah* together at home. There is a famous saying which says that "Families who pray together, stay together." Not only is it a means for increasing the bounties and blessings of Allah in a household, but it is also a way for spouses to connect with each other spiritually. Other activities can be reading the Qur'ān together, or discussing the traditions of the Prophet ﷺ and his Ahlul Bayt ﷺ.

Our spiritual lives are at the foundation of our emotional and psychological health and well-being, and spiritual health built

---

[17] Noble Qur'ān, Sūrah Ṭāhā (20), Verse 132.

together between couples will bring about good emotional and psychological health in a marriage.

Think about the other ways you can connect spiritually with your spouse on a daily basis.

Presence versus Being Present: Healthy Family Activities

إذا أنفـق الرجـل علـى أهلـه نفقـة وهـو يحتسـبها كانـت لـه صدقـة.

Prophet Muhammad ﷺ said: *"When a man spends something on his family, intending to receive [God's] reward, it will be regarded as charity for him."* [18]

Spending money is not the only way you can give something to your family - spending time is often even more important.

Quality presence is much more needed and beneficial for one's spouse than just physical presence which does not have any meaningful results.

There is a big difference between presence and being present. You may be sitting at home with your family, but you may have no presence because you are fixated on your computer, tablet, smartphone, TV, or talking on the phone. Being present is therefore not enough. Learn to focus on your spouse and children with complete presence if you want to have a healthy family.

Communication is key for a healthy marriage, and often technology - which is supposed to facilitate communication - becomes a barrier to this as it creates bubbles which can lead to mental distance between couples.

A good way of being present is to focus on activities that you can both do together, such as cooking, lawful board games, nightly

[18] As-Suyūṭī, Jalāl ad-Dīn, *Ad-Durr al-Manthūr fī Tafsīr al-Mathūr*, 6 Vols., (Qum: Kitāb-Khānayi Ayātullāh Marʿashī Najafī, 1404/1983), Vol. 1, P. 337.

walks, or listening to religious lectures. These kinds of activities will build strong bonds through mindful presence and good communication.

Feed Your Spouse with Admiration and Compliments

من لم يشكر المخلوق لم يشكر الخالق.

Imām ar-Riḍā ﷺ said: *"A person who does not thank the creations (other people) has not thanked the Creator."* [19]

The expression of gratitude and thankfulness is a quality of righteous people. It is a well-known tradition of Prophet Muḥammad ﷺ and his Household to always thank other people. If we want to see positive results in our marriages, then we must start with compliments and gratefulness toward our spouse.

Start Your Conversations with Praise

كـن كالنحلـة إذا أكلـت أكلـت طيبـا، وإذا وضعـت وضعـت طيبـا، وإذا وقعـت علـى عـود لـم تكسـره.

Imām ʿAlī ﷺ said: *"Be like a bee: When it consumes, it consumes something good (nectar). When it gives, it gives something good (honey). When it lands upon a reed, it does not break it."* [20]

When a bee comes to a flower, it takes what is best (nectar); but when a fly comes, it takes the worst (excrement). A honeybee gives the best - which is honey, whereas a fly gives disease. When a honeybee sits on a flower, that flower's life grows by one and a half times; but

---

[19] Shaykh Ṣadūq, *ʿUyūn Akhbār ar-Riḍā*, 2 Vols., Ed. Mahdī Lājurdī, (Tehran: Nashr-i Jahān, 1378/1958), Vol. 2, P. 24. This tradition also comes in a slightly different version: *"A person who does not thank the granter of blessings from among the creations has not thanked Allah, Exalted is He."*

[20] *Ghurar al-Ḥikam*, P. 532.

when a fly sits on a flower, then its lifespan can be reduced to a half.

We should be like honeybees in our marriages, and give the best we have to offer; we must not be like flies.

The most successful communication in marriage always begins with praise. People are most impressionable at the beginning of their conversations, for it sets the mood on how the rest of the interaction is going to be like. Starting your conversation on a positive note and tone will generally set a beneficial and upbeat feel with your spouse for the rest of the day. On an alternative note, do not be shocked when things go downhill if you start off talking with criticism. The first words of your day will tend to have a domino effect for everything else.

Therefore, always be gentle like a bee. Bring and take with you what is the best and sweetest.

Improving Your Marriage When You are Apart

Answer When Your Spouse Calls

وَإِذَا حُيِّيْتُمْ بِتَحِيَّةٍ فَحَيُّوْا بِأَحْسَنَ مِنْهَا أَوْ رُدُّوْهَا ۗ إِنَّ اللّٰهَ كَانَ عَلَىٰ كُلِّ شَيْءٍ حَسِيْبًا

"And when you are greeted with a greeting, greet with a better one than it, or return it (in a similar manner); indeed Allah takes account of all things." [21]

Communication is an essential part of marriage. Due to busy lives and schedules, couples often have to be away from each other. However, through technology we can keep communicating with one another even though we may be physically apart. Based on the teachings of the Qurʾān, if someone approaches us with a greeting, it is obligatory for us to return the greeting. This applies to long distance communication via text or phone calls as well. It is our duty

---
[21] Noble Qurʾān, Sūrah an-Nisāʾ (4), Verse 86.

to respond to other people, especially our spouses.

Do your best to pick up the phone when your spouse calls. If you do this, then the underlying message you give to your spouse is that they are important. This will go a long way in the prosperity of your marriage.

We are quick to pick up the phone if our boss calls. However, our boss will not be with us whenever we need them, but our spouses most likely will be. Making our spouses feel like they are a priority in our lives is a feeling that will most often end up being reciprocated by them.

Of course, if you are in a tight situation you may not be able to pick up the phone at that moment. However, make sure to call your spouse back when you are immediately free thereafter. Do not wait until you get back home to catch up with your spouse, unless you have an understandable and valid reason.

Be With People who Support Your Marriage

قال رسول الله (صلّ اللّه عليه وآله وسلّم): المرء على دين خليله فلينظر أحدكم من يُخَالِل.

Prophet Muḥammad ﷺ said: *"A person will follow the religion of one's friend, so look at whom you befriend."*[22]

Make sure to surround yourself with people (especially friends and family members) who do not entice you to compromise your etiquettes (*akhlāq)* and compassion, when it comes to your spouse.

Many marriages would have worked out well if it was not for the ill advice and bad encouragement of other people.

Having a good friend or companion can save a person's marriage, and make one's future better for years to come.

[22] *Al-Kāfī*, Vol. 4, P. 122.

General Recommendations

5 Tips on How to Forgive Someone

من لا يَرحم لا يُرحم.

Prophet Muḥammad ﷺ said: *"A person who does not show mercy (to others) will not be shown mercy [by God]."* [23]

If we want God to forgive us for our many sins, then we must be willing to forgive the sins of others.

There is nothing more destructive to your soul (*nafs*), your faith (*īmān*), and your spirituality than the constant remembrance of the wrongs that were done to you by someone else. By this, it means the inability to forgive someone by holding resentment against them. As was mentioned earlier, forgiveness does not imply that you have to forget what a person did to you (as that is almost impossible), but forgiveness means to not continue to have resentment toward them.

The remembrance and resentment against wrongs that builds up is a poisonous fruit of unhealed anger. Oftentimes, it will open the door to several other sins.

When people remember injustices that were done to them, and they become contemptuous, their anger and resentment will make them more prone to slander, gossip, listening to forbidden music, and commit other sins - small or big.

The constant remembrance and resentment of wrongs that others did to you contradicts what we seek from God for ourselves.

Prophet Muḥammad ﷺ taught us to recite the following prayer:

اِغْفِرْ لَنَا حُوْبَنَا وَخَطَايَانَا أَنْتَ رَبُّ الطَّيِّبِيْنَ

Which means: "(O God) Forgive us our sins and trespasses, You are the Lord of the pure ones."

[23] *Man lā Yaḥḍuruhu al-Faqīh*, Vol. 4, P. 380.

Here are some tips to help you forgive the wrongs done to you:

1. Remember your own sins, and how you want God to forgive you.
2. Remember how other people have forgiven you for the wrongs you did to them. Then think about your own hypocrisy in not forgiving the wrongs that other people committed against you.
3. Ask the person who wronged you for forgiveness, and be the first to say sorry even if you are not guilty. Try to teach others about forgiving others when they have been wronged. In this way, you may feel a little hypocritical and your "inner self" may try to reshape itself so that it can forgive.
4. Every time you remember the wrongs that a person has done to you, ask God to forgive you for your sins.
5. Finally and most importantly, talk to God about your weakness and inability to forgive. Ask Him to help you, and grant you the transformative grace needed to heal the spiritual sickness within you and allow you to truly forgive the person who has wronged you.

True forgiveness does not happen all of a sudden. It is a long and difficult process, and will happen one step at a time. Therefore, do not despair if you still have some resentment left in you.

Here is an interesting point: A true sign of whether or not you have forgiven a person is when a calamity befalls that person, you feel pity for them.

Relationship Maps

ليس منا من لم يحاسب نفسه في كل يوم.

Imām al-Kāẓim ﷺ said: *"A person is not from [among] us if*

they do not inspect themselves [in regards to their good and bad actions] every day."[24]

A critical aspect of marriage is to have checks and balances, along with goals and expectations.

Try mapping out your relationship by asking your spouse to make a list of five things that would make a great marriage. Discuss the points that are important to your spouse (not just you), and listen and reiterate those points as much as you can.

Have your spouse do the same.

Then create a new list which is acceptable to both of you (even if it is just one point) and build upon it. Stick it on the fridge so that neither one of you forgets to uphold it.

These maps will go a long way to help improve your marriage.

The Limits of an Outsider's Marital Advice

فَاسْأَلُوا أَهْلَ الذِّكْرِ إِنْ كُنْتُمْ لَا تَعْلَمُونَ

"Ask the People of the Reminder if you do not know."[25]

It is very important to refer to experts in matters concerning our lives. However, one of the worst mistakes that a person can make is referring to people who have partial or incomplete knowledge as they can often misunderstand things, and get the situation all wrong by only knowing one side or a fraction of the story. This is a downfall that one must avoid.

A potential problem with seeking marital advice from outsiders is that they often base their judgments and recommendations on limited evidence without knowing the entirety of the picture from both parties.

Marriage problems are usually in a gray zone, but how it may seem to others - especially people who are not qualified for marriage

[24] *Al-Kāfī*, Vol. 4, P. 269.

[25] Noble Qur'ān, Sūrah an-Naḥl (16), Verse 43.

counseling - is a picture that is largely black and white filled with disconnected anecdotes from a biased and emotional source.

It is always good to seek advice from others, but do not take it as the gospel truth or something that is completely correct as chances are that their recommendations may be as weak as their knowledge of the events in your marriage.

Try to read good marriage counseling books, or listen to good lectures on the internet, and learn the proper tools on how to manage your marital problems, and grow together as a result. With the proper knowledge, disposition, humility, and introspection into your own faults, you will be surprised at how good of a job you can do in repairing and improving your marriage.

Six Things to Avoid in a Conversation

وَلَا يَغْتَبْ بَعْضُكُمْ بَعْضًا

"And do not backbite one another."[26]

Marriage is beyond just spending time together or even a general friendship. Marriage covers all aspects of life, including the task of spiritual growth. Therefore, marriage must promote moral and spiritual discipline; and boundaries need to be observed that must not be crossed.

In your marriage conversations, take the following six points into consideration:

1. Do not talk about others.
2. Do not talk about past bitter events.
3. Do not talk about issues you do not have enough knowledge about.
4. Do not talk about known weaknesses.

[26] Noble Qur'ān, Sūrah al-Ḥujurāt (49), Verse 12.

5. Do not talk about sensitive issues and topics.
6. Do not talk about promises that you cannot fulfill.

When Honesty is Lacking in a Marriage

من عرف بالكذب لم يقبل صدقه.

Imām ʿAlī ﷺ said: *"One who is known for lying, [even] their truth will not be accepted."* [27]

Below are some of the consequences of lying in a marriage:

1. Your spouse will not be able to trust you even when you are telling the truth.
2. Even strong proofs will not be convincing enough.
3. Your spouse will be suspicious and distrusting of everything you do or say.
4. You will lose your respect and dignity at home.

Dishonesty comes with short term rewards but long term pains; and honesty comes with short term pain but long term rewards.

There is however, an important point to keep in mind. Being honest does not necessarily mean that you always have to say everything. There are instances when it is best to refrain from saying what you know, feel, or think. Here are some examples:

1. Revealing the secrets of other people.
2. Ruining someone's reputation.
3. Creating corruption (*fitnah*) or problems among other families.
4. Making fun of people.
5. Something that may put the other person or someone else in danger.

[27] Al-Laythī, ʿAlī ibn Muḥammad al-Wāsiṭī, *ʿUyūn al-Ḥikam wa al-Mawāʿiẓ*, Ed. Ḥusayn Bīrjandī, (Qum: Dār al-Ḥadīth, 1376/1997-1998), P. 430.

6. Big or little lies.
7. Jokes that are based on lies.

Things should always be in balance and one must avoid extremes.

Making Promises that You Cannot Fulfill

One day, Prophet Sulaymān (Soloman) ﷺ was watching two pigeons, one male and one female. The male pigeon said that he could bring the moon and the sun to the throne of Sulaymān. The female pigeon did not believe him so the male pigeon came to Prophet Sulaymān and started to complain to him. The Prophet was surprised that he made such claims. The male pigeon responded that this was just husband-wife talk. Prophet Sulaymān ﷺ answered that this kind of talk is sometimes okay, but eventually it will lead to a husband losing his credibility.

Respect and trust must be at the root of a healthy marriage. When a person makes promises that one cannot fulfill, then they will erode their own dignity in front of their spouse's eyes and decrease the respect and trust between the two of them.

Dignified character brings admiration in a marriage. To enhance this, make promises that you will be able to fulfill, and do your best to keep them. It is natural to fail sometimes, but your spouse should see that at least you tried your best.

3

Marriage as a Process of Transformation

From an Islamic perspective, there are four major purposes for marriage:

1. Peace and tranquility;
2. Spouses completing each other;
3. Spiritual and emotional growth, and satisfaction;
4. Bearing children and having a progeny.

If these four purposes have a common denominator that glues them together, then it will be a mission and vision in life that seeks for self-improvement and reformation of the soul. Without setting transformation as the ultimate goal of a marriage, one's relationship will not thrive. This is why people who base their marriages solely on lust often become disappointed, and sometimes even end up in divorce.

There are countless ways and approaches that one can take for self-transformation from the Islamic perspective. However, if we were to highlight three important fundamentals for transformation in the context of marriage, they would be the following things:

1. The nature of one's thoughts;

2. The capacity of patience in a person;
3. The ability to see the positive in people.

Let us elaborate on this more:

1. <u>Your Thoughts are the Foundation of Your Marriage</u>

When God created Prophet Ādam ﷺ, He created him from nothing. When he was presented to the angels, the angels bowed down to him. Then God asked Ādam ﷺ about how he felt being in such an elevated position as the representative of God on Earth. He had everything: position, health, youth, and possessions. Ādam ﷺ responded that he did not have any purpose, peace, or tranquility in his life. So in response to this, God created Lady Ḥawwāʾ (Eve) for him and married her to him. God then asked again how he felt after he held her hand, to which Ādam ﷺ responded: "O God, now I am in complete peace and tranquility." [1]

وَقُلْنَا يَا آدَمُ اسْكُنْ أَنْتَ وَزَوْجُكَ الْجَنَّةَ

"And We said: 'O Ādam, dwell you and your wife in paradise...'" [2]

Thoughts are the foundation of our relationships, and this includes our relationships with our spouses. Manage your thoughts and you will manage your relationships.

Our thoughts shape our perception of this world, along with our behavior and reaction toward it and the people dwelling therein. With our thoughts, we create the subjective world that we live in.

If our thoughts are positive, then we will be hopeful and gracious toward other living beings, including our spouses. Our relationships with others will also follow suit. On the other hand, if your thoughts are dark and negative, then chances are that is all you will find in life as well.

If your world and relationships are in a dark place and you want

---

[1] *Biḥār al-Anwār*, Vol. 9, Pp. 115-120.

[2] Noble Qurʾān, Sūrah al-Baqarah (2), Verse 35.

to change those dynamics, then start by observing the quality of your thoughts. Modify them and you will alter the world you live in through your mind.

2. Coming to Terms with True Patience

علامة الصابر في ثلاث: أولها أن لا يكسل، والثانية أن لا يضجر، والثالثة أن لا يشكو من ربه تعالى، لأنه إذا كسل فقد ضيع الحق، وإذا ضجر لم يؤد الشكر، وإذا شكا من ربه عز وجل فقد عصاه.

Prophet Muḥammad ﷺ said: *"The signs of the patient are three: the first is that a person is not lazy; the second is that one does not get irritated; and the third is that one does not complain against one's Lord, the Exalted. This is because if a person is lazy, then they will forfeit the truth; if one becomes irritated, then they will not be grateful; and if an individual complains against one's Lord, the Exalted, then they have disobeyed Him."* [3]

A hard, but true lesson in patience (*ṣabr*) in Islam is not when you are patient after being reprimanded for something you actually did, but when you are reviled for something that you are innocent of.

We are often able to be patient with our spouses when they scold us for something we obviously did wrong. However, in our community, it is not uncommon to see spouses being reprimanded for having done the right thing.

People are willing to forgive and be patient with their spouses when they scold them for their obvious mistakes, but it is very painful and hard to bear when they are criticized for doing the right thing or accused of having committed something wrong that they are innocent of.

In such cases, your greatest enemy will be anger. In order

[3] Shaykh Ṣadūq, *ʿIlal ash-Sharāʾiʿ*, 2 Vols. (Qum: Kitābfurūshī-i Dāvarī, 1385/1966), Vol. 2, P. 498.

to counter the anger and truly be patient, you must make your mind "compassion oriented." Compassion and forbearance are the antidotes to anger, and the foundation of patience in Islam.

What practical steps can we take in order to become compassion oriented? Here are a few guidelines to keep in mind:

1. Give your spouse the benefit of the doubt that they may be confused or may have misunderstood something. Perhaps you would have made the same assumption if you were in their position.
2. Your spouse is going through a really hard time and is not thinking straight.
3. Your spouse may have been negatively influenced by someone.
4. Your spouse may be basing their assumption on a particular offense that was repeated multiple times in the past.
5. Pick a good time when both of you are calm to discuss the matter further. If not, create a space where each of you can take turns talking without any interruptions.
6. Only state the facts that are in your defense. Do not, under any circumstances, attack your spouse's character or personality because of a false accusation.
7. If the matter is too heated or very serious, then have a religious counselor who is well versed in marriage issues to arbitrate your problem.

These are only some examples of various guiding ideas. There are many more that can fit into different kinds of scenarios. But there is one common denominator and underlying factor which will determine whether or not you will be able to get through the problem or not, and that is the management of your anger through compassion and patience.

In this sense, you can see how even difficult moments like these can become opportunities for increasing in patience and compassion, and thereby help you grow closer to God. As difficult as living in this world can be, the gift of redemption by God for the wrongs done to us in this world is always plentiful and present if we look carefully.

Make Excuses for Your Spouse

يَا أَيُّهَا الَّذِينَ آمَنُوا اجْتَنِبُوا كَثِيرًا مِنَ الظَّنِّ إِنَّ بَعْضَ الظَّنِّ إِثْمٌ ۖ

"O you who believe, avoid much suspicion. Indeed, some suspicions are sins." [4]

Do not despair when you experience or suffer heavy trials in this life at the hands of people. They are necessary for the upliftment of one's spiritual life. Try to see how you can blame yourself, but make excuses for your neighbor. Be humble and take ownership of your mistakes - no matter how small they may be.

If you can have this kind of an attitude toward trials, then above all it will be a test in humility, and you will be able to reduce the sway of your ego and pride over your heart. By practicing this kind of humility, you will acquire the blessings of the Almighty in your spiritual life which can then facilitate your ascent toward Him.

ജ്ഞ

In this next chapter, we are going to discuss a number of puzzles which have to do with these aspects of marriage and self-transformation with the following perspectives in mind: One must see marriage as a blessing and not a burden; one must change one's paradigm of marriage; and finally one must keep the end goal of marriage in mind - that it is not just a means of happiness, but salvation and spiritual growth.

---

[4] Noble Qur'ān, Sūrah al-Ḥujurāt (49), Verse 12.

Marriage: A Blessing or a Burden?

يا هشام! لو كان في يدك جوزة و قال الناس في يدك لؤلؤة ما كان ينفعك و انت تعلم انها جوزة و لو كان في يدك لؤلؤة و قال الناس انها جوزة ما ضرك و انت تعلم انها لؤلؤة.

Imām aṣ-Ṣadiq ﷺ said: *"O Hishām, if there is a walnut in your hand, but the people say that what is in your hand is a pearl, that will not benefit you because you know (for a fact) that it is a walnut. Similarly, if there is a pearl in your hand, but the people say that it is a walnut, then that will not harm you because you know (for a fact) that it is a pearl."*[5]

There is a popular sentiment in society that sees marriage as a burden. People often do not cherish the blessings of marriage until it is too late. They believe what they have in their hands is a walnut, but fail to see that it is actually a pearl. In other words, they only see the bad in marriage and what is lacking in it, thus they end up missing the blessings that are right in front of them. This section is about giving a different perspective on marriage, and how overall marriage is a great blessing with all of its difficulties and joys.

A Person who Loves God will Welcome Criticism

المؤمن يحتاج إلى توفيقٍ من الله، وواعظٍ من نفسه، وقَبولٍ ممن ينصحه.

Imām ʿAlī ﷺ said: *"A believer is in need [of three things]: [1] Divine providence, goodness, or success (tawfīq) [granted] from God; [2] admonishment or spiritual guidance from one's (own) soul; and [3] accepting the advice of one who advises them."*[6]

A person who truly loves God will welcome and benefit from both

[5] *Biḥār al-Anwār*, Vol. 75, P. 300.

[6] *Tuḥaf al-ʿUqūl*, P. 457.

praise and criticism. When praised, one will become more committed (to continue to do that good action); and when criticized, one will find an opportunity to repent and grow spiritually. However, when our egos and arrogance take center stage in the praise/criticism binary, that is when we need to re-examine the quality of our love for God.

There will be no real transformation unless we let go of our egos. There will be no betterment in our relationships or closeness to our Creator if we resist criticism or advice, and refuse to repent. Repentance does not need to be just about big things, it can be about small things as well, including matters where we are at fault - even if they account for a just small fraction of the reason.

By letting go of our egos and welcoming criticism, blinding veils will be lifted from our hearts, and we will be able to enter a new loving relationship with God and by extension, we will have a healthier relationship with our spouses as well.

True love is not possible for someone who has an ego.

Making Good Deeds a Harmonious Flow

وَإِنَّكَ لَعَلَىٰ خُلُقٍ عَظِيمٍ

"And indeed, you [O Muḥammad] possess great character."[7]

إنّما بعثت لأتمّم مكارم الأخلاق.

Prophet Muḥammad ﷺ said: *"Indeed I was sent to perfect the morals (and good character of people)."*[8]

What makes a person beautiful? Their deeds must not be random, single acts here and there, but one must create a beautiful and flowing story. This is why isolated acts of goodness are not enough to save marriages, and oftentimes they are not enough for the kind

[7] Noble Qur'ān, Sūrah al-Qalam (68), Verse 4.

[8] *Biḥār al-Anwār*, Vol. 16, P. 210.

of salvation that everyone desires in the Hereafter.

The word for manners in Arabic is *adab*. The word '*adab*' is also at the root of the word *adabiyāt* which means 'literature' in Arabic. This is because *adab* in Arabic means 'to put things in their right place.' In the world of literature, it means 'putting words in their right place.' In writing stories, *adab* is 'not only respecting grammatical rules, but also respecting the proper flow and logic of the story that one is writing.' In manners, it is 'to do, and say the right things in the right place and at the right time.'

We must all do our best to maintain our *adab* by reacting in the right way, in the right place, and at the right time. In each moment of our lives - whether it is desirable or not - we must strive to observe *adab* and not break 'the flow of our story.' If we do break the flow somehow or another, then we must correct ourselves. Through practice, we will get better and better at writing the story of our lives.

By observing proper etiquette in our *adab*, we will create beautiful life literature, and become the exemplary people that God intended us to be. [9]

Why was Prophet Muḥammad ﷺ considered as the best and most perfect human being? It was not just his outward appearance, rather it was because his entire life was a life of perfect harmony and synchrony. His life and complete existence was the perfection of *adab*.

When Criticized for Doing Something Right

وَالْكَاظِمِيْنَ الْغَيْظَ وَالْعَافِيْنَ عَنِ النَّاسِ وَاللّٰهُ يُحِبُّ الْمُحْسِنِيْنَ

"And those who restrain their anger, and excuse [the faults of] the people, and God loves the virtuous ones." [10]

---

[9] Throughout this book, most of our recommendations have been about how to uphold proper manners and etiquettes with our spouses and families.

[10] Noble Qur'ān, Sūrah Āl 'Imrān (3), Verse 134.

When you interact with someone, especially on a daily basis, it is obvious that you will make some common mistakes and run into routine problems. We tend to forgive those whom we do not have much interest in, and those who do not hold a lot of value in our lives, but when it comes to people of true value in our lives, we are often not too willing to forgive them.

One of the hardest feelings to deal with is to be scolded, criticized, attacked, or even betrayed by your spouse for having done something right. It is very discouraging and can often lead people to despair. However, it is important to note that from a spiritual perspective, such a situation can be a gift and gem in disguise. It is a rare opportunity for spiritual growth; and an opportunity to forgive and pray for someone who has clearly transgressed against you.

Forgiveness does not mean justifying your spouse's misdeeds, but it is letting go of resentment and praying that God will give the best to the person who hurt you. This may be an extremely difficult task, but try remembering all of the times that you sinned or did something bad, and were nevertheless forgiven by the All-Merciful Creator, and the people whom you hurt.

Therefore, be courteous enough to extend that kindness to others when they make mistakes, even when they do not admit to them or ask forgiveness for them. Try complaining less, and be humble enough to acknowledge your own faults as well. By forgiving and praying for your spouse, as well as recognizing your own faults and weaknesses, you will open the doors of the special grace of God, and immeasurable blessings will fill your life.

Be Grateful for Your Spouse's Criticisms

أحب إخواني إلي من أهدى إلي عيوبي.

Imām aṣ-Ṣādiq said: *"The most beloved of my brethren is the one who points out my flaws."* [11]

---
[11] *Al-Kāfī*, Vol. 4, P. 687.

We live by a faulty paradigm. We do not accept positive feedback, let alone criticism from our spouses or anyone else. We often take them as attacks against our personality even when they are not meant to be as such. If we change our paradigms toward building the best possible character and manners, then criticisms from our spouses - let alone positive feedback -will make us more mature and get us closer to our goal of personal transformation. It will actually make us grateful to our spouses for their criticisms.

However, spouses should also learn to criticize respectfully, and not insult the other person's character.

An important part of why we are sane is because we outsource a great deal of our sanity to others. This is one of the advantages of marriage in that our spouses act as constant checks in our behavior, reminding us that a certain joke is inappropriate, or such a phrase or action should or should not be done.

An ideal function of marriage is to keep us from becoming too eccentric in our behavior. So even when we think that our spouses are sometimes mean (of course, within reasonable limits), we should at least be grateful to them if they are fulfilling the role of helping us transform ourselves to become better human beings.

Success With God is Success With Marriage

ما بنى بناء في الاسلام أحب إلى الله من التزويج.

Prophet Muḥammad ﷺ said: *"Nothing in Islam has been established which is more beloved to God than marriage."* [12]

The mindset of doing everything for the sake of God will also change your perception about your successes and failures, particularly in your relationship with your spouse.

Doing what the Almighty wants you to do in the affairs you encounter on a daily basis will set the standard of seeing how

[12] *Man lā Yaḥḍuruhu al-Faqīh*, Vol. 3, P. 383.

successful you are and how you are leading your life.

With this kind of a mentality, you will find yourself more patient, polite, loving, and gentle, even when things are not going well. For example, if you are in a situation where your spouse or children make you angry and you respond with patience for the sake of pleasing God, you will feel successful.

But this is not just limited to a feeling. It will give you success in both religion (*dīn*) and this world (*dunyā*); and if you think about it, success in *dīn* and *dunyā* go hand in hand.

So what is the net result one may wonder?

Eventually, the pleasure of God will become so near and dear to you that you will use Islamic core values in every aspect of your life without having to think about it. It will become second nature through practice.

In conclusion, because your actions are based on the fact that you want to please God, you will find inner peace in everything you do. You will feel much stronger when you deal with disappointment and grief in life.

Changing the Paradigm of Marriage

Pray for Your Spouse Even When They Hurt You

وَالَّذِينَ يَقُولُونَ رَبَّنَا هَبْ لَنَا مِنْ أَزْوَاجِنَا وَذُرِّيَّاتِنَا قُرَّةَ أَعْيُنٍ
وَاجْعَلْنَا لِلْمُتَّقِينَ إِمَامًا

"And those who say: 'Our Lord! Give us from among our spouses and offspring comfort to our eyes, and make us a leader (an example) for the righteous ones.'" [13]

Even when you are severely hurt by someone, then whatever you do, do not respond in a similar way in deed or word. Go immediately toward God and pray for Him to help you, and recall all of the people

[13] Noble Qur'ān, Sūrah al-Furqān (25), Verse 74.

whom you have hurt or sinned against in the past. Then ask God to forgive you for your trespasses, and pray to Him for the worldly and spiritual success of the person who hurt you.

If the offense of the person was clearly sinful, then ask God to forgive that person with compassion and humility, not with a sense of arrogance and superiority. You will be surprised at how effective this can be in reducing potential resentment in your heart.

Transformation is a Long and Slow Process

يَا أَيُّهَا الَّذِيْنَ آمَنُوا اصْبِرُوْا وَصَابِرُوْا وَرَابِطُوْا وَاتَّقُوا اللّٰهَ لَعَلَّكُمْ تُفْلِحُوْنَ

"O you who believe! Be patient, and endure (stand firm), and be closely tied together, and be conscious of God so that you may be successful." [14]

One of the markers of a dignified person in Islam is the ability to see small incremental changes in people in a positive direction. These changes are - at first glance - hard to see but they show over time.

This is an important point to consider when we emotionally react to our spouse's mistakes. Yes, they will make them over and over again, but we need to be on the watch out for these little noticed positive changes. Perhaps not this year, but over the years (maybe even after a decade) - with your patience and help - you will see your spouse transform into someone better. This is how a life-long friend in marriage is acquired, not through abandoning them on the short run. Ten years of patience may be rewarded with 20 or 30 years of bliss.

From a Qur'ānic perspective, there is a reason why Allah's guidance is often symbolized as *Ṣirāṭ al-Mustaqīm* (the Straight Path) ...a path is something that people travel on at different paces - some fast, and some slow depending on the circumstances, such

---

[14] Noble Qur'ān, Sūrah Āl 'Imrān (3), Verse 200.

as: traffic, car crash, model of the car, etc. You can probably find appropriate analogies for these in your own spiritual life and realize that not everyone, including your spouse or children, goes at the same speed as you.

When I was in Qum, I asked my teacher how long I have to have patience with my spouse, He replied: *"You should be patient for a hundred years, after that you should be okay."* When further asked what this meant, he responded: *"You are not perfect either, so you need to have patience with her, just like she is being patient with you."*

Peace Comes with Letting Go of Grudges

فَاعْفُ عَنْهُمْ وَاصْفَحْ ۚ إِنَّ اللَّهَ يُحِبُّ الْمُحْسِنِينَ

"Forgive them and forebear (their mistakes), indeed God loves the virtuous ones." [15]

One of the greatest factors that can destroy our inner tranquility are the grudges we hold toward other people. The heart will not be able to be at peace until it wants good for those who have wronged it.

Marriage is not always easy. It is an on-going process that has its ups and downs, and its joys and heavy difficulties. This is natural as marriage is the union of two opposite egos. Our spouses will hurt us, and they will do so over and over again. That is a natural part of marriage.

But we must not let the hurt turn into grudges. Grudges are fertile grounds for revenge and resentment, two important ingredients in the destruction of not only our marriages, but also for peace and tranquility in our hearts. In this sense, our grudges will hurt us the most in this world.

Our heart will only know peace if we let go of grudges, and want the best for our spouses.

[15] Noble Qur'ān, Sūrah al-Mā'idah (5), Verse 13.

The End Result of Marriage

Change Yourself, Change Your Spouse

إِنَّ اللَّهَ لَا يُغَيِّرُ مَا بِقَوْمٍ حَتَّىٰ يُغَيِّرُوا مَا بِأَنْفُسِهِمْ

"Indeed God will not change what is in people (their condition) until they change what is within themselves."[16]

People look for change on the outside. But change cannot happen on the outside until what is within us also changes.

In other words, if we want to change the world, then we must change ourselves first. Oftentimes, the evil that we point out in the world is the same evil that runs through our own hearts. We cannot change the world for the better with corrupt hearts. Let us first begin with ourselves, then our immediate families, then our relatives and friends, and slowly expand from there. If one was to ask: *"Where is the best place to start from?"* The response would be: *"Work on your own manners and etiquettes (akhlāq), recite your prayers on time, and create a daily schedule,"* then see what happens.

Neuroscience teaches us that we have "mirror neurons." [17] By acting a certain way, the people who are close to us imitate or "mirror" our states of being. If you are having trouble with your spouse's behavior, sometimes the best way to change them is by changing yourself. Our spouses often reflect how we are, and vice versa, without us even being aware of it.

[16] Noble Qur'ān, Sūrah ar-Ra'd (13), Verse 11.

[17] Acharya, Sourya, and Samarth Shukla, *"Mirror Neurons: Enigma of the Metaphysical Modular Brain." Journal of Natural Science, Biology, and Medicine* 3, No. 2 (2012): Pp. 118-24.doi:10.4103/0976-9668.101878.

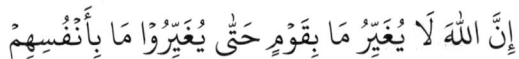

Bear Your Sufferings with Patience

ليس الشديد من غلب الناس إنما الشديد من غلب نفسه.

Prophet Muḥammad ﷺ said: *"The strong (ones) are not those who defeat (other) people. Rather, the strong (ones) are those who defeat their own egos."* [18]

We often think that success is found in ease, but true success is found in problems and suffering. With patience, through difficulties people can reach the highest levels of spirituality. Therefore, success can truly be found through hardship, patience, duties, and responsibilities.

Try to be steadfast when you are facing difficulties or suffering in your life, and try to defeat your ego, that way you will not only be at peace with yourself, but you will bring peace to others as well, including your spouse and your family.

However, if you keep on complaining, then you will lose the battle against your ego and lose that peace within yourself. You may, perhaps, even lose your salvation because this attitude will lead you to become ungrateful in life, dissatisfied with others, and ultimately resentful toward God. Reacting in an angry and selfish way will destroy your relationship, and further deteriorate your mind and soul.

Remember, one of the meanings of a *kāfir* in classical Arabic is an "ingrate."

Your Spouse's Problems can be Spiritual Medicine

وَعَسَىٰٓ أَن تَكْرَهُوا۟ شَيْـًٔا وَهُوَ خَيْرٌ لَّكُمْ

"It may be that you dislike something while it is good for you." [19]

[18] 'Ajlūnī, Ismā'īl ibn Muḥammad, *Kashf al-Khafā' wa Muzīl al-Ilbās*, (Maktabat al-'Ilm al-Ḥadīth, nd), Vol. 2, P. 197.

[19] Noble Qur'ān, Sūrah al-Baqarah (2), Verse 216.

Marriage is not just a remedy for lust, or for attaining temporary desire. Rather, it is a lifetime commitment and partnership for building the best in our worldly life (*dunyā*), and the hereafter (*ākhirah*). But commitment comes with challenges and sufferings. A person who launches a startup company will go through a lot of obstacles, but through these trials one will grow exponentially in experience and wisdom.

Sometimes God brings people into our lives to cause us problems in order to bring about patience and humility in our hearts. Unfortunately, instead of being grateful, we become angry and refuse to be reformed. It is like refusing to give thanks to a parent who gives a child bitter medication when they are sick.

Marriage is a process of transformation and reforming ourselves to become better individuals. This transformation cannot happen without dealing with ups and downs, and growing from the difficulties and conflicts that we experience with our spouses. If we approach marital tensions the right way, then the most important spiritual skills which we will develop are patience and humility—two key spiritual dispositions for union with the Almighty.

Just reflect your own past experiences: think of a time when you were in a situation which caused you a lot of stress or was a struggle for you, then look at how that helped you become a better person or helped you grow. Even small experiences or changes in our lives have ripple effects that affect so much more than we are often aware of.

Emotions Do Not Care about the Facts

وَجَعَلَ بَيْنَكُم مَّوَدَّةً وَرَحْمَةً

"And He (God) placed between you [husband and wife] love (affection) and compassion." [20]

[20] Noble Qur'ān, Sūrah ar-Rūm (30), Verse 21.

People usually pay more attention to emotional information rather than facts, so beware of your perception of reality when you are in an intense argument with someone, or when you are going through a difficult time.

In other words, if things are tense enough, then your spouse's emotions will not care about your facts. During these sensitive times, logical discussions will usually be counterproductive.

Instead, practice patience, compassion, and empathy. Think of the times when you were overwhelmed with emotions and how they prevented you from understanding or acknowledging facts. Use this empathy to actively listen to your spouse, and understand the emotions that they may be going through, instead of thinking about how "irrational" their emotions are at the moment.

This compassionate and empathetic support will not only help your spouse see things clearer later on, but it will also help develop your skills for compassion and empathy.

Remember that one of the Names of God is *ar-Raḥmān*, the All-Compassionate. For God, compassion or mercy (*raḥmah)* is part of His Essence. Although God has given us the quality of compassion in our souls, it is nevertheless a faculty that we need to develop through practice. By perfecting it, we will transform ourselves, and grow closer to God.

What better way to practice these qualities than with your spouse?

Marriage is There to Help You Grow

ليكن احبّ النّاس إليك من هداك الى مراشدك و كشف لك عن معايبك.

Imām ʿAlī ﷺ said: *"The most beloved among the people to you should be the one who guides you to right conduct, and discloses your faults to you."*[21]

[21] *Ghurar al-Ḥikam wa Durar al-Kalim*, P. 548.

Mistakes and flaws are part of human nature. Striving for perfection means that we should assist each other in correcting our imperfections.

In relation to the purpose of creation, the purpose of marriage is also to reach closeness and proximity to God (*qurb*), and in doing so, we need to help each other identify our faults and then overcome them.

Constructive feedback and accepting it is one of the tools for reaching the goal of our creation, namely, meeting God (*Liqāʾ Allah*).

A spouse supplies you with a pair of extra eyes, ears, and hands to help you be aware of your actions, and remind you of the purpose of creation even if they do so unconsciously. Accepting feedback, reflecting upon it, and attempting to apply it will take us one step closer to our ultimate goal.

Once we realize that our spouse is our helper, we will be more ready to accept and welcome critiques that come our way.

Do Not Love Codependently, Love Completely

لَّيْسَ عَلَيْكَ هُدَاهُمْ وَلَٰكِنَّ اللَّهَ يَهْدِي مَن يَشَاءُ وَمَا تُنفِقُوا مِنْ
خَيْرٍ فَلِأَنفُسِكُمْ وَمَا تُنفِقُونَ إِلَّا ابْتِغَاءَ وَجْهِ اللَّهِ وَمَا تُنفِقُوا مِنْ
خَيْرٍ يُوَفَّ إِلَيْكُمْ وَأَنتُمْ لَا تُظْلَمُ

"It is not up to you to guide them; rather it is God who guides whomever He wishes. And whatever good any of you spend, it is for your own benefit, as you do not expend but to seek God's pleasure, and whatever good you spend shall fully be repaid to you, and you will never be wronged." [22]

Codependence is a relationship phenomenon in which people depend on others for their sense of self-worth and dignity. They are happy if others are happy with them, they feel good about

[22] Noble Qurʾān, Sūrah al-Baqarah (2), Verse 272.

themselves if others feel good about them. It is a painful life to live. When codependent love happens in relationships, they can often turn into a disaster.

Codependent behavior in a marriage is not a form of respect, nor is it respected. Spouses will go out of their way to make the other partner happy and please them because they may want to manipulate their spouses into validating them and making them feel worthy. The driving factor behind such behavior is often toxic shame that grows worse, especially if the spouse in question suffers from childhood trauma where attention and approval were scarce growing up, and as a child they had to "perform well" in order to get their parents' love.

People consciously or unconsciously pick up on this kind of codependent or conditional love, and they do not like it. They often feel repulsed and sense that the love and kindness in question is not fully genuine.

So, what should a person do? First, an individual must repair one's own sense of dignity. One must learn that God is the source of absolute, unconditional love. He is the One, Who through His love, is the real giver of dignity and honor to human beings. Knowing this and believing it are two different things. It takes effort, reminders, and contemplation to internalize this fact. Second, one needs to love and be kind without expecting anything in return. A person should only expect the approval and grace of God. To put it differently, a person should love, be kind, and show compassion to one's spouse without being attached to any results. The only result one should anticipate is to attach oneself to God's pleasure.

This is not an easy thing to do. One will have lots of failures, but with each failure and mistake (no matter how embarrassing) one will learn and grow more. Over time with the practice of this virtue, God will in His own time allow a person to love more, love unconditionally, and thus love more freely. This is the only kind of true and genuine love and respect; not only will this make you as an individual happier, but others will also feel it.

A note of caution: You can assume codependence for yourself as you know yourself and your intentions. But do not assume your spouse to be codependent as you do not know that for sure. This assumption may lead to false judgment and blaming your spouse for something that is not true. When it comes to judging others, do so in the best manner. Keep judgments to yourself and not others.

4

Family and Raising Children

هُوَ الَّذِي بَعَثَ فِي الْأُمِّيِّينَ رَسُولًا مِّنْهُمْ يَتْلُوا عَلَيْهِمْ آيَاتِهِ وَيُزَكِّيهِمْ
وَيُعَلِّمُهُمُ الْكِتَابَ وَالْحِكْمَةَ

"It is He who sent to the unlettered people a Messenger from among themselves, to recite to them His verses, and to purify them, and teach them the Book and wisdom." [1]

One of the main purposes of marriage is to bear children and uphold the survival of humanity. Islam, like any other Abrahamic religion, emphasizes the importance of parental responsibilities toward children. It is quite clear that our understanding about caring for our families, tending to our marriages, and raising our children has evolved tremendously over the course of history. What we have today are the cumulative experiences of caring for our families from the time of Prophet Ādam ﷺ up until today.

In light of so much knowledge which has been gained, we know that any healthy development of a child must be holistic in nature. There are a myriad of factors which play into the holistic development of a child - from the household to society, peers, religious practices, school, technology, media consumption, and so much more. True strength is acquired by a child through considering the different

[1] Noble Qur'ān, Sūrah al-Jumuʿah (62), Verse 2.

parallel realms that they live in, from the spiritual and intellectual realms to the physical and cognitive ones.

If Prophet Muḥammad ﷺ taught us wisdom (*ḥikmah*) as the above verse states, it is the wisdom of the proper implementation of awareness (*maʿrifah*) and knowledge (*ʿilm*) in one's life. This comes from adopting a holistic approach toward existential development, and the transmission of that approach to the next generation. The purpose of this chapter is, to the best of our knowledge and understanding, an attempt to explain this process.

Our Personal Histories and the Self

Our personal histories - meaning the people and places in our lives - shape our brain's development. As Bruce D. Perry explains: "Our life experiences shape the way key systems in our brain organize and function," and consequently each of our brains becomes unique, and so do the ways each of us see and understand the world.[2]

Our life experiences in this world start in the womb. A child's fetal brain development is influenced by an array of factors, including the mother's diet, activity, stress, substance, and medication use. From the moment of conception, a child's life is intricately tied to other people, the mother obviously being the primary source of that relationship.

While growing up, Perry explains that a child experiences the world through the filter of adults. Even when a child does not understand language, they sense non-verbal communication such as the tone of a voice, and can feel anger, hostility, and even exhaustion, despair, and depression in speech from the parents. Since in the first years of life there are innumerable associations about how the world works, early experiences, and the 'emotional tone of the environment' one lives in, these will have the largest

---

[2] Perry, Bruce D. and Oprah Winfrey, *What Happened To You? Conversations on Trauma, Resilience, and Healing,* (New York: Flatiron Books, 2021), P. 29.

impact on an infant and young child.[3]

The home is the crux of much of what will shape a child's emotional and spiritual health in adulthood. The emotional and spiritual aspects go hand-in-hand. A nominally 'religious' home that is an emotionally hostile environment will produce poor emotional health in the child, and thus poor spiritual health. An emotionally healthy environment devoid of spiritual nourishment will not only lead to poor spiritual health, but it may also lead to poor emotional health as the primary human relationship that makes a human whole is a strong relationship with God.

The core of healthy and thriving communities begin with healthy families. Healthy families are predicated on successful marriages, and successful marriages are predicated on people who were raised emotionally intelligent and compassionate. It is a circle of life in which all elements support and feed into one another.

In this chapter, we will outline some of the major observations and techniques in what we believe contribute to healthy parenting, and the development of an emotionally and spiritually intelligent child. In this endeavor, we are guided by the teachings of Islam as promulgated by Prophet Muḥammad ﷺ, and the Imāms of his Holy Household, the Ahlul Bayt (a). We have also reviewed the expert opinions of a series of authors and specialists in the field of child development and human relations who have useful insights on this subject, including Marshall B. Rosenberg, Leonard Sax, Daniel J. Siegel, and some others.

As long as you have children, even if they are adults, these tools can always be helpful. But these insights are not just restricted to parenting, they are useful tools for cultivating compassion in any relationship, including those with other children, spouses, and friends. Compassion and emotional intelligence are not just tools for better living in this world, but they are essential ingredients for

[3] *What Happened To You? Conversations on Trauma, Resilience, and Healing*, Pp. 32-33.

a proper relationship with God and a prerequisite to real closeness (*qurb*) to Him.

Philosophy and Mindset of Raising Children

Introduction

It is common to see four different parenting styles in our community which can range from different levels of strictness, religiosity, and understanding. The first are those extreme religious types who isolate themselves and their kids from almost everyone and everything. The second are the permissive types with no boundaries. The third are those who robotically follow whatever psychology books tell them without even questioning them; and the fourth ones are the lost types who have no plan, no philosophy, and no balance when it comes to raising families.

These are the realities on the ground, and we as parents must strike a healthy balance and be holistic. We must have plans and a guiding philosophy for rearing our children. We should be religious, but not extreme. We should be open to what scientific research may tell us, while also being aware that scientific studies are not the be-all-and-end-all of knowledge. Children are trusts given to us by God and it is our duty to prepare them to have a healthy adulthood, and good afterlife.

Families are Founded on Marriages - Not Children

وَمِنْ آيَاتِهِ أَنْ خَلَقَ لَكُم مِّنْ أَنفُسِكُمْ أَزْوَاجًا لِّتَسْكُنُوا إِلَيْهَا
وَجَعَلَ بَيْنَكُم مَّوَدَّةً وَرَحْمَةً ۚ إِنَّ فِي ذَٰلِكَ لَآيَاتٍ لِّقَوْمٍ يَتَفَكَّرُونَ

"And among His signs is that He created for you mates from among your own selves that you may find tranquility in them, and He placed between you love and compassion. Truly there are signs in that for people who reflect."[4]

[4] Noble Qur'ān, Sūrah ar-Rūm (30), Verse 21.

The foundation of your family is not your children, but your marriage. You will ruin your marriage if your primary focus is your children, and thereby you will end up ruining your children as a consequence. If you want to have healthy children, then put your marriage and your spouse first. Work on creating **tranquility** in the marital relationship so that your children will benefit from it.

The primary source of a child's mental, spiritual, psychological, physical, academic, and emotional well-being comes from stability at home. Parents may have an excellent relationship with their children, but the children will sense it immediately if there is something off between the parents; and this will hurt and affect the children.

For all of the six development factors mentioned above, a child needs - above all - a sense of security. A child's sense of security comes from stability in the home which is founded on the stability of the relationship between the child's parents.

It is stability which will give a child the sense of security, to be curious enough to explore and take risks, to love compassionately and accept love, and to trust others, as well the ability to grow up with confidence, motivation, and a healthy sense of self-esteem. Usually, the best performing students even at school are the ones who come from stable marriage homes.

Studies have confirmed that children who witness abuse at home carry the same risk to their mental and physical health as if they had been abused directly. Brain imaging shows that infants - even when they are sleeping, or in the womb of their mothers - will have their brain wired differently by abuse at home when it happens to one of their parents. In fact, children who witness abuse at home sometimes show the same pattern of PTSD (Post-Traumatic Stress Disorder) as war veterans. Psychologists say that domestic violence can feel scarier to children than a war.[5]

[5] O'Donnell, Jayne and Mabinty Quarshie, *The Startling Toll on Children who Witness Domestic Violence is Just Now being Understood*, accessed July 30th 2020, https://www.usatoday.com/story/news/health/2019/01/29/domestic-violence-research-

Abuse is not just physical violence, it can be verbal and emotional as well, and the effects of all of them are similar, but at times some can be worse.[6]

The effects of witnessing such abuse are not temporary, and can last for even 20 years down the road, perhaps even the entire span of a person's life.[7]

Trauma at home can also happen from neglect. Just as children can be traumatized by parental neglect at home, they can also be traumatized if they see one parent neglecting the other and thus face adverse developmental experiences.

Do not underestimate the primacy of a strong and loving marriage between parents. If you value your children, then you must put your spouse first.

Do Not Always be Serious with Children

من كان عنده صبي فليتصاب له.

Prophet Muḥammad ﷺ said: *"Whoever has children in their presence should act like them (in a childish way)."* [8]

The main objective of parents is to guide their children to be good moral and spiritual citizens. Harshness, too much seriousness, and being too dry will make kids lose their connection to their parents and themselves. They may feel unsafe and unloved. Even if children listen and are obedient, they will hold grudges and resentment inside, and rebel later on in life.

---

children-abuse-mental-health-learning-aces/2227218002/.

[6] There is a whole subfield of psychology that deals with this phenomenon. It is often known as CPTSD (Complex Post-Traumatic Stress Disorder). See for example Pete Walker, *CPTSD: From Surviving to Thriving: A Guide and Map for Recovering from Childhood Trauma,* (Scotts Valley: CreateSpace Independent Publishing Platform, 2013).

[7] Ibid.

[8] Al-Ḥurr al-ʿĀmilī, Muḥammad ibn Ḥasan, *Tafṣīl Wasā'il ash-Shīʿah ilā Taḥṣīl Masā'il ash-Sharīʿah,* 30 Vols., Ed. Mu'assasāt Āl al-Bayt (Qum: Mu'assasāt Āl al-Bayt, 1409/[1988-1989]), Vol. 21, P. 486.

Seriousness is only needed when it is absolutely necessary. It can be useful in some ways - sometimes it is a quick solution to a life-threatening problem, sometimes it is needed for long-term important life issues, and at other times it is helpful to prevent major disasters. However, too much of it is counterproductive.

Appropriate humor with your kids or spouse can quickly lighten tense situations. Across several chapters, we have written about the importance of humor with our spouses. But sometimes we forget that humor is just as important with our children. Many parents make the mistake of treating their children like adults, and for them this means being serious almost all of the time. When parents are too serious, children feel emotionally abandoned, and this can be a recipe for many future mental and emotional health problems.

Humor is very important for a child's emotional and spiritual sustenance. Humor makes them feel loved, safe, and secure. Humor is a necessary ingredient for mental, emotional, and spiritual health, but like all things, it too must not be overdone.

Abuse is More than Just Hitting

ليس المؤمن بالطعان، ولا اللعان، ولا الفاحش، ولا البذي.

Prophet Muḥammad ﷺ said: *"A true believer is not involved in taunting, or frequently cursing (others), or in indecency, or abusing."* [9]

There was a story about a boy who first started school, he would get into trouble like many boys his age. As a punishment for his misbehavior, one of his teachers put him in a room all alone. As the lights in that room were automatic, they turned off and he was trapped in a dark room. Out of fear and terror, he ended up peeing in his pants. Although this was not done on purpose, the ensuing effects of this last until today.

[9] *Nahj al-Faṣāḥah*, P. 658.

This event was so traumatic for him that it eventually led to serious emotional problems and even learning disabilities in his teens. This story highlights the importance of holistic development with children, and how although we may do things with good intentions without the purpose of abuse (physical or emotional), actions which are done from ignorance can still be abusive and lead to long term consequences and effects.

It is important to remember that physically beating a child is not the only kind of abuse. There are other kinds of non-hitting discipline that can be just as damaging - if not more - than physically hitting a child. This can include humiliation (such as ridicule, comparison, etc.), neglect, prolonged isolation, ignoring, yelling, making threats, using foul language, intimidating facial expressions, or expressions of disgust.

Not only are these non-hitting forms of discipline abuse, but they are also potentially traumatic. Humiliation, screaming, or ignoring a child can have long lasting psychological and physical health effects - all the way into adulthood even.

Even directing these non-hitting types of discipline toward other siblings of the child, or verbally abusing one's spouse can carry the same traumatic effect as if they were done to the child directly.

These forms of discipline terrorize a child's soul and teach them to focus on the parent's reaction and how to manipulate it so as to avoid future terror, rather than encouraging the child to reflect on their own behavior and how to change it.

Fear-based Upbringing Corrupts Morality

إن النفس لجوهره ثمينة من صانها رفعها ومن ابتذلها وضعها.

Imām ʿAlī ﷺ said: *"Indeed the soul (nafs) of a person is a precious gem, and whoever protects it, exalts it; and whoever humiliates it, debases it."* [10]

[10] *Ghurar al-Ḥikam*, P. 227.

Any kind of abuse (physical or non-physical), inflicting terror, or any other fear-based upbringing of a child will create weak character. It will make children fearful and prone to anxiety in the long term. Children will become afraid of authority figures, will become approval seekers, people-pleasers, and lose their own identity in the process. They will become frightened by angry people, and will not be able to tolerate any personal criticism as adults. As a result, they will learn to suppress their feelings and have lower self-esteem.

Out of the fear of punishment, children learn to lie in order to avoid it. They learn to be dishonest, distort the truth, and manipulate people and their surroundings to make their environments safe, even when they do not have to do this. They learn to be hypervigilant at all times which keeps their bodies at high stress levels. This means that children's bodies will have unregulated stress hormone levels for extended periods of time which can lead to depression, anxiety, and autoimmune disorders.

Regular abuse or scaring children forces them to create masks, be fake and inauthentic which prevents moral growth and inhibits healthy and trusting relationships with others. Wearing masks prevents other people from seeing what truly lies beneath them.

A fear-based upbringing, although it can bring about quick results, will have long term effects on the physical and emotional growth of a child, and may even turn children into abusers in the future. Due to this fear, they lose their confidence and cannot optimize their own potential. This makes them easy targets to predators.

The Downstairs Brain vs. The Upstairs Brain

ما من تكبر أو تجبّر، إلا لذلّة وجدها في نفسه.

Imām aṣ-Ṣādiq ﷺ said: *"No one would be arrogant or haughty unless one feels a flaw in oneself."*[11]

[11] *Biḥār al-Anwār,* Vol. 70, P. 225.

Threats do not always have to be verbal. They can be anything scary that is also non-verbal, like the contorted facial expressions of anger, tone, and/or posture.

A child who misbehaves or is emotionally aroused is usually in a dysregulated state. Daniel S. Siegel states that when we become threatening, or when we act in emotionally dysregulated ways, we further trigger a child's "reactive downstairs brain." He identifies this area as the reptilian part of the brain, as opposed to the rational part of the brain which he calls the "upstairs brain."

The downstairs brain includes the lower regions of the brain which control our functions such as our heartbeat and breathing, as well as our impulses like hunger, and emotions like anger and fear. The upstairs brain controls our rational mental faculties and processes such as planning, decision-making, self-awareness, empathy, and morality.[12] Since the downstairs brain controls our fight, flight, or freeze responses, as well as our other impulsive emotional reactions, our upstairs brain functions to regulate emotions, instill calmness, helps with better decision-making, and regulates the emotions of the downstairs brain. When the upstairs brain is functioning well, then a person is more likely to be able to slow oneself down, think before acting, regulate emotions, self-soothe, and be understanding toward the feelings of others.[13]

When we as parents react in a dysregulated state, meaning when we react with our own downstairs brain, what we are essentially doing is "poking the lizard" in the child with our angry or panicked states.[14] What inevitably happens is that the emotions escalate for both the parent and the child by further activating *both* downstairs brains.

---

[12] Karen Pace, *Understanding the "Upstairs" and "Downstairs" Brain,* accessed June 7th 2021, https://www.canr.msu.edu/news/understanding_the_upstairs_and_downstairs_brain.

[13] Ibid.

[14] Siegel, Daniel S. and Tina Payne Bryson, *No-Drama Discipline,* (Bantam Books: New York, 2016), P. 47.

Siegel recommends that instead of reacting in this way, we can appeal to a child's more sophisticated brain by "demonstrating respect for our child, nurturing them with lots of empathy, and remaining open to collaborative and reflective discussions." [15] By communicating no threat, the child has the opportunity to relax their reactive brain.

There are several ways that a parent can do this. First, it is by bringing the child physically closer. Second, allow the child to talk about their feelings and what they are upset about without interrupting them except for asking clarifying questions (such as what the child is feeling). The act of naming and describing their feelings forces the upstairs brain to become activated. Asking a child exactly where they feel their emotions (such as in the chest or stomach) further activates the upstairs brain.

The process of inviting a child to physical closeness when possible, and discussing their feelings and events in a non-judgmental way from the parent elicits calm, a sense of safety, and more rationality from the child. Once this is established and the upstairs brain is properly engaged, the child will be more receptive to listening to the parent and making better choices and decisions.

Threats on the other hand, shut down the upstairs brain because they trigger the downstairs brain even more. When the downstairs brain is more active and the upstairs brain is less active, it is very difficult, and sometimes even impossible, to have the child learn any lesson from you.

This is true even more so if a child is afraid of the parent. The child may be outwardly calm and not reactive due to the threat, but internally they have just frozen out of fear. A state of fear means increased downstairs brain arousal which will not allow for proper rational processing and understanding of events.

Think about your own past experiences, when you are very upset or emotional, are you able to process situations in an optimal

[15] *No-Drama Discipline,* P. 47.

manner? Do things even properly register in your mind when you are very emotional?

Pick up Crying Children from Their Bed

إن الله عز وجل ليرحم العبد لشدة حبه لولده.

Imām aṣ-Ṣādiq ﷺ said: *"Surely God, the Exalted and Majestic, will have mercy on His servant due to the intense kindness and affection that a person (the believing servant) has for one's child."*[16]

When a baby cries, it usually means that they need something. This can be a physical need and/or an emotional one. Crying is one of the main ways that a baby is able to communicate one's needs to their parents.

There has been an on-going debate on whether or not a baby should be picked up whenever they cry. It seems that current research has put an end to this debate: Babies should be picked up every time they cry, especially until they are six months of age.

In adulthood, people who were not cared for when they were younger tend to be more stress reactive, and have a harder time calming themselves. The more parents responded to their infant's cries, the safer and more secure they felt later on in life. These children grew up being "healthier, kinder, less depressed, more empathetic, and more productive" according to a study of more than 600 adults. [17]

According to new research by the University of Notre Dame psychology professor Darcia Narvaez, it is "impossible" to spoil a baby by picking them up when they cry. In fact, the opposite is true, letting them cry can ruin their development.[18]

[16] *Al-Kāfī,* Vol. 6, P. 50.

[17] Jessica Schrader, *Should You Pick Up Babies Every Time They Cry?* accessed December 23rd, 2021, https://www.metroparent.com/newborn-care/should-you-pick-up-babies-every-time-they-cry/

[18] Ibid.

It is understandable that parents are tired and may want to sleep, but how we relate to our children in their early stages, especially during the first few months of life can have lasting effects. Caring for and showing affection to our children will bring its rewards many times over in the future when they grow up as stable and healthy adults.

Reality of Upbringing Children

Upbringing is a process which is slow and long. We need to understand the dynamics, circumstances, required flexibilities, and have lots of patience when raising our children. The holistic development of a child means that the development and upbringing of a child is not **just** physical or about academics or emotions or spirituality, rather it is all of these put together, and so much more.

Each stage of development has its own approach and certain needs for healthy growth, and this does not depend on age. If a child is fully developed in one cognitive or emotional area, it is possible that they have stymied in another, and would thus require nurturing relevant to the level that they are at. For example, if a child is in the fifth grade, but their reading level is at the first grade, one cannot expect to change them in a day or even a month. There is no magical solution, and one would need an intervention plan so that they could catch up on their reading. This means that the child would have to go through first, second, third, and fourth grade level reading processes, step by step.

The same goes for cognitive and emotional developments, and milestones for healthy growth in what Bruce D. Perry developed as the *Neurosequential Model of Therapeutics (NMT)*. The neurosequential approach holds that "children need patterned, repetitive experiences appropriate to their developmental needs." For people who missed important neurodevelopmental milestones, it refers to the needs that reflect the age at which they missed important stimuli or had been traumatized, not their chronological age." [19]

For example, infants who were not touched or held much during infancy can stagnate in certain areas of brain development and thus emotional growth. This can lead to depression and various types of anger tantrums that are uncharacteristic for older children and teenagers. Instead of ignoring them, or asking the person to "grow up," it may be helpful to have a targeted therapy to help the affected brain area in the order that it was "affected by neglect and trauma (hence, the name neurosequential)." [20] In the case of a child for whom touch and holding was neglected, it may mean being lovingly held and touched through specific forms of massage therapy. The goal is thus to help match one's biological age with one's developmental age.

When we see emotional, academic, or any other functional issues with children, it is important for parents to be compassionate. Often enough, negative behaviors are rooted in pain and suffering that can be resolved through loving action and patience.

Our Children will Inherit Our Emotions

انظر فی ای نصاب تضع ولدک فإن العرق دساس.

Prophet Muḥammad ﷺ said: *"Be mindful with whom you have a child with, for what is bred in the bone will come out in the flesh."* [21]

It is of utmost importance to manage the chaos of your thoughts. This is because children will inherit our thoughts and our emotions.

---

[19] Perry, Bruce D. *The Boy Who was Raised as a Dog: And Other Stories from a Child Psychiatrist's Notebook - What Traumatized Children can Teach Us about Loss, Love, and Healing,* (New York: Basic Books, 2017), P. 152.

[20] Ibid., P. 153.

[21] This tradition has not been translated literally as its meaning is quite difficult to render into English. The English expression: *"What is bred in the bone will come out in the flesh"* signifies that a person's behavior and character will often be inherited by one's children. See *Ghurar al-Ḥikam*, P. 266.

Thoughts are meant to be used - they are not meant to possess us. Emotions are meant to guide us - not destroy us.

There is a lot of discussion about how our children do not listen to what we say, but they will do what we do. This is correct, however there is less discussion on how our children and spouses also imitate and mirror our thoughts and inner states of being as well.

Constant worry, anger, sadness, and other mental and emotional states are often inherited by children, or learned from their parents.

Sometimes it is not so obvious though. A parent who may be a religious extremist can have a child who will grow up to be a secular or liberal extremist. But in essence they are the same. The parent who tried to mask his emotional problems with religious extremism may have a son who also inherited the father's emotional problems (that of toxic shame), but tried to mask it with other forms of extremism. Even though at face value both seem to be completely different, they are in fact rooted in the same thing which is often unmet needs, shame, or other kinds of trauma.

Learn to heal your mind and heart because your thoughts and emotions may be inherited for generations to come.

Give Space for Growth and Rejuvenation

رحم الله من أعان ولده على بره قال قلت كيف يعينه على بره قال يقبل ميسوره ويتجاوز عن معسوره.

Prophet Muḥammad ﷺ said: *"May God have mercy upon the person who assists one's child in doing good." He was asked: "How can a person assist one's child in doing good?" The Prophet responded: "Accept what they are capable of, and do not be too hard on them."* [22]

In regards to your children and spouse, be careful not to overburden them. Water is the essence of life in a garden, but you can kill or

[22] *Al-Kāfī*, Vol. 11, P. 450.

hurt a plant by giving it too much water. Similarly, not giving enough space to your loved ones can also have a negative effect on them. It will make them feel like they are a prisoner, or it will suffocate them.

From time to time, people need space, solitude, and silence. This kind of space is needed for people to feel free in order to be with themselves, contemplate, and be rejuvenated.

A plant that is allowed to grow naturally will always be stronger and more beautiful than one which was grown artificially through force.

Give your spouse and children the space that they need, and they will be more welcoming of you when you enter it at the right time.

It is also important to remember that just like suffocating our loved ones can be a problem, so can abandonment. A healthy balance is always necessary, and such is our duty and responsibility. A parent should not neglect the supervision of a child for the sake of giving them free space, yet on the other hand, a parent should not micromanage every aspect of the child's life.

Children Follow the Religion of Their Friends

المرء على دين خليله فلينظر أحدكم من يُخَالِل.

Prophet Muḥammad ﷺ said: *"A person will follow the religion of one's friends, so let every one of you be mindful of who they befriend."*[23]

We live in a society where it is all too easy to slip away from being a pious and practicing Muslim. A major factor which will shape our religious lives is the kind of company and friends we keep. Our children are no exception to this.

This is why it is very important that our children grow up in

[23] *Al-Amālī*, P. 518.

an environment which includes a strong Muslim community, hence the importance of attending a *masjid* or an Islamic center. If centers are not possible, then the next best thing is to have an environment where there are other people who share your same values. You may not get along with everyone in a center, but you can always find a strong friend, or group of friends to surround yourself with.

Stepparents: Prioritize Marriage over Kids

يَا أَيُّهَا النَّاسُ اتَّقُوا رَبَّكُمُ الَّذِي خَلَقَكُم مِّن نَّفْسٍ وَاحِدَةٍ وَخَلَقَ مِنْهَا زَوْجَهَا وَبَثَّ مِنْهُمَا رِجَالًا كَثِيرًا وَنِسَاءً ۚ وَاتَّقُوا اللَّهَ الَّذِي تَسَاءَلُونَ بِهِ وَالْأَرْحَامَ ۚ إِنَّ اللَّهَ كَانَ عَلَيْكُمْ رَقِيبًا

"O people! Be wary of your Lord Who created you from a single soul and out of it created its mate, and out of the two spread a multitude of men and women. Be wary in Whose name you plead for rights, and heed the ties of kinship. Indeed, God is always watchful over you."[24]

In another section, we talked about how by putting our spouses first, we are helping our children. In other words, it is strong marriages which will positively affect children the most, not direct strong relationships with the children themselves (although this is very important as well).

Prioritizing the children over the spouse will often end up weakening a marriage, and thereby affect the children in return.

Children often become the center of a parent's attention after divorce, especially for the parent who holds custody of the child/ren or the majority of it. An important question one may ask is regarding the role of stepparents if the parent remarries, and what to do if the child has been used to being the primary source of the parent's attention, but that parent now has another spouse?

---

[24] Noble Qur'ān, Sūrah an-Nisā' (4), Verse 1.

This rule applies to a new stepparent as well. This does not mean that one cares less for the child - of course not - both parents, especially the new stepparent should show a lot of affection, positivity, and love toward their new stepson or stepdaughter. There should not be the impression that a child will be neglected because there is a new spouse in the picture.

But prioritizing marriage is more important than prioritizing children. The strength of your family is not built around the primary attention you give to your children, but it is built around a strong marriage between a husband and a wife.

If you neglect your marriage for the sake of your children, then your marriage will suffer; and if your marriage suffers, then so will your children; and this will in turn be more troublesome for any child.

Now, in cases where a stepparent comes into the life of a child after a divorce, it is important that the strongest marriage possible is presented to the child as an example. This is because the child already witnessed one failed marriage, and to see another failed marriage will be disastrous in multiple ways. Most importantly, the child will not be given stability or a proper marriage model to follow and emulate.

This child will grow up one day, and eventually will no longer live with their parents anymore. If a child moves out of a home where the second marriage was also a failure, then they will be left with bad examples to look up to, and will be more likely to have a failed marriage as well.

For stepparents, it is important to take care of your stepchildren as if they are your very own. By getting married, you get blessings from God, and you will get even more rewards by bringing stepchildren under your care. In such a relationship, it is of utmost importance to give the same kind of care and affection to our stepkids as if they were our own. Sometimes in fear of lawsuits, or worrying about the biological parent, we keep our distance or neglect the children for the sake of our other spouse, but our duty as Muslims is to follow the traditions of Prophet Muḥammad ﷺ, and care for such children regardless of any other circumstances.

Speak Gently with Your Daughters

مـن كان لـه أنثـى فلـم يبدهـا ولـم يهنهـا ولـم يؤثـر ولـده عليهـا، أدخلـه اللـه الجنـة.

Prophet Muḥammad ﷺ said: *"Whoever has a daughter and is not abusive or disrespectful to her, and does not favor one's son over her, God will enter them into Paradise."* [25]

It is not uncommon to hear complaints from daughters that their fathers shout at them. When we ask fathers, they deny that they ever shouted. A possible reason why there is a disagreement between father and daughter may lie in biology.

According to Leonard Sax, for the average boy to hear, as well as the average girl, you have to speak eight decibels (dB) more loudly. Women, on average, "are more sensitive to sounds than boys or men of the same age. Also, children and teenagers are more sensitive to sounds than middle-aged people are." [26]

To be a bit more precise, the most comfortable listening level for females between the ages of 19 and 25 years was 36.2 dB, and for males it was 42.1 dB. In other words, males like to speak six dB louder than what females are comfortable with. Similarly, the tolerance for background noise is about seven dB respectively.[27]

This means that a male may be speaking normally to a female, but the female may interpret it as shouting when in fact he is not. It is also true that an age gap makes a difference as well. A younger

---

[25] Muḥaddith Nūrī, *Mustadrak al-Wasā'il*, Vol. 15, P. 118.

[26] Sax, Leonard, *Why Gender Matters*, 2nd Ed., (New York: Harmony Books, 2017), Pp. 19-20.

[27] *Why Gender Matters*, Pp. 320-321.

girl may be more sensitive to louder voices than a boy, and a middle-aged man may speak even louder than younger males due to his age - thus compounding the problem.

To fathers: your daughter may not be aware of this, or may be too young to understand this reality. For this reason, you should try to put in a conscious effort to speak more gently with your daughters. If your daughter wants to speak, then give her the right to speak first and listen attentively.

The tone of voice and the way words are used are, of course, even more important. When Prophet Muḥammad ﷺ or Imām ʿAlī ؑ used to come home, they could kiss and hug all of their children. Lady Zainab ؑ for example, would be caressed by her grandfather, the Prophet ﷺ and her father, Imām ʿAlī ؑ. Some girls may not like this physical interaction and that is okay, but the general point here is the gentle care, love, and attentiveness toward our daughters.

Avoid Lecturing

رب سكوت أبلغ من كلام.

Imām ʿAlī ؑ said: *"Sometimes silence is more meaningful than words."* [28]

A common instinct among parents is to immediately start lecturing their children or teenagers when they misbehave. Most of the time, there is not much value in this.

When a person is in a dysregulated state, their minds are in chaos. They are overwhelmed with emotions. This means that most of what a parent says will not even register in the child's mind. They are biologically incapable of processing this kind of information when the brain is so overwhelmed.

If the situation is a precarious one, then the parent's job is to take the child out of that situation, sternly even, if need be. The

[28] *Ghurar al-Ḥikam*, P. 382.

parent can then ask questions to the child in an inquisitive manner, meaning asking them to explain what happened. The process of asking questions and letting the child talk instead will help to calm them down.

Sometimes a parent must allow enough time to pass so that the child can become in a calm and receptive state. Once they are is in this state, then the parent can proceed to talk and give advice to them.

The goal of discipline is to teach a child to make better choices. Lecturing is counterproductive in many cases. This is even more true when the parent is dysregulated. If a parent is emotionally dysregulated, it is best to calm down first, then proceed to have a serious conversation with the child.

Your Children will Make Mistakes

احـــب الصبيـــان لخمـــس: الأول: أنهـــم هـــم البـــكاؤون. والثّانـــي: يتمرّغـون بالتّـراب. والثالـث: يختصمـون مـن غيـر حقـد. والرابـع: لايدّخـرون لغـد شـيئا. والخامـس: يعمـرون ثـم يخربـون.

Prophet Muḥammad ﷺ said: *"I love kids because of five (characteristics that they possess): First, they cry a lot; second, they play with dirt; third, they fight with one another but do not hold any grudges (they forgive one another instantly); fourth, they do not save anything for tomorrow; and fifth, they play and then they destroy (meaning that they are not attached to anything)."* [29]

All parents love their children, and they are usually on the lookout to improve them. But if done incorrectly, then it can come at a hefty cost. It is important to keep children under reasonable and consistent standards. Some parents may punish their children for

[29] ʿĀmilī, Muḥammad al-Ḥusaynī, *Al-Mawāʿiẓ al-ʿAdadīyah* (Muʾassasāt al-Balāgh, 2002), P. 340.

having an emotional breakdown, yet turn a blind eye on the fact that they as parents also have emotional breakdowns from time to time.

Like adults, children are fallible, emotional, and will make mistakes. Consistent frustration is not the solution. Compassion and putting oneself in the child's shoes is what needs to be done. Holding a child to a higher standard than one's own self can be destructive to a child's sense of self-worth.

When it comes to mistakes, we should be lenient with some of them, and stricter with others. We must be careful to avoid double standards. We should not expect higher standards from our children than from ourselves. We should also ensure that we do not treat one child at a different standard than another, such as in issues related to gender where we expect more from our girls than our boys.

Giving Orders is Not a Conversation

ألا اخبركـم باشـبهكم بـي؟ قالـوا: بلـى يـا رسـول اللّـهِ. قـال: احسـنكم خلقـا و الينكـم كنفـا و ابركـم بقرابتـه و اشـدّكم حبـا لاخوانـه فـي دينـه و اصبركـم علـى الحـق و اكظمكـم للغيـظ و آحسـنكم عفـوا و اشـدّكم مـن نَفسـه انصافـا فـي الرضـا و الغضـب.

Prophet Muḥammad ﷺ said: *"Should I inform you about the most similar of you to me?" They said: "Yes, O Messenger of God." He continued: "Whoever has the best ethics, is more lenient toward others, helps one's relatives the most, keeps one's brothers/sisters in faith as friends, is most patient on the Truth, is the most controlling of one's anger, shows the most forgiveness, and is the most fair in happiness and sadness [is the person who is most similar to me]."* [30]

[30] *Wasāil ash-Shīʿah*, Vol. 21, P. 485.

Simply giving commands and orders to your children is not conversing with them, it is just shouting orders. Learn to talk to them in a kind and gentle manner, but use calm, yet assertive energy when need be. By having regular respectful dialogues with the parents, children are more likely to grow up to be confident, tranquil, and well-mannered adults.

Sometimes our mindset is that a conversation is simply talking. A conversation is a balanced interaction between two parties. For example, if we speak for two minutes, then we should listen for **at least** two minutes for there to be mutual understanding and compassion. For a conversation to take place, both parties need to be at, or reach to a path of regulation and connection. Conversations also need to be just, so when speaking to children we should speak to them as children, not adults; and when addressing teenagers, we need to speak to them as such, not like children.

Tone of Voice can Matter More than Words

إذا غضبت فاسكت.

Prophet Muḥammad ﷺ said: *"When you are angry, be silent."*[31]

Your tone of voice speaks louder than your words. Psychologists say that people respond more to the tone of your voice than the actual words which are said. In other words, how you say something may be more important than what you say.[32] A good tip to level your tone of voice is to look at the person whom you are talking to eye to eye, breathe well, and be aware of your body language which is often a precursor to your tone of voice.

If your child is sitting, then sit down as well, and it may even be a good idea to hold them. If they are standing, you should still sit as this communicates peace and calmness.

---

[31] *Biḥār al-Anwār*, Vol. 70, P. 272.

[32] Knaus, Brian, *It's Not What You Say - It's How You Say It!* Accessed October 16th, 2020, https://www.psychologytoday.com/us/blog/science-and-sensibility/201311/it-s-not-what-you-say-it-s-how-you-say-it

Some Advice for Husbands and Fathers

من لم يتغافل ولا يغض عن كثير من الأمور تنغصت عيشته.

Imām ʿAlī ؑ said: *"A person who does not overlook or forgive the many things that will happen around them, their life will become miserable."*[33]

Many people do not understand the pain and energy that mothers invest in their children. They do it from the bottom of their hearts; and they are very giving.

It is not easy being a mother and working with kids at home. Mothers generally have the best interest of the family at heart. If the home is sometimes messy, it is not because they are careless, it is due to the difficulty of being with children. They miss out on sleep and do not get proper rest. Men and women are quite different and so are their needs. This was made obvious by the Covid-19 pandemic. How many men were stressed out by working from home with kids around them?

Husbands and fathers need to be supportive, caring, appreciative, and grateful for all that women do. If the men are not compassionate and understanding with what the women do, then they will suffer tremendously in the long run.

Here are some important tips:

1. One cannot expect the same level of cleanliness and organization that existed before children.
2. One must reduce their standards.
3. A husband should put in extra effort to understand his wife. If he does not do that, then it will fuel a fire in the home.

One very important thing to remember is: Never fight in front of your children. Children are smart and quickly pick up on such tensions. Avoid fighting or arguing, especially when your wife is

---

[33] *Ghurar al-Ḥikam*, P. 451.

pregnant, as the fetus will pick up on these tensions and it will affect them in ways that you cannot even imagine.

Families should Exercise Together

علِّموا أولادكم السباحة والرماية.

Prophet Muḥammad ﷺ said: *"Teach your children swimming and archery."*[34]

It is important as a family to exercise together if possible. Not only will this help families stay mentally and physically fit, but it will also contribute to strengthening family bonds. Families who perform sports activities together regularly are happier at home. Children who grow up this way are less likely to want to hang out with questionable peers who may have negative influences upon them.

Sports do not need to be intense; they can simply be going to the park together for easy exercises, or even going for a walk or a bike ride.

Learning vs. Regretting Consequences

ازجُرالمُسي ء بثواب المحسن.

Imām ʿAlī ﷺ said: *"Punish the sinful one by rewarding the good doer."*[35]

The goal of discipline is 'to teach and transform.' That is what the word literally means. In Arabic, its equivalent term *tarbiyah* also means 'to nurture or to teach.'

Some parents confuse discipline with punishment. They believe that since their child may have stopped acting out in ways which they disapprove of, their approach has been a success. But success

[34] *Al-Kāfī*, Vol. 11, P. 442.

[35] *Nahj al-Balāghah*, P. 501.

is not always guaranteed.

Often, when we are quick to punish, our children do not learn to regret their actions, they learn to regret the consequences. They do not learn that what they did was inappropriate or immoral, they learn to fear the consequences and punishment instead. As a result, children do not learn to grow and become better human beings, they simply learn to hide their misbehavior better and become more fearful and manipulative.

In many cases, it is important for parents to sit with their child, connect with them through empathy and compassion, and use their action of misbehavior as a teachable moment.

Real discipline is not just outward, rather it has to be inward as well. It is emotional and spiritual. The militaristic style of discipline focuses on the outward, but real discipline is a form of inner compassion - it covers both realms.

Misusing Time-Outs and Encouraging Time-Ins

إن رسـول اللـه (صـلّ اللّـه عليـه وآلـه وسـلّم) كان فـي الصـلاة و إلـى [أحـد] جانبيـه الحسـين بـن علـي فكبـر رسـول اللَـه فلـم يُجِـر الحسـين (عليـه السـلام) التكبيـر، ثـم كبـر رسـول اللّـه فلـم يُحـرِ الحسـين التكبيـر، ثـم لـم يـزل رسـول اللَّـه يكبـر و يعالـج الحسـين التكبيـر، فلـم يُحـر حتـى أكمـل سـبع تكبيـرات، فأحارالحسـين فـي السـابعة.

Imām aṣ-Ṣādiq ﷺ *narrates that one day as the Messenger of God* ﷺ *stood up for prayer, Ḥusayn ibn ʿAlī* ﷺ *[who was a young child at that time] was next to him. When the Messenger said the takbīr,*[36] *Ḥusayn tried to say the takbīr, but he could not. The*

[36] The *takbīr* refers to the statement "*Allāhu Akbar*" (God is Greatest above everything) which Muslims say before they begin their formal ritual prayers, and other times to glorify God.

Messenger repeated the takbīr again, but Ḥusayn still could not pronounce it. The Messenger kept repeating the takbīr until the seventh time when Ḥusayn was finally able to recite it. [37]

Time-outs can sometimes be useful tools in discipline. It can give children time to cool down, self-regulate, and be more receptive to learning.

Daniel S. Siegel argues that sometimes time-outs can often be misused in what he calls "punishment time-outs." [38] He states that time-outs are meant to help children calm down, self-regulate, and perhaps even reflect on their behavior. But when misused, what ends up happening instead is that the child grows angrier and becomes more dysregulated.

Even worse, it may instill a feeling of abandonment in the child, especially if they are dysregulated and already out of control. Siegel notes that it may send a subtle message to the child that if they are not perfect, then the parent does not want to be near them. It teaches the child that the parent will only be in a relationship with them if the child is "good" and "happy," but will withhold love and affection when the child is not.[39]

Although we may not always agree with Siegel, this observation of his is noteworthy.

In other words, children feel the most unsafe when they are acting out of control and dysregulated. It is during these moments that they need connection, compassion, comfort, and love. As Gabor Mate argues, when time-outs are misused, children are taught that their sources of security (parents) are unavailable when they are at their most vulnerable. They are taught that when they feel unsafe, they are not lovable and they are only lovable when they act in a

---

[37] *Biḥār al-Anwār*, Vol. 43, P. 307.

[38] *No-Drama Discipline*, P. 26.

[39] Ibid., P. 29.

way that parents accept.[40]

This form of discipline can be damaging to future relationships as well. It can teach kids to ignore and neglect important people in their lives when their behavior is not pleasing to them, and only show love and compassion when their spouses or friends behave in a way that is pleasing to them. It also instills toxic shame in children who later grow up believing that they are inherently flawed. This will lead to many other emotional illnesses.

Siegel recommends that parents sit down with the child instead. They can give the child some time to calm down, but sit with them, talk, and comfort them instead. When children feel the most unsafe, it will be the active role of the parents that will be the most important to help them out.

This does not mean that a parent should allow one's child to act however they want to, and be shielded from any consequences. Children may need to still face consequences, yet feel safe, loved, and connected with their parents; they are not mutually exclusive. What connection, love, and **presence** do is that they allow a child to reflect on their behavior more deeply, thus increasing moral, spiritual, and emotional intelligence in the long run.

All children, of course, should not be treated the same way. They have different cognitive and logical capacities, as well as different levels of emotional development as was mentioned earlier. Each child is unique in their own way.

Teaching Your Child Self-Regulation

يَٰٓأَيُّهَا الَّذِيْنَ اٰمَنُوْا قُوْٓا أَنْفُسَكُمْ وَأَهْلِيْكُمْ نَارًا وَقُوْدُهَا النَّاسُ وَالْحِجَارَةُ

"O you who believe! Guard yourselves and your families

---

[40] See Gordon Neufeld and Gabor Mate, *Hold On to Your Kids: Why Parents Need to Matter More than Peers*, (Ballantine Books: New York, 2014).

against a Fire whose fuel is people and stones." [41]

Strong emotions can be a good thing. They are opportunities for growth. When a child is dysregulated, helping them regulate themselves through calm energy will teach them to process their emotions and give them the skills they require to regulate themselves automatically in the future. Shouting or punishing a child will have the opposite effect, it will teach them confusion, fear, and compulsive behavior which may prime them for future mental and emotional difficulties like depression, anger management issues, and anxiety disorders.

Parents must also emulate this approach with each other because children will learn from them as well. Shouting at a spouse will teach children that shouting is an appropriate response. Children will imitate whatever they see at home.

Avoid Reacting Negatively to a Child's Dysregulation

رحم الله من أعان ولده على بره قال قلت كيف يعينه على بره ويتجاوز عن معسوره ولا يرهقه ولا يخرق به

Yūnus ibn Ribāṭ narrates that Imām Jaʿfar aṣ-Ṣādiq ﷷ quotes the Messenger of God ﷺ as having said: *"God has mercy on the parent who helps one's child to do righteousness." So I asked [Imām aṣ-Ṣādiq ﷷ]: "How does a person help one's child in righteousness?" The Imām ﷷ answered: "By accepting what is easy for the child, and not expecting something that is difficult for them, and by not burdening or breaking them."* [42]

Parents go through a lot of stress nowadays. The world is unpredictable and not easy to live in. When a child misbehaves, it is

[41] Noble Qurʾān, Sūrah at-Taḥrīm (66), Verse 6.

[42] *Wasāil ash-Shīʿah*, Vol. 21, P. 481.

easy for a parent to snap at their child. The fact that some parents did not learn proper emotional regulation from their own parents does not help at all either; they respond to their children the way they were responded to when they were younger.

A good strategy to keep oneself away from 'reacting' and instead 'acting' is to increase awareness and compassion. When a child becomes out of control emotionally, know that the child is in a disintegrated state. As Siegel argues, one should recall that "Chaos and losing control are signs of blocked integration, where the different parts of the brain are not working as a coordinated whole. Since connection creates integrative opportunities, connection becomes the way we comfort. Integration creates the ability to regulate emotions." [43]

So when a child is dysregulated, behind the screams and rude behavior is a desperate call to have you help them regulate themselves and become calm again. It might not seem so, but that is what these intense emotions are. They are feelings of unsafety, and calls for safety. If a parent can see this through all of the chaos, then they will be more likely to cultivate compassion and act with calmness and integration.

A good example is when a child hurts oneself. If they cut themself, do we yell at them or attend to their needs and help them heal from the wound? The same thing applies to emotional hurt. We want to attend to the emotional wound with love, care, and healing.

When these experiences are repeated over and over again with an emotionally responsive parent or caretaker, then the child will more easily be able to "self-regulate and self-soothe over time," and thus become more independent and resilient.[44]

Remember, true tranquility is rooted in love and compassion. Your true goal is not to end the child's misbehavior, it is to be

---

[43] *No-Drama Discipline,* P. 85.

[44] Ibid., P. 86.

emotionally present with the child so that they can heal and grow.

Bring Yourself to Your Child's Eye-Level

إنا معاشر الأنبياء نُكلم الناس على قدر عقولهم.

Prophet Muḥammad ﷺ said: *"We, the community of Prophets, speak to humankind in accordance with the level of their intellect and understanding."* [45]

Whenever Prophet Muḥammad ﷺ would communicate with children, he would crouch down and bring himself to their eye-level. This strategy is very important when it comes to calming down a child. This position communicates a safe space to the child and gives them a sense of control. Siegel argues that such a posture not only communicates calmness to the child, but it also calms down the parent.[46] Posture is very important in the animal kingdom as well, when an animal lies down and shows its belly, it communicates non-aggression.

Physical posture plays an important role in the regulation of our emotions, mind, and soul. There is a reason why in Islam we exercise various postures during the daily ritual prayers because each of the positions - if one is mindful and present with the movements - is designed to have an effect on the believer's heart.

The energy we give off to our children is not restricted to words, touch, and tone, but even other non-verbal cues such as our posture.

Connect with Your Child's Feelings

لا تقسروا أولادكم على آدابكم فإنهم مخلوقون لزمان غير زمانكم.

Imām ʿAlī ﷺ said: *"Do not force your own traditions and culture upon your children because they were created and*

---

[45] *Biḥār al-Anwār,* Vol. 1, P. 251.

[46] *No-Drama Discipline,* P. 120.

born in times other than your own." [47]

How we feel is not in our hands, and sometimes it is not even in our control. Have you ever been in a tough and tricky situation, and were able to turn off your feelings? Can you make yourself feel happy when you are extremely sad? If we could completely control our emotions and feelings, then we would have no need for other people, or a community; and there would be no requirement to improve ourselves or our lives.

The reality is that we have little control over our emotions and how we feel. What we do have control over is **how we behave**. This is why when we speak about patience (*ṣabr*) in Islam, it is not an absence or control of our emotions, rather it is a control of our behavior. When we tell a child **how to feel**, we are invalidating their emotions, and as Siegel says: "We invalidate their experience."[48] To add to this, when we invalidate a child's emotions by making them not matter, what the child understands is that they themselves do not matter.

Doing this can have very negative consequences on the development of a child. It will prevent the child from learning how to process their emotions. It will make them feel that there is something inherently wrong with them, which as a result will teach them to be ashamed of who they **are**, rather than understanding that what they **did** was something wrong. Every person is a creation of God who is loved in His eyes, and self-shame or toxic shame will only teach a child that they are inherently defective and of low-worth. This will then create a cycle of toxic relationships with the self, and with others in the present and the future.

What then should a parent do?

According to Siegel, the parent must first recognize the child's feelings. The parent can say: "That made you really angry, didn't it?"

---

[47] *Sharḥ Nahj al-Balāghah,* 10 Vols., Ed. Muḥammad Abū al-Faḍl Ibrāhīm (Qum: Maktabat Āyatullāh al-Marʿashī al-Najafī, 1404/1983), Vol. 20, P. 267.

[48] *No-Drama Discipline,* P. 127.

This validates the child's emotion and helps create awareness about what they are feeling. It will give the child emotional intelligence and help build their vocabulary.

The second step for the parent is to let the child know that they understand their feelings, basically that they "get it." This form of validation will relax the child back from extreme tenseness to a greater sense of calm within them.

Validating emotions does not mean that one is validating the actions or behavior of someone. It does not mean that one is allowing the child to do whatever they want. It does not mean that there will be no consequences for the child's actions. It shows understanding that when a child misbehaves, it is often due to dysregulated emotions.

When you touch the heart of a child, they will trust you, feel safe, and be open to change. This will not happen through lecturing - it will happen through connection and compassion.

Challenges and Opportunities for Raising Children

Introduction

Opportunities and challenges will always be there. You will never be able to master raising children, it is always a learning experience. Remember that the challenge is not necessarily the behavior, it is what is happening inside of the child. We cannot expect to raise our children the same way we, as parents or caregivers, were raised. Many of our challenges were not the same at all.

When dealing with your child, we should not guess the situation, nor should we generalize it, or be quick to judge and blame. Oftentimes, the point of discipline is to make us as parents happy, but that is not really correct. Discipline is to help the child become a holistic adult.

Parenthood is Not Pausing Marriage

فدارها علي كل حال واحسن الصحبة لها فيصفو عيشك.

Imām ʿAlī ﷺ said: *"Always be tolerant and patient with your spouse, sit with them in kindness and goodness so that your life may become serene and felicitous."*[49]

A common practice with some parents is that they pause their marriage while they raise their kids. Pausing a marriage means to stop investing in your relationship. It is to stop trying to sustain it or make it better. This can include a variety of different ways of neglect, such as making no efforts in intimacy, not spending quality time with your spouse, or not engaging in meaningful conversations.

Pausing marriage is to stop tending to the needs of our spouses. Child rearing is indeed very difficult. We worry about our children, and put in a great deal of energy in nurturing them. It is natural that by the end of the day, we feel quite tired, and sometimes it is hard to tend to our spouses.

But this is not good at all and can be very dangerous. Leaving the crumbs of your energy for your spouse will most likely damage your marriage, and cause even more damage to your kids. As was mentioned before, the most important thing for a child's mental and emotional well-being is not the direct relationship that a person has with one's child, but it is the quality of one's marriage. Stable marriages are what positively feed our children their sense of security and emotional well-being. This is an established fact.

So what should we do?

You do not need to be a perfect parent. Your energy is limited, and you do not need to dedicate all of your energy to your kids. Reducing your involvement in a <u>responsible manner</u> will not damage your kids. They will survive. But neglecting your spouse will put your children in jeopardy, and could put them at risk for

[49] *Man lā Yaḥḍuruhu al-Faqīh*, Vol. 3, P. 556.

dangerous behaviors, or mental and emotional illness when they are older.

If possible, have your spouse share some of the responsibilities for the children. If that does not work, then that is okay as you cannot control what your spouse does, but you can control what you do. Improving your relationship with your spouse by prioritizing them will make them more likely to help out at home or in other areas. Reacting with resentment and anger at your spouse's unwillingness to help will damage your marriage and your kids.

Cooperative relationships take a lot of time and effort to establish.

Some people fool themselves into thinking that after the kids grow up, then they will start focusing on their spouses. This is a very dangerous approach. It takes many years for couples to develop a stable, comfortable, and transformative relationship together. Once we get into a comfort zone of marital neglect, it is difficult to change and revert back to a nurturing relationship.

Many marriages are often put on pause for years until the children grow up. The net effect of pausing means that the parents learn to lead parallel and separate lives which become deeply ingrained habits that then become very difficult to change. Once their children grow up and leave, parents fall into conflict because they have nothing that strongly binds them together.

Pausing your marriage will not have a good outcome. Prioritize your spouse, and your kids will flourish.

Dividing Parental Duties "50/50" Does Not Work

كان أمير المؤمنين (عليه السلام) يحتطب ويستقي ويكنس،
وكانت فاطمة (عليها السلام) تطحن وتعجن وتخبز.

Imām aṣ-Ṣādiq ﷺ said: *"The Commander of the Faithful (Imām ʿAlī)* ﷺ *used to collect the firewood and clean the house,* and Fāṭimah 🌺 used to grind the wheat, make the dough, and bake the bread."⁵⁰

Dividing up parenting into percentages (especially the very dangerous 50/50 principle) is a recipe for disaster. There is no reasonable way to even keep track of what percentage you are following. You will find it very difficult to say that you took care of the kids, for example, 57% of the time! Some people recommend that if you want to divide parenting duties between the mother and father, then do it on the basis of "enough and not-enough." In other words, what is acceptable or satisfactory in terms of division of duties and responsibilities will differ between couples and families.

This will eliminate confusion and unrealistic expectations that often fuel conflict and resentment.

Responsibilities come with circumstances and conditions, and everyone's conditions are different. If a father is working and a mother is at home, then the conditions are different. If both spouses are working or none are working, then the conditions will be different. What is important is not who is doing what and how much time one is putting in, rather it is about establishing an enjoyable environment where all parties appreciate what is being done. It is living in gratitude.

Children Who have Lost a Parent

إذا بكى اليتيم اهتز له العرش.

Imām aṣ-Ṣādiq 🌺 said: *"When an orphan cries, the Throne of God shakes."* ⁵¹

A topic that is seldom talked about in our community is how a parent should raise a bereaved child when they have lost their spouse. Each

---

⁵⁰ *Jāmiʿ Aḥādīth ash-Shīʿah*, 31 Vols. (Tehran: Intishārāt-i Farhang-i Sabz, 1386 H.Sh/2007), Vol. 25, P. 508.

⁵¹ *Man lā Yaḥḍuruhu al-Faqīh*, Vol. 1, P. 188.

year, we have some children in our community who lose a parent. We know that a child's psychological and emotional adjustment is strongly associated with the living parent's ability to adjust oneself to this unfortunate reality.

A noticeable tragedy is how there are very few resources to help such parents cope with these realities in our community. At this time, the only advice we can give is what we recently read in a magazine from the British psychoanalyst, Donald Winnicott, who argued that perfect motherhood or fatherhood was neither "possible, nor desirable" in these moments. What we need is a "good enough" mother or father. While nothing can really make up for a lost parent, Winnicott argued that what a child needs the most from a grieving mother or father is "love, connectedness, structure, and a parent who is present and in the game with them."

When a child loses one of their parents, the other parent will also be in great difficulty. This loss can be followed with long bouts of illness. The best situation for the remaining parent is to seek healing from the loss, exercise patience, and learn gradual acceptance. Oftentimes even, the right kind of counseling may be needed to handle the situation properly. What is important is to give the child a sense of emotional safety and security. By being with a child in this manner, the process of grieving will be more successful. If you tell a child not to cry, or neglect them due to your own sorrow, then it will cause trauma that will viciously backfire. Healing from the traumatic effects of loss requires processing emotions together and being present with one another. Imām ʿAlī ﷺ, for example, would take his children to the grave of Lady Fāṭimah az-Zahrāʾ ﷺ, and together they would mourn for her.

Giving the child spiritual explanations, such as talking about heaven, and expanding social networks and connections is very crucial. Letting the child cry without being present is neglect. Not allowing a child to grieve is also abuse.

Sometimes damage is done with good intentions. As we

mentioned, for a child to heal from trauma it is important for them to process their emotions with a regulated adult. Some parents try to distract their children from grieving by distracting them with toys and sweets. A child may stop crying for some time, but those emotions will bottle up inside and intensify. They may even turn into various forms of emotional illnesses for years to come.

Grieving appropriately is healing. Only time coupled with real parental presence will help a child process trauma in a healthy manner.

Relaying Consequences in a Nurturing Manner

يسروا ولا تعسروا وبشروا و لا تنفروا.

Prophet Muḥammad ﷺ said: *"Be easy-going and not demanding, and give glad tidings and do not avert (others)."*[52]

Kids should know that there will be consequences, either disciplinary or natural, however parents should deal with consequences in a nurturing and compassionate manner.

Reduce lecturing and inadvertent shaming, such as telling them: "I told you so." Instead, do the following things:

1. Show empathy (example: "Your clothes are dirty, that must be uncomfortable").
2. Comfort them, but do not rescue them (example: "A change of clothes might help").
3. Most importantly: validate their feelings (example: "That must have been quite embarrassing").

By making your child feel secure with you, they will be able to develop trust and emotional self-awareness which are necessary ingredients for happiness in adult life.[53]

---

[52] Abī Jumhūr, Muḥammad ibn Zayn al-Dīn ibn, *'Awālī al-Laālī al-'Azīzīyah fī al-Aḥādīth ad-Dīnīyah*, 4 Vols., Mujtabā 'Irāqī (Qum: Dār Sayyid al-Shuhadā' lil-Nashr, 1405/[1984-1985]), Vol. 4, P. 386.

[53] A resource with some useful tips can be found in: Adele Faber and Elaine Mazlish, *How to Talk So Kids Will Listen and Listen So Kids Will Talk,* (New York: Scribner, 2021).

Limit Violent Video Games and Social Media

يَٰٓأَيُّهَا ٱلَّذِينَ ءَامَنُوا۟ قُوٓا۟ أَنفُسَكُمْ وَأَهْلِيكُمْ نَارًا وَقُودُهَا ٱلنَّاسُ وَٱلْحِجَارَةُ

"O you who believe! Save yourselves and your families from a Fire whose fuel is people and stones."[54]

Children and teens who are addicted to video games and social media are less likely to develop healthy hobbies and interests. They are also less likely to develop the social skills needed to succeed in life.

Children and teens who play a lot of violent video games for extended periods of time also become less patient in life. These games teach them to shoot away at nuisances and obstacles, yet one cannot do this in real life so this often leads to frustrations, alienation, and a difficulty in being patient.

For example, children who play games like *Call of Duty* generally become - after a few years of playing - more hostile, less honest, and less kind.[55]

Similarly, children who spend a lot of time on social media posting pictures of themselves are more likely to become less humble and more selfish.[56] This may breed the kind of insecurities that will negatively impact their relationships as adults later on in life.

Parents often get resistance from their children when they try to limit their hours or access to these gaming and social media venues. But redirection is not supposed to be easy. Although children may know what is pleasurable for them, they do not always know what will give them success in life. Children usually do not understand this, so it is a parent's job to direct their child toward what will bring them success, and keep them away from what may potentially

[54] Noble Qur'ān, Sūrah at-Taḥrīm (66), Verse 6.

[55] Sax, Leonard, *The Collapse of Parenting,* (New York: Basic Books, 2016), P. 145.

[56] Ibid., P. 171.

destroy their lives in the present and the future.

Life is changing. The amount of screen time on our gadgets is not as obvious as before. We are so immersed that we often lose track of how much our screen time actually is. This is obviously having a huge impact on our emotional well-being, yet having no screen time is no longer possible in this twenty-first century. Only guided time, combined with suitable replacements that are fun and exciting, will work for most people.

Teach Your Children Humility

وَعِبَادُ الرَّحْمَنِ الَّذِيْنَ يَمْشُوْنَ عَلَى الْأَرْضِ هَوْنًا وَإِذَا خَاطَبَهُمُ الْجَاهِلُوْنَ قَالُوْا سَلَامًا

"And the servants of the All-Merciful are those who walk humbly on the earth, and when the ignorant address them, they say: 'Peace!'" [57]

Many parents in this world confuse virtue with worldly success.[58] Failure to achieve great financial success and power is considered to be one of the worst of human failures for some people.

One of the most important skills and true markers of success that parents can teach their children is humility. Humility does not mean that a person should denigrate oneself, rather one should respect oneself and accord the same respect to others. Humility means that one should consider others as equals, and always be open to learn something from them that one may not know. It is being open to the thoughts of others without ego and arrogance. Humility is believing that everyone has something to offer in skills and/or experience even though we may think that they are not "educated."

Leonard Sax lists many detrimental consequences for people who lack humility in life. For him, people who have a "puffed

---

[57] Noble Qur'ān, Sūrah al-Furqān (25), Verse 63.
[58] *The Collapse of Parenting*, P. 160.

up ego" at ages 8 or 14 can become resentful by their twenties, something which does not spell well for overall happiness and stable relationships.[59] Unfortunately, much of social media is about self-promotion which often leads to arrogance and puffed-up egos.

Since lack of humility can lead to resentment and misery in the future, a culture of humility can lead to gratitude, appreciation, and above all, contentment.[60] As all religions teach, the fundamental key to happiness in life is contentment (*riḍāʾ*) and gratefulness (*shukr*).

More fundamentally, it has been shown that gratefulness is in itself a cause of happiness, psychological well-being and a "sense of personal mastery." This becomes very difficult to achieve for people who have been indoctrinated in their "own awesomeness." [61]

An important question that may come up is: How do we teach our kids to walk humbly on the earth? Islam teaches us that one of the keys to humility is charity to others. Charity is not only giving money, but it is serving others with big and small things. Charity can be a smile intended to uplift another person, or helping others physically when they are in need of help. Of course, all of this must be done with the intention of pleasing God.

A recommendation Sax gives to instill humility in children is limiting kids' use of social media. The culture of social media is the antithesis of the culture of humility. Social media, Sax writes: "Are all about self-promotion: '*Here I am. Look at me.*' It is all about broadcasting and aggrandizing the self." [62]

Even though social media can be used for good, that is not how kids use it for the most part. According to family experts like Sax, social media with its subversion of humility is creating a culture of disrespect toward peers, parents, and other adults.

We should optimize our children for success both in this world

---

[59] *The Collapse of Parenting*, P. 160.

[60] Ibid.

[61] Ibid.

[62] Ibid., P. 170.

and the next. There is nothing more pleasing to God than a truly humble servant.

Partner with Your Child for Behavior Solutions

وَشَاوِرْهُمْ فِي الْأَمْرِ ۖ فَإِذَا عَزَمْتَ فَتَوَكَّلْ عَلَى اللَّهِ

"And consult them in the affairs, and once you are resolved, then put your trust in God." [63]

When a child does something wrong, deep down inside they are likely to realize why they broke the rule after they calm down. When they are emotionally dysregulated, they will blame almost anyone and deny that they did anything wrong. They may rebel in anger or withdraw in shyness. Good solutions should be discussed with the child once they have calmed down.

When a child misbehaves, it is important for a parent to teach the child how to regret the action, not the consequence. The parent should teach the child **how** to respond better in the future, not hide their misbehavior.

This means that parents should not always tell their children directly how to behave. They should ask the child questions (if they are old enough) and help them think about what the best course of action is. With proper guidance, this will teach the child how to become a better decision-maker who will then strive toward making independent good choices in the future.

Learning from the Experience of Others

Introduction

لا حليم إلا ذو عثرة ولا حكيم إلا ذو تجربة.

Prophet Muḥammad ﷺ said: *"There is no fortitude unless one*

[63] Noble Qur'ān, Sūrah Āl 'Imrān (3), Verse 159.

has stumbled and blundered, and there is no wisdom unless one has experience."[64]

It is important to understand that life skills, and having a proper system of livelihood are the result of a combination of experience, knowledge, and wisdom. It is not always about degrees and certificates. Life experiences, even when one has little formal education, can have as much, if not more worth and value than a degree. Experience is gold.

Anxieties Should Not Make Us Forget Our Families

حُسن الظن من أفضل السجايا و أجزل العطايا.

Imām 'Alī said: *"Thinking positively is one of the greatest qualities, and the best of gifts."*[65]

In moments of resentment, we sometimes only see the negatives without looking at the positives. We even do this in petty things. As a consequence, we miss out on being present with family, and forget the good things because of the small bad things in life.

Anxiety attacks can bring chaos to one's emotions and severely damage social relations, the biggest victims being your spouse and children. On your deathbed, it is likely that you will regret having spent so much time dwelling on fears and not actually "having lived" and appreciated those precious God-given moments with your family.

As a religious cleric, I have conducted countless funerals and have been to innumerable deathbeds. In those times, people did not regret finances, social status, or anything else materialistic. What

---

[64] *Nahj al-Faṣāḥah*, P. 675.

[65] *Ḥusn aẓ-ẓann* is thinking positively in a holistic sense. It can mean giving the benefit of the doubt to people as well as thinking optimistically about God's help in this world. See *Ghurar al-Ḥikam*, P. 345.

they regretted the most was missed relationships.

With this in mind, a good "hack" on how to deal with anxiety attacks is not to look toward the unknown future from the present moment, but to look at the present from the perspective of your future deathbed which is certain.

The remembrance of death, and the shortness of life will teach you to appreciate what you have now, and reduce your worldly anxieties.

The Importance of Regularly Playing with Children

يستحب غرامة الغلام في صغره ليكون حليما في كبره.

Imām al-Kāẓim ﷺ said: *"It is commendable that a person is loving toward a child when they are young, so that they (the child) may be gentle and patient when they are older."* [66]

Some parents believe that it is beneath their dignity to play with their children. The teachings of Islam show us the exact opposite, in that one of the most dignified actions of a Muslim is to play with one's child. 'Playing' is not limited to one thing, it can be physical like wrestling, intellectual games like mind puzzles, or social games like board games, or recreational activities like sports, hiking, camping, picnic, or spiritual games like religious quizzes. The point is not the games themselves per se, but the bonding experience which takes place through this playing. Fun is one of the best ways to come down to the level of your child and create a harmonious relationship.

The bonding experience between a parent and a child when they play is a critical component of psychological health. Among other things, it helps to develop social and emotional skills for children within a structured context that helps children to be able

[66] *Wasāil ash-Shīʿah*, Vol. 11, P. 479.

to maturely relate to society. It teaches them the limits, and the dos and don'ts of how to engage in society.

Playing with one's parents also raises the oxytocin levels in children. Research shows that the release of oxytocin in the body increases compassion, trust, safety, connectedness with others, calmness, and generosity in children.[67] In fact, it is often called the "love hormone." and it has also been shown to have positive effects on people with PTSD (Post-Traumatic Stress Disorder).[68]

By becoming more compassionate, trusting, and empathetic beings, your children will grow up being a positive spiritual influence in the world. But remember, playing with them occasionally may not have that many positive effects. Children need consistency and regularity. By playing regularly with your child (them and those around them in their immediate and future lives) will reap the full rewards of the time that you spent with them.

Preserve Your Child's Unconditional Love For You

أحبـوا الصبيـان وارحموهــم واذا وعدتموهــم شـيئا ففــوا لهــم فإنهــم لا يــدرون إلا انكــم ترزقونهــم.

Prophet Muḥammad ﷺ said: *"Love children and be compassionate with them; if you promise them something then fulfill that promise, for they do not know of anyone but you who provides for them their sustenance."* [69]

This love is unconditional. If we do not optimize it properly, then this love will be deviated, and the children will see their parents

---

[67] Kristin Neff, *The Physiology of Self-Compassion*, accessed July 31st 2020, https://www.psychologytoday.com/us/blog/the-power-self-compassion/201207/the-physiology-self-compassion

[68] Sharon Palgi, Ehud Klein, Simone G. Shamay-Tsoory, *Oxytocin improves compassion toward women among patients with PTSD in Psychoneuroendocrinology*, 2016; 64: 143 DOI: 10.1016/j.psyneuen.2015.11.008

[69] *Al-Kāfī*, Vol. 11, P. 449.

as unsafe to be with. They will channel the love elsewhere looking for safety, such as with bad friends, inappropriate relationships, or addictions. The innate nature of everyone gravitates toward peace and love. It is part of who they are, and it needs to be expressed somehow.

One of the greatest treasures a person can ever have in this world is having children who grow up to love you unconditionally. People often do not appreciate this until they are old and lonely, but by then it is too late.

Let us not squander this wealth by ignoring our kids, or worse, not showing them the kindness and love that they need and deserve. Initially, your children will naturally love you unconditionally, but you must preserve this love by spending quality non-distracted time with them and showing them kindness, not yelling or incessantly scolding them, or God forbid, hitting them.

Listening to What is Not Being Said

فَبَشِّرْ عِبَادِ الَّذِينَ يَسْتَمِعُونَ الْقَوْلَ فَيَتَّبِعُونَ أَحْسَنَهُ

"So give good news to My servants who listen to the word [of God] and follow the best [interpretation] of it." [70]

God gave us two ears and one mouth and a large mind to understand, and a heart to process our emotions. Therefore, before preaching and talking, one should listen, understand, and process, then speak.

If you want to communicate with a disruptive child (or a teenager), learn to hear what is **not** being said. The same rule applies to your spouse.

Sometimes people do not have the words or vocabulary to express their feelings and needs. At other times, people do not have sufficient emotional self-awareness to really understand what they need, let alone express them.

[70] Noble Qur'ān, Sūrah az-Zumar (39), Verses 17-18.

At other times, people are afraid to express what they really think or feel.

What ends up happening is that our family members end up avoiding the topic, or they communicate in all of the wrong ways. They either vent their feelings in the context of seemingly irrelevant topics, become cold and distant, or just speak in an ambiguous and vague manner.

What a parent or spouse should do is look at body language cues. Look for tension and ask relevant questions. Do not look to refute or debate your loved ones, rather become an investigator and ask curious questions at the right time and place when your child or spouse is more likely to open up and be honest with their feelings and concerns.

A Healthy Family is One who Forgives

إرحم تُرحم.

Imām ʿAlī: *"Have mercy (on other people), so mercy will be shown to you."* [71]

Forgiveness is one of the greatest virtues that a Muslim can practice. Often sour relationships and animosity lead to a point where we do not want to forgive because the resentment is too much to let go. The net result is that this destroys our souls, and often even our own bodies through various illnesses.

According to the teachings of the Holy Household of Prophet Muḥammad, family members should not be able to rest or sleep properly until they are back to peaceful terms. We should strive to mend relationships; not argue to see who the winner will be.

We should understand that forgiveness is not just an intellectual activity, but an emotional one as well. Lack of forgiveness will lead

---

[71] Nishābūrī, Muḥammad ibn Aḥmad al-Fattāl al, *Rawḍah al-Wāʿiẓīn*, 2 Vols., (Qum: Intishārāt-i Raḍī, 1375 H.Sh/1996), Vol. 2, P. 370.

to resentments, and resentments are rooted in the emotion of anger which is not always directly under our control. There are certain actions which we can take that can influence our emotions when we approach resentment with mindfulness. In families, resentment and lack of forgiveness often happens through conflict. In most cases of conflict, this happens because compassionate and real listening does not take place. We seek to be understood before we understand the other person. If we could try to reverse this and sincerely understand the other person before being understood, then it would resolve many of the emotional blockages that prevent forgiveness.

If these temporary blockages occur, then we should not feel shame. No matter how much we try to avoid it, sometimes we will develop resentment against certain individuals. What is key in our growth is how mindful we are of our resentments and the practical steps we take to heal them.

Forgiveness is but one step. We should also respond with goodness, acknowledge our own mistakes, and apologize when necessary. This not only extends to our spouses, but also to our children. By acting like this, we set ourselves as examples for good character and humility. We often make the mistake of being arrogant in front of our children so that we can exert authority and righteousness, but by doing so we only perpetuate ego in them all the way into their adulthood.

Be an Authoritative Parent, Not Authoritarian

إنه من لا يَرحم لا يُرحم.

Prophet Muhammad ﷺ was kissing Imām Ḥasan ؑ when Aqraʿ ibn Ḥābis saw him and said: *"I have ten sons and have never kissed any of them."* Prophet Muḥammad ﷺ said: *"A person who does not show mercy (to others) will not receive mercy."*[72]

[72] *Wasāil ash-Shīʿah*, Vol. 21, P. 485.

Parents are the guardians (*awliyāʾ*) of their children and the pillars for their growth. They are their sources of stability: emotional, financial, educational, and cognitive. Parents should not be tyrants, they should be humble and responsible guardians who keep the best interests of their children in mind. They are to train them holistically, not just in one area of life.

There are three types of parenting styles: authoritarian, authoritative, and permissive. Authoritarian parents are those parents who are too hard and very strict. They often make unrealistic demands and rarely show any kindness and love. Children who are brought up by authoritarian parents are more likely to become abusive parents themselves as adults. They may also have difficulties in sustaining healthy marriages.[73]

Permissive parents show love and kindness to their children, but they are often not good at setting strict boundaries or rules, nor enforcing them. Permissive parents sometimes try to treat their children as adults, and think that giving them choices and freedom to do as they want is healthy. Unfortunately, children and even teenagers do not know what is best for them. Permissive parents may mean well, but they often confuse pleasure with fulfillment.

Kids may know what brings pleasure to their lives, but most often they do not know what will fulfill them and turn them into responsible and happy adults in the future. By growing up in a permissive environment, kids learn to do as they please without learning restraint and patience. For this reason, children who grow up with permissive parents are more likely to suffer from depression as adults. They are also more likely to have problems with drugs and alcohol abuse, struggle financially, and live within their means; and they are more likely to be convicted of a felony.[74]

Authoritative parents are those who set strict boundaries and

[73] *The Collapse of Parenting*, Pp. 140-141.

[74] Ibid.

limits for their children, but also show them kindness, love, and respect. Research shows that the children of authoritative parents do better in school, are less likely to do drugs and alcohol, and are less likely to engage in unsafe sexual practices, both in their teenage years, as well as adults.[75]

Strict boundaries obviously should not be unrealistic and suffocate a child, they should be realistic, practical, and with purpose.

Your Child's Lash-out is Not Rudeness

شـكوت إلى، أبي، الحسـن، موسـى (عليـه السـلام) ابنـا لـي فقـال،:
لا تضربـه واهجـره ولا تطـل.

One of them said: *"I complained to (Imām) Mūsā (al-Kāẓim)* about a child of mine,"* so he replied: *"Do not strike them, but rather isolate them, but not for too long."*[76]

One of the natural reactions of a child who is not yet mature and lacks experience is to lash out. When a child is lashing out, those who are mature and experienced should not compare themselves with the child. Rather, they should take this as a great opportunity to connect, understand, evaluate, and come up with a good solution which can shape the future of the child. Suppressing lash outs by force is counterproductive.

Children (and even teenagers) are not adults. They do not have fully developed brains, nor do they have the experience that adults have. It is to be expected that children will not have the ability to regulate their emotions and impulses like many adults can. This means that when kids face disappointments and upsetting situations, they will react in ways we find unhinged and unacceptable, such as kicking, screaming, or crying.

It is important for parents to understand that this is not because

---

[75] *The Collapse of Parenting*, P. 140.

[76] *Biḥār al-Anwār*, Vol. 101, P. 99.

the children are ill mannered, or that the parents are bad, but reacting in such ways is normal. Children often do not have the biological capacity or experience to react in ways that we as adults are expected to react like.

When a child lashes out, it is usually the case that they are having a difficult time processing emotions and are in need of help. The parent's task is to be gentle with the child, and show them love and compassion, such as by hugging them, or stroking their hair, and generally letting them know that they understand their emotions, then proceed to calm them down.

This will teach a child to regulate oneself so that during adulthood, they can respond to the stresses of life in a balanced state of mind.

Giving Orders is Not Talking and Connecting

قَوْلٌ مَّعْرُوفٌ وَمَغْفِرَةٌ خَيْرٌ مِّن صَدَقَةٍ يَتْبَعُهَا أَذًى ۗ وَاللَّهُ غَنِيٌّ حَلِيمٌ

"An honorable reply [in response to the needy] and forgiveness is better than a charity followed by injury. And God is All-Sufficient, All-Forbearing."[77]

Orders and demands are not healthy forms of communication. Healthy communication is the expression of love and needs. The ultimate purpose of healthy communication is not correction, but the creation of a safe environment for a child.

For many parents, the easiest solution is often to tell their children what to do. This can often result in their adult children growing up and having difficulties making the right choices and decisions. It is common to see adults make rash decisions based on fear and anger, which almost always leads to regret.

Sometimes the reason behind this kind of attitude goes back to childhood. As children, they were not taught to be good decision

[77] Noble Qur'ān, Sūrah al-Baqarah (2), Verse 263.

makers. Their parents gave them orders and commands without any healthy communication. This was especially true when the child became emotionally dysregulated. Some parents think that shouting commands like "STOP!" or "BE QUIET!" or even "CALM DOWN!" are appropriate forms of discipline. However, with reactions like these, children do not learn how to calm themselves down and make rational decisions. They only learn to react, which is to freeze in fear, or fight back in anger.

Good decision making is part and parcel with emotional regulation. You cannot have good decision making in the long run with emotional dysregulation, if so, it is exceedingly rare.

Good decision making with emotional regulation means that the parents set boundaries and choices, and allow the child to decide and operate within those boundaries and choices. It means calmly discussing those choices with the child, and coming down to the child's level.

As was mentioned earlier in the chapter, behind every want there is a need. We want to attend to the needs that are behind the wants, which are love, connection, and safety.

So, when a child is dysregulated, helping them process their emotions and weigh their decisions will become an opportunity for deeper insight and growth, as well as a healthy integration of the heart and mind - the prerequisites for connection and closeness to God.

Your Family Associations and Spiritual Growth

جالسوا من تذكركم بالله رؤيته ولقائه، فضلا عن الكلام.

Prophet ʿĪsā (Jesus) said: *"Sit with those who remind you of God just by seeing and meeting them, let alone speaking with them!"*[78]

---

[78] *Biḥār al-Anwār*, Vol. 97, P. 84.

We live in a world where we interact with all sorts of people. Islam asks us to be respectful and mindful of all of them. We do not want to live in extremes where we cut off everyone who we do not agree with; but on the other hand, we cannot closely associate with anyone regardless of their moral status.

It is important to keep in mind that whoever we befriend or interact with will affect our behavior, morals, and spirituality in some way or another. We have stated many times throughout this book that our relationships with our spouse and children are a deeply spiritual one. We get married and have children primarily for spiritual growth and becoming closer to God, not just to be happy. Happiness is a consequence of how we choose to live, not a tangible thing that we can directly aim for and grasp, otherwise everyone would be happy.

Therefore, if we **closely** associate and befriend people who are of dubious morality or live lives that counter the principles through which God asks us to live by, then their way of life will affect our own spirituality and that of our children without us realizing it. If we are to grow and improve as sincere Muslims who submit to the laws of God, then it is important that the people who we interact with are those who will help us improve spiritually and morally.

Takeaways

With the grace of God Almighty, we were able to discuss some of the important practical points of raising a family holistically. Life is not always easy. Our health challenges, conflicts with our spouses, difficulties at the workplace and the greater world leave us emotionally depleted. The tensions between traditional values and the modern world can sometimes leave us confused. Unfortunately, our children face the brunt of the accumulated tensions that we carry. But as difficult as these challenges are, they must not come in the way of nurturing our children.

Before we conclude this chapter, we would like to end off with a few takeaway points on the types of challenges which may get in the way of nurturing our children and their potential consequences.

Teaching Our Kids to Avoid Sins is Not the End-Goal

The idea behind *aṣ-Ṣirāṭ al-Mustaqīm* (The Straight Path) as stated in the opening chapter of the Qur'ān is not simply to avoid sins, but to rise up spiritually and develop one's relationship with God. This should be the overarching goal of any parent who wishes to teach one's child about Islam.

Removing sins from one's heart is like taking weeds out of a garden, but to prevent the weeds from growing again and keeping the garden from just looking like a flat land of dirt, we must sow fruitful plants in their place in order to make the garden beautiful.

This means that we should teach our kids the fundamental Islamic virtues that lead to the purification of the heart and closeness to God. These include maintaining the regular prayers in their appropriate times, giving charity, being altruistic, caring for others, acting with humility, never boasting, and always speaking the truth even when it goes against our own interests. The list of spiritually affirming actions is too long to list here, but the point is that avoiding sins, and being proactive in performing virtuous actions go hand-in-hand in the teaching of Islam to our children.

Sins do not come out of nowhere. They are rooted in emotional, physical, and spiritual disturbances. It is not enough to just teach our children about sins, but to give them the awareness of how sins come about and why we get tempted to perform them, parallel to giving them the appropriate tools to counter them. Sin is not simply a mistake, it is deviating from one's purpose in life. The root meaning of one of the words for sin in Arabic is *khaṭā'* which is an arching term meaning "to miss the mark."

The Consequences of a Child Living in Fear

A child lives in fear because they feel insecure, this can be from their own mistakes, or the behavior of their parents. They may feel that their parents will abandon them, or fear that they will not be able to properly express their thoughts and emotions. If a child cannot be comfortable with their parents, then they will live in fear.

A child living in an environment of fear at home will face devastating long term consequences. Sometimes there is an environment of fear because a parent is emotionally unstable, but at other times the parent thinks that they are being a good disciplinarian. Although discipline, rules, and consequences are good and needed for a healthy upbringing, there are cases where in some homes it goes to the extent of instilling a reign of fear and terror in the child's life.

As a survival mechanism, such children learn to persistently lie and speak half-truths - not because they are bad or naughty - but they do so as a survival mechanism in a hostile environment. These children grow up to lie in exchange for temporary safety and comfort. They also learn that through lying and purchasing that comfort, they are able to manipulate people and the world. But obviously what they do is just make things worse.

The practice of buying temporary comfort at the price of submitting to fear, when it becomes a habit, creates a lifetime of anxiety, humiliation, and eventual depression. Lying warps a person's soul and makes them weaker, begets loneliness, and alienates people - including family - from oneself. It turns an already problematic world to an even more hostile place to live in, thereby requiring more lies which just makes things even worse. If your child lives in fear of you, then you may want to consider the kind of person you are molding into adulthood and sending out to the world.

Your Spouse has Priority Over Your Family

We need to shift our paradigm. When we have children, we are often tempted to make our spouses secondary. If we want to see the well-being of our children, we have to put our spouses first. Even if our relationship with our spouse is not good, we should at least make it a priority to be respectful to each other in order to make the children feel safe.

The first relationship God ever created was the relationship between a husband and wife. According to Islam, a spouse's first responsibility is to one's spouse. All other relationships, including one's relationship with the children, siblings, friends, coworkers, uncles, aunts, grandparents, and even parents must be secondary.

Many of the conflicts and even divorces that happen in our community are due to the prioritization of other relationships over the marital relationship. Although our duties can be immense toward other family members, including our parents and children, they cannot override the priority of our duties toward our spouses.

If this primacy is not managed properly, then it can lead to despair and burnout from one or both spouses.

The nucleus of the family is the husband and wife. If you do not build and strengthen this nucleus you cannot invest in your children. If you are not on the same page, then you cannot nurture your children properly. We must respect others like we respect our own parents, grandparents, and other family members, but the nucleus is the husband and wife. This is the root and the foundational well-being of emotional, spiritual, and even physical health for our children, and for generations to come.

Prophet Muḥammad ﷺ used to say "I love you" to his wives in front of his family. Unfortunately, we express love to co-workers, neighbors, and others more than to our own spouse, and this has become the seed for so much of our despair and unhappiness in life without even realizing it.

Responsibilities Toward Parents vs. Spouse

يَا أَيُّهَا النَّاسُ اتَّقُوا رَبَّكُمُ الَّذِي خَلَقَكُمْ مِنْ نَفْسٍ وَاحِدَةٍ وَخَلَقَ مِنْهَا زَوْجَهَا وَبَثَّ مِنْهُمَا رِجَالًا كَثِيرًا وَنِسَاءً ۚ وَاتَّقُوا اللَّهَ الَّذِي تَسَاءَلُونَ بِهِ وَالْأَرْحَامَ ۚ إِنَّ اللَّهَ كَانَ عَلَيْكُمْ رَقِيبًا

"O humankind! Be conscious of your Lord who created you from a single soul, and from it created its mate, and spread many men and women from the two. And be conscious of God when you make requests from each other and concerning [your] womb-relations. Indeed, God is Ever-Watchful over you." [79]

Husbands and wives are the nucleus of their families and humankind. When God created Prophet Ādam ﷺ, He commanded all of the angels to prostrate to him. God then asked Ādam ﷺ how he felt about it, and he responded that he did not have peace and tranquility inside. God then created Eve and married her to him. God then asked Ādam ﷺ to hold Eve's hand and when he did so, tranquility entered into his heart.[80]

[79] Noble Qur'ān, Sūrah an-Nisā' (4), Verse 1.

[80] The background of this story is narrated by Imām aṣ-Ṣādiq ﷺ who describes the details of their creation: *"When God, Exalted is He, created Ādam from mud, He ordered the angels to prostrate to him. Then He placed him (Ādam) in a deep sleep, and started creating a new creature for him. Then He placed Ḥawwā' (Eve) near him, and this was so that women would go along with men. When Ḥawwā' started to move, her movement woke Ādam up. At this moment, Ḥawwā' was told to move away from Ādam. When Ādam saw her, he realized a beautiful creation just like himself with the difference that she was a female. He started talking to her. Ḥawwā' responded with his language. Ādam then asked her: 'Who are you?' Ḥawwā' responded: 'As you can see, I am a creature who God created.' Ādam asked God: 'My Lord, who is this beautiful creature that when I get close to or look at her, she makes me feel calm?' God said: 'This is My [believing] servant, Ḥawwā'. Would you like her to be your companion and partner, and talk to you and follow you?' Ādam said: 'Yes, and as long as I am alive, and I will thank You for this bounty and glorify You.' God, Exalted is He, said: 'Ask her to be your bride as she is My servant and is proper for your desire.' Then God created the faculty of lust in Ādam while He had informed him of such faculty before. Then Ādam said: 'O God, I will ask her hand in marriage, what will please*

Ādam ﷺ felt completely at peace, and responded to God that now he felt that he had purpose in life. God then told him: *"O Ādam, dwell you and your wife in paradise."*[81] Then Ādam ﷺ had children and became parents, thereafter their children moved out, and the concept of the family as we know today was created. Then grandchildren came and when their numbers were great enough, society as we know it today came to be. The nucleus and foundation of all of humanity today is the relationship between a husband and wife.

Parents are an important part of life, but our main responsibility is toward our spouses. If in one way or the other you have concerns about your parents or the parents of your spouse, these matters should be discussed before marriage such as one's outlook on living in a joint family where you feel that your parents should live with you. Imposing these things after marriage is not advisable. A wise and faithful servant of God is a person who lives in balance with one's family and society. The parents have their own place and so does one's spouse. The relationship between husband and wife is unique because they share each other's private lives, secrets, and intimacy. You know your spouse's secrets, weaknesses, and strengths. Your whole life and family may fall apart if you do not honor your responsibilities toward each other.

Your spouse is not just a means for lust, sexual desire, or financial sustenance, rather your spouse is the main element and component of peace and tranquility in your life. Although Prophet Ādam ﷺ had peace in God, it was through holding his wife's hand that a different level of peace and tranquility was created. This is why most of

---

You?' God replied: 'My pleasure is for you to teach her the principles of My religion.' Ādam responded: 'If that is what You want, then I will do so.' God said: 'This is what I want. I have made her your wife, so call her to yourself.' Ādam said: 'Come to me (O Ḥawwā').' Ḥawwā' replied: 'You come to me.' Then God told Ādam: 'You go to her.' So Ādam got up and went toward her, and if it was not like this, then women would go asking men to marry them, and would ask their hands in marriage.'" *Biḥar al-Anwār*, Vol. 11, Pp. 220-221.

[81] Noble Qur'ān, Sūrah al-Baqarah (2), Verse 35.

the Prophets got married - despite the difficulties that come with marriage - as it was an important part of their relationship with God and their own souls.

Some parents often feel that they will be left out and vulnerable once their child gets married. However, sometimes it is the incoming spouse who feels a sense of inferiority, insecurity, or jealousy with the in-laws. Parents should treat their son-in-law or daughter-in-law as if it is their own child. Similarly, spouses should treat their parents-in-law as if they were their own parents.

To couples: If you want to live your life with peace and love, then prioritize your spouse. They are the foundation of your life and society.

To in-laws: Our humble request to you is **not** to judge your son-in-law or daughter-in-law on a few things you see here and there. Do not look at them with doubt or judge them for their mistakes. Rather, look at the true needs behind their wants, give them space, respect, and your unconditional love, then you will see good results.

When I first got married, my parents told me: "My son, your wife is my daughter, and now you are my son-in-law." This was a strong message to my wife that she had their unconditional support, and that I as her husband could not escape my duties. Later on, I found out that my own mother-in-law told my wife that: "Now you are my daughter-in-law, and Nabi Raza is my son." That completely changed the mindset and equation between us to the extent that when I had complaints I went to my mother-in-law, and when my wife had any concerns she went to my mother. This was a powerful message for both of us.

The 7-7-7 Prophetic Principle in Raising Children

الولـد سـيد سـبع سـنين وعبـد سـبع سـنين ووزيـر سـبع سـنين، فـإن رضيـت أخلاقـه لاحـدى وعشـرين وإلا فاضـرب علـى جنبـه فقـد أعـذرت إلـى اللـه تعالـى.

Prophet Muḥammad ﷺ said: *"Treat your child as a master] for the (first) seven years, a servant for (the next seven years, and a counselor and advisor for (the last) seven years. Then if you are content with their character at twenty-one, (then it is good); otherwise let them be, as you are excused by God, the All-High."*[82]

People often misunderstand the above tradition. They take it literally in that we should play with our children and treat them as kings for the first seven years (0-7), then teach them for the next seven (8-14), then finally advise them for the last seven years (15-21). The reality though is that we cannot compare a one year old to a three year old, or someone who is sixteen with a twenty-one year old. The Prophetic tradition does not mean that we should forgo any of the stages, or that we should cease in disciplining them. It means that we should train our children to be well-rounded people in all areas of life. In the first stage we teach them self-confidence and to be leaders; in the second stage we teach them to be humble, to be servants, workers, and followers; and in the last stage we teach them how to become advisors for the betterment of society.

As well-rounded adults, the idea is not to "treat" them in different ways depending on their age, but to train them so that they can take on different roles in life as needed - be it at home, in the community, at work, or in greater society at large. This in turn will help our children grow in emotional intelligence, and in their ability to regulate themselves as well-rounded adults who can be of benefit for all of humanity.

---

[82] *Jāmiʿ Aḥādīth ash-Shīʿah*, Vol. 25, P. 848.

5

A Realistic Mindset in Marriage

If we were asked what is one of the biggest crises people face in marriages, we would have to say it is people's expectations. Expectations are the gaps between what is and what should have been. The danger lies in the fact that the frustration and resentment that is born out of this expectation gap dilutes one's power to constructively do something about the issues of life.

Expectation-related disappointments have a knack for sidetracking your creative mind, and keeping you from solving your problems.

Learn to master yourself by mastering your ability to have a realistic mindset, and it is only then that you can take a real step toward being a free person and having a better marriage.

Changing Your Spouse will be Slow

A lot of marital conflict comes from focusing on things we cannot do or achieve in our lives. This leads to anger and bitter resentment. The key to happiness in life is: 1) be content with what you have, 2) believe that what you have will improve and get better over time, and 3) believe that what you have is not deficient. On a side note, it is also important to realize that happiness comes from the mindset that you yourself are not perfect.

Sometimes these expectations are from ourselves, and at other times they are from our families and societies. Our expectations should be rational. One of the reasons why our families fall apart is exactly this - our mindsets are not realistic or reasonable.

For example, we often expect our spouses or others to change overnight, but if that is not possible for us, then how is it possible for others? Change is a slow and tedious process. The human soul is very complex.

We do not expect a first grader to acquire a PhD at the end of the school year, but we somehow expect people to have a PhD in their spirituality overnight.

Be patient, and realize that changes take a long time to come about. Above all, learn to enjoy the process of change. Pay attention to subtle cues of change, and you will see what we mean! It is only through enjoying the process of change that you will be able to stick to it.

إِنَّ اللَّهَ لَا يُغَيِّرُ مَا بِقَوْمٍ حَتَّىٰ يُغَيِّرُوا مَا بِأَنفُسِهِمْ ۗ

"God will not change the condition of people until they change what is in themselves."[1]

Where do Unrealistic Expectations Come From?

Unrealistic expectations come from many sources. They primarily come from comparisons which we make that are a waste of our time and precious resources. They come from our imagination where impossible dreams are ponded over.

Unrealistic expectations come from the idea where we implicitly believe that we are perfect, or better than our spouses and we ultimately deserve better.

They also come from not seeing things from all sides. For

[1] Noble Qur'ān, Sūrah ar-Ra'd (13), Verse 11.

example, a person may see the good side of one thing, but blind themselves to its negativities. They can also come from a corrupt environment, bad friends, greed, and of course challenging spouses.

One may ask: How then can we counter this problem? The first solution is to stop comparing our situation to others. Good comparisons do not really exist because every person and situation is unique and different.

Let us unravel this, and look at how we compare our spouses to others.

The first mistake we make is that we compare the good qualities of other people's spouses to the bad qualities of our own spouse, without knowing the bad qualities of those whom we perceive as "good spouses." We do this while we also ignore the unique good qualities of our own spouse. For example, although there may be some qualities lacking in our spouse, we know that in most cases no one will be a more loving parent to our children than our current spouse who is the real parent of our children.

A second mistake which we make is that the so-called good qualities that we perceive in other people may not suit our own lives, and could even become a source of problems for us but sometimes do not think about that. For example, we may want a spouse who is extra tidy, but once we live with such a person who is like that, it may become unbearable for us.

The third mistake we make is that when we compare our spouses to others, we do not consider our own flaws. Unfortunately, the mindset which we often have is that we do not possess any flaws. Here we must make sure that we introspect ourselves. Understanding ourselves will teach us humility which in turn will help tamper down unhealthy expectations.

While being aware of these mistakes, it is also important to take an extra step of having good friends, being in a good environment, and instilling a culture of positivity.

Realism vs. Fantasy

Compassion vs. Perfection in a Spouse

In Duʿāʾ Kumayl, Imām ʿAlī ﷺ supplicates:

اللّٰهُمَّ إِنِّي أَسألُكَ بِرَحمَتِكَ الَّتِي وَسِعَت كُلَّ شَيءٍ.

"O God, I ask You by Your Compassion (Raḥmah) that encompasses everything."

Marriage by itself will not make a person happy. The more you expect marriage to make you happy, the less happy your marriage will be. Conversely, the less you expect from it, the happier it will make you.

Islam sees marriage as a means for discovery, a process of learning about yourself and improving one's self. It is not something that is supposed to make you feel good all of the time. It will teach you how to love and be patient with an imperfect and broken person just like yourself, and understand how God loves all of His imperfect creations.

Marriage, if approached from the right perspective, will set the grounds for learning how to live in the image of God; and it will lay the grounds for teaching you how to have compassion for your enemies as Prophet Muḥammad ﷺ, and his successors, the 12 Imāms ﷺ, taught us.

The key for *Liqāʾ Allāh* (meeting with God) is universal and unconditional compassion for the imperfect and broken ones; but if a person is not able to do this with one's spouse, then imagine how much more difficult it will be to do this with the rest of His creations?

It is this compassion (*raḥmah*) for others that one must have in the heart which will free human beings from the chains of fear, worry, and anger. By shifting one's perspective of marriage, a person can take the first step in learning permanent inner peace and joy. For this opportunity, one should be grateful for one's imperfect spouse.

Do not wait for your spouse to fulfill your needs, learn to be selfless and serve them, and you will be the first person to reap its rewards. That is the Divine promise.

Your Spouse's Perceived Flaws Can Save You

وَعَسَىٰٓ أَن تَكۡرَهُواْ شَيۡـٔٗا وَهُوَ خَيۡرٞ لَّكُمۡۖ وَعَسَىٰٓ أَن تُحِبُّواْ شَيۡـٔٗا
وَهُوَ شَرّٞ لَّكُمۡۚ وَٱللَّهُ يَعۡلَمُ وَأَنتُمۡ لَا تَعۡلَمُونَ

"Yet it may be that you dislike something, but it is good for you; and it may be that you love something, but that it is bad for you; and God knows, while you do not know." [2]

We should be aware of the tendencies and characteristics which we dislike in people because sometimes those things which we dislike the most in some people can show up at the right time and in a mysterious way end up saving us later on.

We may have a desire for our spouses to act and do things the way we want them to, but it is possible that they are simply not capable of what we expect from them, but if they are put in a different situation or context, their true value may come to surface.

For example, the issue of having a spouse devoting themself to be a stay-at-home parent. With some people this can oftentimes lead to severe disagreements due to the financial constraints that it may incur. But depending on the context and temperament of some children, having a full-time parent at home may be the thing that provides the key for their emotional and spiritual growth, whereas the lack thereof may become detrimental to their well-being. So what was a financial difficulty at the time ended up saving the future of one's child.

---

[2] Noble Qur'ān, Sūrah al-Baqarah (2), Verse 216.

Discomfort with People and Eternal Reward

وَيَدْرَءُونَ بِالْحَسَنَةِ السَّيِّئَةَ

"And they repel evil with good."[3]

Your true reward from God will not come from how you behave with those people you are comfortable with. Rather, your real reward will come from how you conduct yourself with those individuals whom you are fundamentally uncomfortable with, and those you dislike for whatever reasons.

It is easy to express love, friendship, and compassion with those people whom you like, or those who have not annoyed you. But true character (*akhlāq*) and faith (*īmān*) is when you are able to show that same kind of love, compassion, and friendship to those who have hurt you, annoyed you, or will never really benefit you in any way.

This is the mark of a true believer as practiced and described by Prophet Muḥammad ﷺ and his Ahlul Bayt ﷺ. In other words, this is what it means to have compassion for your enemies, and those who frustrate or anger you.

Remember that compassion for those who hurt you is a basic requirement for the union of the soul with God. It is a prerequisite for true spiritual success.

If this is how we should react with an enemy, imagine the love and compassion we should show our own spouse. So remember this the next time your spouse frustrates you that your patience and compassion toward them will always work in your favor, and help you to achieve your ultimate goal which is getting closer to God, and uniting with the Lord.

---

[3] Noble Qur'ān, Sūrah al-Qaṣaṣ (28), Verse 54.

Unexpressed Gratitude can Feel Like Ingratitude

من لا يشكر الناس لا يشكر الله.

Prophet Muḥammad ﷺ said: *"Whoever does not thank people has not thanked God."*[4]

Unexpressed gratitude in a marriage can feel like ingratitude, meaning that if a person does not thank one's spouse, then they will feel unappreciated; and if one is not acknowledged for their hard work, then this is a sure ticket to make one's spouse distant and cold in a marriage.

No matter how difficult it may be, or even if you are really tired or down, still take the time to express to your spouse how grateful you are for who they are; then follow it up with some concrete examples of what you appreciate about them. These tangible examples will demonstrate that your appreciation is well-thought, genuine, and not fake.

You will find that when you take the time to think and express how you appreciate your spouse, your mind's perception will change over time, and your positive outlook of your spouse and marriage will grow as the days go by. Your resentments will decrease, and your spouse will notice that as well. Your expectations will change, and your marriage will transform for the better.

Sometimes this gratitude can be expressed in words, by a look, indirect comments, praise, or acts of service; but whichever way it is shown it will have a huge positive impact on your future.

[4] *Man lā Yaḥḍuruhu al-Faqīh*, Vol. 4, P. 380.

Useful Tips

Heart Over Logic: Spouse Perspective

أصدق المقال ما نطق به لسان الحال.

Imām ʿAlī ﷺ said: *"The most truthful word is the [emotional] state [behind your] speech."*[5]

What we consider traits that may bug us in our spouses often depends on our own interpretation of those traits. Think of it in this way: When you first married your spouse, some of those traits might not have bothered you much. Ask yourself these questions: Did you change, or did your spouse change? Were you looking at your spouse through the heart instead of the mind at that time, but perhaps now that is different? Maybe you should start looking at your spouse through your heart again, and that may resolve some of your problems.

Sometimes looking at things only through logic can lead to disasters. We usually become overly analytical, critical, judgmental, and cold. The heart is the seat of compassion. Through the heart, we do not see our spouses as objects, but as loving creations of God. Our spouse's flaws become part of their humanity and creation, and because they are the creation of the Almighty, we learn to love their flaws as well.

At the beginning of your marriage you overlooked many of their flaws, and now you can do it again! Start by taking your spouse out on dates again.

---

[5] *Ghurar al-Ḥikam wa Durar al-Kalim*, P. 212.

Your Spouse's Faults are the Price You Pay for Their Virtues

فدارها على كل حال واحسن الصحبة لها فيصفو عيشك.

Imām ʿAlī said: *"Always be tolerant and patient with your spouse, and live with them in the best manner (with kindness and compassion) so that your life may become serene and felicitous."* [6]

In this world, you will never be able to get someone who is 100% perfect because you yourself are not 100% perfect. People do not come in parts, they come as full and complete packages.

For example, you may be married to someone who is always busy at work, but this is the price you have to pay for having a spouse who is career-oriented, and for them to provide financial security for the family. You may be married to someone who is very devoted to the family, but the price you may have to pay is that this person will also be devoted to their extended family as well.

After years of marriage counseling, we feel that this is one of the most important facts of human life which people must realize so that they can have a better chance at a successful marriage. For fallible human beings, virtues and faults come together.

Another one of the greatest misconceptions which we have in marriage is that we blame the flaws of our spouse's family members and friends on our spouses themselves. We must learn that oftentimes our spouses are innocent of the shortfalls of those who surround them. In a way, the faults of your spouse's family is the price you pay for the virtuous spouse that you have.

---

[6] Miyānjī, ʿAlī Aḥmadī, *Makātib al-Aʾimmah*, 7 Vols., Ed. Mujtabā Farajī (Qum: Dār al-Ḥadīth, 1426/2005), Vol. 2, P. 211.

Compassion Resolves Emotional Needs, Not Logic

إن الرجل ليؤجر في رفع اللقمة إلى في في امرأته.

Prophet Muḥammad ﷺ said: *"A man will be rewarded for lifting a morsel of food to his wife ('s mouth)."* [7]

When people are going through an emotional roller-coaster in their lives, one cannot expect reason to work properly. This is why the Household of Prophet Muḥammad ﷺ taught us to be physical, and touch and hug our loved ones. When people are emotionally distraught, they will not benefit from any logical solutions, instead they need to feel loved and cared for appropriately. They want and need to feel validated.

This is the key to connection. Without connection, nothing can be resolved. But with proper connection, things will automatically resolve.

Furthermore, you should avoid resolving emotional needs with reasoning when you yourself are in an emotional state.

Show Appreciation Without Expectation

الَّذِيْنَ آمَنُوْا وَتَطْمَئِنُّ قُلُوبُهُمْ بِذِكْرِ اللهِ أَلَا بِذِكْرِ اللهِ تَطْمَئِنُّ الْقُلُوْبُ

"Those who believe, and whose hearts find comfort in the remembrance of God. Surely, with the remembrance of God the hearts (rest and) find comfort." [8]

When your spouse is fulfilling their obligations, do not remain silent thinking that it is simply their duty. Remember to thank them and

---

[7] Al-Kāshānī, Muḥsin Fayḍ, *Al-Maḥajjat al-Bayḍā' fī Tahdhīb al-Iḥyā'*, (np: nd), Vol. 3, P. 70.

[8] Noble Qurʾān, Sūrah ar-Raʿd (13), Verse 28.

show your sincere appreciation even if you get nothing in return. When you make someone feel valued, they will inevitably change for the better, and you will be rewarded many times over by God's grace which will manifest itself in your heart and in your relationship.

No good that a person does ever goes in vain; the Lord of the Worlds and His angels will always be the greatest and most important beings to acknowledge and recognize these good actions. The most important reward - namely the granting of tranquility in the heart (*itminān al-qalb*) - will become a greater possibility for you in your lives.

When a person pursues this world, in reality it is a tranquil heart that they are pursuing; and true tranquility of the heart begins with letting go of high expectations.

6
Conflict Resolution

Conflict is a natural and necessary process for the spiritual and emotional development of a human being. Conflict **can be good** because it teaches us that there are other minds and people apart from ourselves, thereby laying the foundation for compassion, empathy, and ultimately love. It is through love that we can reach the depths of our spiritual nature, cleanse our hearts, attain true God-consciousness, and fulfill the purpose of our creation.

يَا أَيُّهَا النَّاسُ إِنَّا خَلَقْنَاكُم مِّن ذَكَرٍ وَأُنثَىٰ وَجَعَلْنَاكُمْ شُعُوبًا وَقَبَائِلَ
لِتَعَارَفُوا إِنَّ أَكْرَمَكُمْ عِندَ اللَّهِ أَتْقَاكُمْ إِنَّ اللَّهَ عَلِيمٌ خَبِيرٌ

"O humankind! Indeed, We created you from a male and a female, and made you nations and tribes that you may know one another. Indeed, the noblest of you in the sight of God is the most God-conscious of you. Surely God is All-Knowing, All-Aware." [1]

Conflicts allow us to understand our differences, cultivate compassion, and ultimately transform ourselves into better human beings. But not all conflicts are good. Just like any other gift that has been given to us by the Lord, it can be misused and have an opposite effect. It can destroy relationships, ruin people spiritually,

[1] Noble Qur'ān, Sūrah al-Ḥujurāt (49), Verse 13.

psychologically, and physically, as well as drive people away from God.

In order to overcome negative conflicts and tensions in our marital lives, and turn them into positive elements, we must understand some of their sources. It is important to note that below are only certain examples, and by no means cover all of the principal sources of conflict.

Psycho-social Well-being

Many of the tensions that we have with our families are the result of our anxieties, which is one aspect of the lack of psycho-social well-being. We fear loss of health, loss of finances, loss of reputation, or what have you. Anxiety ruins our moods, and we often end up behaving erratically with our spouses and children. But keep in mind that life is a struggle and you will have ups and downs, but the negative memories you instill in your children's and/or spouse's mind due to your fluctuating fears and emotions will likely be remembered forever. Make sure to practice God-conscious patience (*ṣabr*) in times of trouble because it is likely that your troubles will ease, but your behavior and examples you set will not be forgotten.

Pessimism and Learning to be Positive

Complaining regularly can rewire your brain to negativity, thereby increasing the chances of depression, chronic anxiety, and other psycho-emotional illnesses. Complaining is sometimes needed and necessary, but be aware of it becoming a habit because it has the ability to destroy your long-term well-being and productivity, and it is often one of the main sources of marital conflict.

Studies on depression show that the onset of depression may often be preceded by extended periods of pessimism.[2] It is safe to

[2] The study looked at the onset of depression among children, see Daniel Goleman, *Emotional Intelligence: Why It Can Matter More Than IQ*, (New York: Bantam Books, 2006), Pp. 243-244.

say that complaining can increase pessimism, and thus create an overall negative mood in life. We know how negative moods can warp our perspectives and abilities to find solutions to different crises in marriage.

Here is a good new habit to try and adopt in our lives: Try being positive, and say affirmative and kind things to yourself, your spouse, and about your life in general. At first, you may feel that you are being dishonest to yourself which is entirely natural. But if you keep at it, those affirmative and positive words will sooner or later take root in your heart, and change your mind for the best.

Forgetting to Pray for Your Spouse

Our relationships often deteriorate because we forget to pray for others; and if we do pray, then we often do not know **how** to pray.

The first and most important means of making peace with those who have hurt you is to pray for them. Praying for those whom you have tensions with holds many benefits if it is done correctly.

In your prayers, first acknowledge your own sins and mistakes. This will help you become more humble, and make you see how you may have contributed to the problem at hand. It is very rare that problems in marriages are black and white, usually both parties share some blame even if one of the spouses holds the lion's share.

Second, ask God to help, bless, and forgive your spouse. This process will help replace inner animosity with compassion toward your spouse. Acting compassionately can go a long way in changing your spouse's behavior.

Finally, prayer will remind you that God has Power over everything, including the state of all of your affairs. By praying, you entrust yourself and your spouse to God, thus making your marriage more receptive to His blessings and guidance, as well as stripping yourself of the feeling of loneliness and helplessness in your struggle for a better life.

Egotistical Feedback and Learning Humility

For many couples, conflicts are not resolved because we lack the ability to communicate feedback positively, or accept feedback that is given to us.

Sometimes couples will not give feedback to help one another, rather they will degrade each other so that they may feel superior over their spouse.

There are a few steps that you should take when preparing to give feedback to your spouse:

1. Being emotionally and mentally prepared. Make sure to check your intentions, and be aware of the negative role your ego and pride may play in this.
2. Before you begin any form of feedback, take a good look at yourself and see your own faults. Be critical of yourself first, before you are critical of others.
3. Use the sandwich method. Do not start with the negative. Start with the positive, give feedback, and then end with a positive. Your spouse will less likely become defensive, and will more likely be willing to listen to what you have to say.
4. You should not constantly use the sandwich method; as your feedback does not always have to be verbal or direct. It can be through you manifesting the desired positive behavior, or speaking about a flaw in general terms without directly referring to your spouse.
5. Your feedback should not be too frequent. Imām as-Sajjād ﷺ taught us that giving too much advice can lead to slander.
6. In all forms of feedback, always maintain your spouse's dignity, and do not actively pick on their faults.

If on the other hand, you are given feedback then make sure to implement it, and be open to the comments from your spouse. That is a form of respect, and it will increase the chances that your spouse will take your feedback positively as well, and try their best to implement them too.

In this chapter, we will look at conflict resolution from three outlooks: 1) the paradigms of conflicts; 2) what to do during conflicts; and 3) considerations to make after conflicts. We will conclude the chapter with general advice that can help resolve present marital tensions.

Paradigms of Conflict Resolution

How Fear and Shame Block Healthy Communication

ايما امراة قالت لزوجها: ما رايت قط من وجهک خيرا فقد حبط عملها

Imām aṣ-Ṣādiq ﷺ said: *"Any woman [or man] who says to one's spouse: 'I have never seen any good from you' will have the merits of their good deeds vanish."*[3]

Fear of shame and anxiety can block couples from communicating in an open and healthy manner. When healthy communication is blocked, it will lead to resentment and contempt. When people are afraid of expressing their true feelings as a means of avoiding shame and anger from one's spouse, meaningful conversation will then go out the window. Furthermore, couples will stop listening to each other, and often end up blowing up at one another in arguments or humiliating each other into submission as an ironic way of escaping feeling worthless.

In this state of heightened fear and unsafety, our perceptions of what our spouses say also become distorted. For example, when the husband speaks, the wife may shut out, blur, or distort what he is actually saying. Behind the words that he is saying, she may

[3] *Man lā Yaḥḍaruhu al-Faqīh*, Vol. 3, P. 440.

hear something like: *"Blah, blah, blah, I don't really love you; blah, blah, blah, I only care about myself; blah, blah, blah, I won't take care of you; blah, blah, blah, you're not safe with me; or finally, blah, blah, blah, I don't care about your wants and emotions."*

The perceived conversation will lead the wife to feeling unsafe, unloved, and unprotected.

Alternatively, when a wife speaks to her husband, he may shut out, blur, or distort what she is saying when he is in a state of anxiety and fears shame. For example, if the wife speaks, he may perceive the following behind her words: *"Blah, blah, blah, you can't meet my needs; blah, blah, blah, I wish I had married someone else; blah, blah, blah, you're not good enough for me, you're not a man; or blah, blah, blah, you're a loser, a bad and lousy sorry excuse for a man."*

The perceived conversation will lead a husband to feel worthless and unvalued. As a result, he may snap back in anger, and dismiss or shame his wife in return. This can make her feel scared, isolated, and alone - further deteriorating their relationship.

When we deny each other's needs or wants without really listening, we make the other person feel as if their emotions are not important which they may take as if **they are not important.** This is in addition to **actual** hurtful words that are often used in an argument.

As couples when we communicate, we need to do so in a way that preserves the dignity of the other spouse. Feelings and the needs behind the wants should be communicated in a safe manner. This means that we need to make an effort to not say absolute statements (such as always, never, etc.); or attack the person; or even belittle the other spouse's desires no matter how irrational they may seem. Behind most wants there is a need, although all wants cannot be addressed, but human needs are basic, and they can be met. A spouse must address the feelings and issues at hand of the other partner. This means listening and trying to understand the emotion, not listening in order to come back with a response.

Try the following exercise: When your spouse speaks, hold back your response, and try summarizing back what they said. Once they acknowledge your summary as accurate, then proceed to ask them about the feelings behind the issue at hand. After they respond, you will notice that they feel heard, and more often than not it will lead to a dramatic reduction in tensions, and bring down the defensive barriers that may distort or blur communications.

We understand that sometimes it is very difficult to go behind someone's wants and find their needs. It often happens that a spouse may really emphasize on a want that is not feasible or possible for the other spouse to meet. Sometimes the want and demand may be irrational. If a compromise is not possible, then it is recommended that the couple refer themselves to a trusted third party or counselor for further help.

Healthy Couples Fight as Much as Unhealthy Ones

ٱدْعُ إِلَىٰ سَبِيلِ رَبِّكَ بِٱلْحِكْمَةِ وَٱلْمَوْعِظَةِ ٱلْحَسَنَةِ ۖ وَجَٰدِلْهُم بِٱلَّتِى هِىَ أَحْسَنُ ۚ إِنَّ رَبَّكَ هُوَ أَعْلَمُ بِمَن ضَلَّ عَن سَبِيلِهِۦ ۖ وَهُوَ أَعْلَمُ بِٱلْمُهْتَدِينَ

"Call to the way of your Lord with wisdom and good admonition, and dispute with them in a manner that is best. Surely, your Lord knows (very well) those who have gone astray from His way, and He knows (very well) those who are guided." [4]

Unhealthy couples fight as much as healthy couples, but the difference between them is that good couples are more mindful in what they say and do during and after a fight. One important tool conscious couples use are "repair mechanisms." A repair mechanism is a word or an action that helps ease tensions between spouses.[5]

[4] Noble Qur'ān, Sūrah an-Naḥl (16), Verse 125.

[5] For more on this, you can refer to John M. Gottman's research. We do not agree with all of his approaches, but some of his forms of conflict resolution can be useful.

For example, one spouse makes a funny gesture during a fight and makes the other spouse laugh, or they say something nice. This is important as it prevents escalation and resentment. Repair mechanisms are "custom made" for each couple, thus you need to find out what works and what does not work for the two of you.

The last part is very important because making the wrong joke at the wrong time can make things worse. Unfortunately, there is not always a perfect way to approach it, it only comes through understanding your spouse better with trial and error.

After a fight, good couples know not to take what was said and done too personally, and they understand that the overall health of the marriage and relationship is more important and greater than the issue that was fought about.

Reflect: What are some repair mechanisms between you and your spouse, what are some things you can incorporate to be more mindful when you fight?

Do Not Hide from Arguments

القول الحسن يثري المال و ينمي الرزق و يُنسئ في الأَجل و يحببالى الاهل و يدخل الجنة.

Imām as-Sajjād ﷺ said: *"Speaking in a good manner will extend one's wealth, increase one's sustenance, delay one's death, make one dearer to the family, and (allow a person to) enter into Paradise."* [6]

None of us are identical to anyone else, nor are we devoid of our own personal emotions and intentions. We are all unique with our own ways of thinking, likings, dislikings, and how we express ourselves. As such, having arguments or talking about differences is a sign of a healthy relationship and a means of growth for individuals.

---

[6] Shaykh Ṣadūq, *Al-Khiṣāl*, 2 Vols., Ed. ʿAlī Akbar Ghaffārī (Qum: Jāmiʿ-yi Mudarrisīn, 1362 H.Sh/1983), Vol. 1, P. 317.

However, if we feel that **only** our own thinking or way of life is what matters, then that can lead to serious tensions.[7]

It is a common misunderstanding that couples who do not fight are healthier ones. That is not always the case for most people. If a couple never fights (by this we mean have arguments, not physical fights) it may be that they are so withdrawn from each other that they have just stopped caring altogether. It could also mean that their relationship is too formal so it may blow up at another time. God forbid, it could even mean that they have lost all hope and are looking for a way out.

Fights or arguments are ways of addressing underlying issues and tensions; so in this sense, arguments can be a healthy part of a marriage. However, what makes it healthy or unhealthy is "**how**" you fight or argue in your marriage.

Do not run away from arguments or fights. If you hold back on problems or big questions in your life that affect both of you, then they may build up over time and become very bad. One can only bottle up issues for so long until they blow up, or end up in extreme resentment. Have you ever noticed that when you bottle up something for long enough, it manifests itself in different ways? You may have one big problem with your spouse, but then start picking on them about small petty things? Picking on small things is often a manifestation of unaddressed inner tensions regarding bigger problems.

Therefore, try to address your problems in a calm and civilized way before they build up and get worse. Choose the right time and space to talk about them, but do not wait for too long.

---

[7] We must always be cognizant that there are certain moral lines in Islam. If we are in doubt about such matters, then it is important to refer to a scholar.

Criticizing vs. Non-judgmental Notices

المؤمن مرآة المؤمن.

Prophet Muḥammad ﷺ said: *"A believer is the mirror of another believer."* [8]

A mirror does not make you look worse or better, it shows you exactly how you are. Mirrors do not contain judgments, and they do not put you down, nor do they tell you about your past. They show you the present reality. Criticisms should be like mirrors, they should show reality respectfully and not nag.

Nagging at your spouse or child is a sure way to cause annoyance and spitefulness. It will not bring about the desired change you want in a person, in fact it may make matters worse or dent your relationship. Try taking the non-judgmental "notice" approach. For example, instead of saying: *"Why are your socks on the floor, didn't I tell you a hundred times to pick them up??!?!?!"* ... try saying: *"I noticed that your socks are on the floor."* Perhaps the first time it may not work, but over time most people tend to react positively to non-judgmental notices, and eventually comply.

Reflect: Think of a recent complaint you had against one another, now think about how to make that complaint non-judgmental.

Dangers of Jokes and Sarcasm

إن الرجل ليتكلم بالكلمة يضحك بها الناس يهوي بها أبعد من الثريا.

Prophet Muḥammad ﷺ said: *"Verily, a person might speak a word to make people laugh (now), but that may plunge them further [into Hell] than the star of Pleiades."* [9]

Most people are aware of how damaging insults can be. Yet how is it that people often feel insulted in the absence of direct insults?

[8] *Tuḥaf al-'Uqūl*, P. 173.

[9] *Biḥār al-Anwār*, Vol. 69, P. 257.

One way we insult others is through sarcasm and jokes. Sometimes we think that they are funny, but it is not so for those who are the recipients of the sarcasms and jokes.

Sarcasm is an insult disguised as a joke. It is often triggered by hidden or manifest resentment, annoyance, anger, or what have you. It is meant to put another person down in a way that can give plausibility to some that it was just a "joke" and not something serious.

Jokes can also be a problem. No matter how funny it may look to the person making the joke, it often comes at the expense of degrading a person's dignity through making fun of them.

So, beware of sarcasm and jokes directed at your spouse or your children, as they can often be very hurtful and breed resentment.

Your Home is Not a Courtroom

وَمِنْ آيَاتِهِ أَنْ خَلَقَ لَكُمْ مِنْ أَنْفُسِكُمْ أَزْوَاجًا لِتَسْكُنُوا إِلَيْهَا
وَجَعَلَ بَيْنَكُمْ مَوَدَّةً وَرَحْمَةً ۚ إِنَّ فِي ذَٰلِكَ لَآيَاتٍ لِقَوْمٍ يَتَفَكَّرُونَ

"And among His signs is that He created for you mates from your own selves that you may take comfort in them, and He placed between you affection and mercy. Indeed, in that there are signs for people who reflect." [10]

Our homes are not courtrooms. We are not tasked to be judges, lawyers, or prosecutors for our families. A family must have certain principles and foundational pillars, and forgiveness is one of them.

If a household does not have a culture of forgiving, then this household will not be able to withstand the storms of life. A culture of forgiveness is not one that asks for forgiveness, but rather one that is merciful with the mistakes of others, and does not give in to resentment.

According to the traditions of Prophet Muḥammad ﷺ and his Ahlul

[10] Noble Qur'ān, Sūrah ar-Rūm (30), Verse 21.

Bayt ﷺ, family members should not rest or sleep properly until they get over their differences and are back on peaceful terms.

We should strive to mend relationships, not argue to see who the winner will be. Arguing is often an attempt to control people which almost never works in the long term.

As we have said many times before, the question you need to ask yourself is the following: Do you want to just be right, or do you want to have a good relationship?

Some Thoughts on Conflict Prevention

Do Not Bottle Things Up

ليس منا من لم يحاسب نفسه في كل يوم.

Imām al-Kāẓim ﷺ said: *"A person who does not judge (or take account of) oneself every day is not from us."*[11]

When couples first get married, there are certain issues that they do not want to bring up because of some reasons, or because they are considered to be unimportant at that time. However, unaddressed problems will not go away on their own, and little things will always accumulate and eventually make a person blow up.

When issues come up with your spouse, do not bottle it up. If you feel strongly about a situation, do not lie to yourself in regards to it. In any marriage, problems will happen, and your spouse will do things that you dislike. Express your feelings respectfully, but do not let them linger on as it will only make things more explosive in the long term.

Sometimes it may be difficult to confront a person face to face, so try sending an email or writing a letter by hand and deliver it to your spouse. This is a better platform than texting because emails and letters are better thought through, and are less susceptible to

[11] *Al-Kāfī*, Vol. 4, P. 269.

misunderstandings. It is important to make sure that you are not criticizing the person, but rather the action (or the issue), otherwise it will lead to defensiveness and only make things worse.

Another way is to take your spouse out to an open space where by default you cannot scream, like walking in a park or a quiet coffee shop where you can express issues in a better manner. If things are really tense, then it is important to have a qualified marriage counselor as an arbitrator who understands your culture, Islam, and marital conflicts.

Avoid Lectures if Your Spouse Makes a Mistake

أحب إخواني إلي من أهدى إلي عيوبي.

Imām aṣ-Ṣādiq ﷺ said: *"The most beloved brother (or sister) of mine is the one who makes me aware of my faults."*[12]

Mistakes are expected to be performed by all of humanity. No one is perfect except for the immaculate ones (*Maʿṣumīn*). We need to point out the mistakes of our loved ones as a means of trying to help them reform, and in the manner of giving a 'gift.' How does one do this? When you give a gift, you give it with respect, and at the right moment.

When your spouse makes a mistake, respond with kindness, and avoid blaming them, or giving lectures. Have humility and think of your own mistakes, and listen to them without offering any advice. Ask sincere questions to help you understand the situation, and make your spouse feel heard. You are more likely to get your spouse to rectify their mistakes this way, thereby giving you a happier and healthier marriage.

Blame games, judgments, and accusatory tones will often lead to defensiveness, and your spouse will likely turn the tables around and mention the mistakes that you have made. Things then will

[12] *Al-Kāfī*, Vol. 4, P. 687.

most likely spiral out of control, and you will be in a worse situation than you were beforehand.

The Origin of Anger

أشجع الناس من غلب هواه.

Imām ʿAlī ﷺ said: *"The bravest of people are those who overcome their whims and desires."* [13]

When it comes to inappropriate anger, here is a helpful tip in dealing with it and trying to overcome this vice. It is important to distinguish between the causes of anger, and the stimulus to that anger. People do not 'cause' your anger. Anger is an internal process. All that the outside environment can do is be a stimulus.

So how is anger caused within us? Internal anger comes from finding faults, blaming and judging others, or other circumstances. This does not mean that outside people cannot be at fault, or that external circumstances are not objectively unfair, but they are not ultimately the masters of your internal emotions, only you can be.

So next time, try to be mindful when you think of your spouse as the root cause of your anger. You yourself are the cause of your own anger.

Looking at Marital Conflict through Awareness, Not Pride

يَا أَيُّهَا الَّذِينَ آمَنُوا اجْتَنِبُوا كَثِيرًا مِنَ الظَّنِّ إِنَّ بَعْضَ الظَّنِّ إِثْمٌ

"O You who believe! Avoid much suspicion, indeed some suspicions are sins." [14]

Remember that you do not have a monopoly on the truth, nor are you omniscient of the moral culpability of your spouse. Although

[13] *Man lā Yaḥḍuruhu al-Faqīh*, Vol. 4, P. 395.

[14] Noble Qurʾān, Sūrah al-Ḥujurāt (49), Verse 12.

sometimes things may be clear, most of the time fights between spouses are in the moral gray zone. Be slow in making accusations, be compassionate, and understand the context and story that allowed your spouse to hurt you.

If you look at the situation with real awareness, then you may realize that your spouse is not as guilty as you first thought they were, and it could be that you may have done (or not done) things that contributed to the problem.

Therefore, understand that there are many vantage points in judging whether or not something is moral in situations like these. We often see things in black and white because our judgment is clouded by our pride. Learn to be truly aware and put your arrogance aside, and you will see wonders in your marriage.

Choice in Jobs and Legitimate (Ḥalāl) Income

يَا أَيُّهَا النَّاسُ كُلُوا مِمَّا فِي الْأَرْضِ حَلَالًا طَيِّبًا وَلَا تَتَّبِعُوا خُطُوَاتِ الشَّيْطَانِ ۚ إِنَّهُ لَكُمْ عَدُوٌّ مُبِينٌ

"O humankind! Eat from whatever is on the earth (that which is) lawful and good, and do not follow the footsteps of Satan. Indeed, he is a manifest enemy to you."[15]

Earning a livelihood and our jobs are one of the areas which most people spend a lot of their waking hours in. Prophet Muḥammad ﷺ taught us that from where and how we earn our wealth has a direct effect on the blessings (*barakāt*) that we incur in life. Divine blessings are necessary ingredients to a healthy spiritual life, and in turn a healthy spiritual life is essential for a truly peaceful life.

Sometimes marital and family conflicts can be rooted in the fact that the money earned in the home is not from permissible (*ḥalāl*) means. In some instances, the sources of conflicts in marriages are due for these reasons, and spouses will find that when the

[15] Noble Qur'ān, Sūrah al-Baqarah (2), Verse 168.

household's income becomes legitimate (*ḥalāl*), then the spirits will heal through the blessings, and the conflicts that were plaguing them will also eventually vanish.

In some cases, the career or job that is undertaken by a spouse - even though it is permissible - is inappropriate, dangerous, or not compatible with family life, all of which can strain a marriage. Often enough, a change in such careers, when possible, can heal married life.

Creating a Culture of Conversation for Conflict Resolution

وَقُولُوا لَهُمْ قَوْلًا مَّعْرُوفًا

"And speak to them (with) honorable words."[16]

Couples who do not have a good culture of conversation for conflict resolution are rarely successful. But these types of conversations do not come spontaneously, they have to be learned then practiced.

How can this be done? Here are a few suggestions:

1. At least once a week, make an appointment to have a conversation with your spouse.
2. Make sure that your scheduling will not be in conflict with other activities, and it is at a time where both of you are relatively in good spirits.
3. Pick a positive place to speak (a restaurant, or a coffee shop that you both enjoy, etc.). Do not have these meetings at home, or in your bedroom, or at the movie theaters where you will not be able to talk properly.
4. Make sure not to bring your children, or other family members.
5. Create some rules of conversation, such as:
   a. Begin with the positives and praise each other;

[16] Noble Qur'ān, Sūrah an-Nisā' (4), Verse 8.

b. Do not interrupt one another, take turns to speak for five minutes each without being interrupted;

c. Do not criticize your spouse, rather criticize their actions; do not blame or judge them, speak about how you feel;

d. Be aware of how you feel and communicate it respectfully and calmly;

e. Express your needs in a respectful manner; but do not keep bringing up past events;

f. Do not talk about other people, just talk about yourselves;

g. Do not make promises that you cannot or do not intend to fulfill.

Do not worry if your appointment with your spouse gets canceled due to some reason. Sometimes things in life come up, do not let the frustration defeat the purpose of why you are having these sessions. Simply reschedule it for another time.

What can Cloud our Judgments

يَا أَيُّهَا الَّذِينَ آمَنُوا اجْتَنِبُوا كَثِيرًا مِّنَ الظَّنِّ إِنَّ بَعْضَ الظَّنِّ إِثْمٌ ۖ وَلَا تَجَسَّسُوا وَلَا يَغْتَب بَّعْضُكُم بَعْضًا ۚ أَيُحِبُّ أَحَدُكُمْ أَن يَأْكُلَ لَحْمَ أَخِيهِ مَيْتًا فَكَرِهْتُمُوهُ ۚ وَاتَّقُوا اللَّهَ ۚ إِنَّ اللَّهَ تَوَّابٌ رَّحِيمٌ

"O you who believe! Avoid much suspicion; indeed, some suspicions are sins. And do not spy or backbite one another. Will any of you like to eat the flesh of their dead brother? You would hate it. Be conscious of (fear) God; indeed, God is All-Clement, All-Merciful." [17]

Sometimes previously non-existent tensions arise between couples because their perceptions become tainted by outside forces.

For example, certain issues which were initially considered benign by the couple can be dramatized by family members, friends,

[17] Noble Qur'ān, Sūrah al-Ḥujurāt (49), Verse 12.

acquaintances, or even enemies. At other times, propaganda through social media, movies, and other entertainment or informational mediums can warp our perspectives, raise expectations, and change important values that can lead to or exacerbate conflicts inside the family structure.

These factors often ruin marriages and families. Be cautious of the outside judgments you absorb. They may make you feel righteous or victimized, but they can destroy your life and long-term happiness.

Who to Seek Counseling From

ما تشاور قوم إلا هدوا إلى رشدهم.

Imām Ḥasan ﷺ said: *"When people go for counseling (or deliberate on matters) surely they will be guided toward the proper actions."* [18]

When people want to resolve conflicts, getting marital counseling and/or advice through a third party is vital for strengthening their marriage. Āyatullāh Bahjat used to go to his teacher Āyatullāh Marʿashī Najafī for counseling.

Counselors should be qualified both in terms of counseling and Islamic knowledge. Sometimes it happens that counselors - although they mean well - do not have sufficient background information about the values and beliefs of Islam, thus they end up giving erroneous advice.

The advisor should be someone that one can trust and confide in, and who honestly wants to see the marriage succeed, and not have one spouse triumph over the other.

As much as you can, avoid engaging your parents or other close family members as counselors as they will often inherently be biased in favor of you.

People have a misconception that the Qurʾān encourages people

[18] *Biḥār al-Anwār*, Vol. 75, P. 105.

to involve their family members. They usually site the following verse from the Qur'ān:

وَإِنْ خِفْتُمْ شِقَاقَ بَيْنِهِمَا فَابْعَثُوا حَكَمًا مِنْ أَهْلِهِ وَحَكَمًا مِنْ أَهْلِهَا
إِنْ يُرِيدَا إِصْلَاحًا يُوَفِّقِ اللَّهُ بَيْنَهُمَا ۗ إِنَّ اللَّهَ كَانَ عَلِيمًا خَبِيرًا

"And if you fear dissension between the two of them, then appoint an arbiter from his relatives, and an arbiter from her relatives. If they both desire reconciliation, then God shall cause it between them two. Indeed God is All-Knowing, All-Aware." [19]

This verse refers to certain extreme circumstances where counseling is of no help, such as cases of impending divorce (after counseling was sought and did not work), or when someone wants to involve law enforcement or an attorney. The Qur'ān here is saying that perhaps involving family arbitration in these cases may be better.

Be Soft in Speech

وَقُولُوا لِلنَّاسِ حُسْنًا

"And speak to people kindly." [20]

Our verbal and bodily expressions determine the level of harmony we have with others, and ultimately our happiness. How we start a conversation will be a game changer in the harmony we have with other people, and by extension our satisfaction in life.

If you want to address a problem with your spouse and you address them in a harsh tone, then it is highly likely that your spouse will put up walls and become defensive. Once your spouse becomes defensive, then it is likely that your message will not be registered.

Remember that you are not dealing with a robot, you are dealing with a human being whose receptivity to what you are saying largely depends on HOW (and when) you say it. If you start in a

[19] Noble Qur'ān, Sūrah an-Nisā' (4), Verse 35.

[20] Noble Qur'ān, Sūrah al-Baqarah (2), Verse 83.

harsh way, then most likely your argument will end in a harsh way.

On the contrary, if you start off softly, gently, and respectfully, you have a better chance of getting your message across and ending the conversion on a good note. Maybe you will not get 100% of what you desire, but you are likely to get more (maybe even significantly more) than if you were to be harsh.

Even if by chance you were to get what you wanted through harshness, chances are that it will come at the price of resentment, and will eventually backfire in the long term (or maybe even in the short term).

Actionable Puzzles During Conflict

Formulating Criticisms the Right Way

فَلَا تَقُلْ لَهُمَا أُفٍّ وَلَا تَنْهَرْهُمَا وَقُلْ لَهُمَا قَوْلًا كَرِيمًا

"Do not say to them words of disrespect - ugh, nor scold them, but speak to them respectfully."[21]

A critical component of success in marriages is how criticisms are formulated. It is natural to sometimes feel hurt, frustrated, or betrayed, but blaming and attacking another person's character will not solve your problems, it will only make them defensive. In the case of your spouse, once they are defensive, they will no longer listen to you. Instead of listening to your words, they will simply think of come-back responses. If there is enough anger, then even your words will be misunderstood and twisted in a way that you did not intend.

Pay attention to this point: During arguments, logical reasoning does not always solve problems, especially if someone is going through emotional or physical pain. Addressing the emotions is more important than addressing with logic.

[21] Noble Qur'ān, Sūrah al-Isrā' (17), Verse 23.

No matter how good your relationship is, no one likes to be criticized, and it is very likely that the person at the other end of the criticism will become defensive. Does this mean that we should do away with criticism all the time? No, but we need to be tactful about it.

Most couples only spend a minority of the time actually listening to one another. The rest of the time things are misunderstood and not paid attention to which can open a Pandora's box of problems in one's relationships.

So, what is the solution? First of all, stop using the word "you" when you want to express issues that you are facing with your spouse, or at the very least, use it as minimally as possible without accusing. Use the word "I" instead. Try to begin by stating your own feelings as neutrally as possible. Some clinical marriage therapists call this technique: Converting your complaints into "positive needs."

So, for example, let us say that the husband in a particular relationship is tasked with taking out the garbage, here are three possible ways out of many that you can formulate your complaint if they did not take it out when they were supposed to:

- Complaint + Indirect Personal Attack: "Why didn't you take out the garbage?"
- Complaint + Personal Attack: "Why didn't you take out the garage? How many times do I have to tell you before you do anything?"
- Complaint + Heavy Personal Attack: "Why can't you remember anything? Stop being so lazy for once and do what you're supposed to do. I'm not going to ask you again to take out the garbage."

Notice that even lightly complaining, and asking the "why" first will likely put your spouse on the defensive.

Now let us try to turn this into a positive need:

"I'm happy that we agreed on delegating responsibilities, and I'm glad that you took the responsibility of taking out the garbage. I took the responsibility of cleaning the home and was able to fulfill my job. I noticed that you did not have the time or forgot to take out the garbage, please understand that cleanliness is really important for us."

Will 100% of the spouses listen to this? Probably not, but is it less likely to put your spouse on the defensive, and thereby prevent a fight. Is it more likely to get the job done? Of course!

Sometimes it is difficult to convert complaints into positive needs. Instead of rushing to say something, sit down and list your complaint on paper. Through writing, try to convert it into a positive need. This will take some practice, and you will make lots of mistakes, but eventually you will get the hang of it, learn more, and become much better at communicating with your spouse.

Avoid Arguing When in a State of Anger

أول الغضب جنون وآخره ندم.

Imām ʿAlī ﷺ said: *"The beginning of anger is insanity, and its end is regret."* [22]

Anger is like tumultuous waters in a closed container, if you open it, all of it will gush out. But if you let it calm down and then open the lid, nothing will spill out. In the same way, when you are angry you can rarely control what comes out of your mouth and you will end up making a mess, but if you let yourself calm down you will have much more control over what is said.

Arguing is a normal part of married life. What one should avoid though is arguing while a person is in a state of anger. If the matter is pressing and you need to talk and argue the same day, then go out

[22] *Sharḥ Nahj al-Balāghah*, Vol. 20, P. 367.

and take a walk for at least 30 minutes to an hour before you begin to address your concerns.

Walking is one of the best ways to calm your emotions and add clarity to your perspective. If you are angry, then chances are that you will only hear what you want to hear, not what is actually being said; and you will say and do things that you will most likely regret later on because your judgment will be clouded by your anger.

Bite Your Tongue and Do Not Say that Mean Thing

لسان العاقل وراء قلبه وقلب الأحمق وراء لسانه.

Imām ʿAlī ﷺ said: *"The tongue of an intelligent person is at the mercy of one's heart, whereas the heart of a foolish person is at the mercy of one's tongue."* [23]

If you have a choice between saying something mean to your spouse or saying nothing at all, then always opt for the latter.

Not saying anything does not mean that you stonewall (or completely ignore) your spouse, that can be more damaging than saying something hurtful as it is belittling and humiliating them.

What it means is that you can continue speaking, but without the hurtful words. If you are really in a state of anger, then you can politely ask your spouse to excuse yourself to process and think about the tense situation.

To emphasize the point mentioned, sometimes not speaking can be more damaging than saying something hurtful. You can kindly tell your spouse that you want to speak about it later, and request them to allow you to think things over. At this point you can change the subject with the promise that you will visit the topic again once you have had time to process it more.

[23] *Nahj al-Balāghah*, Short Saying #40.

Wait Before Giving Your Side of the Story

عن ابن عساكر قال شبيب بن شيبة رحمه الله من سمع كلمة
يكرهها فسكت انقطع عنه ما يكره وإن أجاب سمع أكثر مما يكره.

On the authority of Ibn Asākir, Shabīb ibn Shaybah said: *"Whoever hears a word that they disapprove of and they remain silent, what they disapprove of will cease. But if they respond to it, then they will hear more of what they disapprove of."* [24]

When you want to give your side of the story in a conflict, sometimes it is better to do so at another time, and just keep silent and listen to what the other person is saying. When people are emotional, they seldom hear what you are actually saying, they only hear what they want to hear and those expectations are often guided by their tumultuous emotions. In this case, giving your side of the story may just make things worse.

Holding off on giving your side of the story also allows you to make your spouse feel heard. When people are listened to, they feel validated and their difficult emotions tend to balance out, making them more open-minded to hear your story when it is relayed to them.

This strategy will also help you understand your spouse better. When we are only focused on trying to explain ourselves, then our minds are not entirely present to what is actually being said by our spouses.

During a fight, it is not the time to have a logical discussion. Your side of the story is important, but if you know that emotions are high, then a logical discussion will probably make things worse because sometimes they are incompatible.

In my own experience, whenever I have conflicts with my wife, instead of arguing logically, I simply hug her and listen to what

[24] Ibn Manẓūr, Muḥammad ibn Mukarram, *Mukhtaṣar Tārīkh al-Dimashq*, (n.d: n.p), Vol. 10, P. 273.

she has to say. After my spouse calms down, then I give my own side of the argument. I always find that she is more receptive to my thoughts after this. At other times, this calmness allows me to see my own mistakes as well, even though I thought I was being logical.

Just Because it is True, Does Not Mean You have to Say it

لا تقـل مـا لا تعلـم، بـل لا تقـل كل مـا تعلـم، فـان اللـه فـرض
علـى جوارحـک کلهـا فرائـض يحتـج بهـا عليـک يـوم القيامـه

Imām ʿAlī ﷺ said: *"Do not say what you do not know. Even more, do not say all that you know, for God prescribed divine precepts to your body parts that will protest against you on the Day of Resurrection."*[25]

The nature of marriage is that you will eventually know each other's pasts and secrets, as well as those of each other's family members. When arguments come up, make sure not to bring up sensitive topics, or things that are irrelevant, or things that have to do with other family members or other people, or anything that is just plain mean, rude, or hurtful.

If you are arguing with your spouse and you want to say something mean (even if you know that it is "true"), it is better not to say anything at all. If your spouse presses you to talk, then one option is to kindly say that you need to think about the situation and get back to them (knowing your spouse, you can figure out a way to avoid giving a mean response if this suggestion is unrealistic).

If you say a mean thing, then chances are that you will forget the mean thing you said, but your spouse will not. Just because your spouse does not bring up the mean things that you said in the past, does not mean that they have forgotten them. Some people just bottle it up and manifest their resentment in different ways. So

[25] *Man lā Yaḥḍuruhu al-Faqīh*, Vol. 2, P. 626.

remember that nothing you say will go without a consequence, you will eventually eat the fruit of your own words one way or another.

Know When to Stop

وَتِلْكَ حُدُودُ اللَّهِ ۚ وَمَنْ يَتَعَدَّ حُدُودَ اللَّهِ فَقَدْ ظَلَمَ نَفْسَهُ

"And these are the boundaries of God, whoever transgresses the boundaries of God has certainly wronged oneself." [26]

It is natural for all couples to argue and disagree. When they do so, it is also common for things to sometimes go beyond what they were intended. How can we know when boundaries are being crossed? Look at your feelings, are you feeling angry? Are you bringing up the past again concerning something you argued about before already? Are you talking about issues that are not even in your spouse's control? Are you going on about other family members? If your answer to any of these questions is yes, then it is best to stop the argument before it gets worse.

Having an argument with your spouse is no casual matter. It involves many emotions like anger, fear, and sadness. It is normal to say things we may not mean, or to say them in such a way that just makes things worse. As bad as arguments often are, they can always escalate and become very intense.

Good couples are aware of their limits, and know when things will start to go downhill. If you see that you are becoming overwhelmed, then pause and find a way to soothe yourself either by sitting down, counting, praying, or leaving the discussion for another time when things cool down a bit. You will eventually know what works best for you. A good example is when there is a heated discussion, and one of the parties who is more emotionally regulated takes the initiative to calm things down. An unhealthy example would be to lead tensions to the point where yelling takes

[26] Noble Qur'ān, Sūrah aṭ-Ṭalāq (65), Verse 1.

place, or false stories are invented which create even more problems in the future.

The Importance of being Heard during Conflicts

جلـوس المـرء عنـد عيالـه احـب الـى اللـه تعالـى مـن اعتـكاف فـى مسـجدى هـذا.

Prophet Muḥammad ﷺ said: *"A man sitting with his wife is more beloved to God than if he were to stay the whole night praying in my mosque."* [27]

Oftentimes we think that by explaining certain things, we are being good and kind, but this can sometimes be wrong. Goodness and kindness come from listening to our spouses.

Your spouse will only listen to you after they feel listened to. One of the primary reasons why communication is so difficult between married couples is because one of the spouses often constantly interrupts the other with defensiveness and explanations. Try to listen to your spouse as if they are talking about themselves and not you. Try to ask questions to show that you are really listening to them. For instance, you can ask them: "Can you give me an example?" By feeling listened to, your spouse will become less defensive and less hostile, thus opening the path for a solution or compromise. If feelings are too tense at a certain time, then try setting up a time later on to discuss the matter. But be precise in your time - even make an appointment so it does not get neglected.

Always Maintain Respect

يَا أَيُّهَا الَّذِينَ آمَنُوا لَا يَسْخَرْ قَوْمٌ مِّنْ قَوْمٍ

"O you who believe! Let not people ridicule other people." [28]

---

[27] *Tafsīre Nūr*, Vol. 10, P. 97.

[28] Noble Qur'ān, Sūrah al-Ḥujurāt (49), Verse 11.

When you are respectful, its results will be vastly different from when you disrespect your spouse.

Respect must constantly be there in a marriage if it is to remain healthy. After some time, many people take their spouses for granted and forget to be respectful to them. Disrespect can be done consciously, as in making fun of or mocking your spouse; or it can be done unintentionally. For example, when you want something, you may yell from the sofa that you want X or Y.

Try to remember that your relationship is something that needs to be nurtured daily. Mocking and shouting orders will not help at all. Instead of shouting at them from the couch, get up and move closer to them, then ask respectfully. You will notice your speech becoming softer and more loving when you take the time to be more respectful.

Do Not Censure during Moments of Animosity

إذا غضب أحدكم فليسكت.

Prophet Muḥammad ﷺ said: *"When one of you becomes angry, you (meaning the other person) should be quiet [and not say anything at the moment of anger]."* [29]

Beware of criticizing people during moments of anger and antagonism. Even if you hide your animosity, people will unconsciously pick up on it because it is hard to control non-verbal cues. The net result is that your fury will clash with their pride, and it can spark a huge fire.

It is better to pause and self-reflect before you censure. Ask yourself about your motivations for censuring. Dig deep and search for the real reason. If your motivations are selfish, then look at your own shortcomings and try to see things from the other person's

[29] ʿAllāmah Majlisī, *Mirāt al-ʿUqūl fī Sharḥ Akhbār ar-Rasūl*, 26 Vols., Ed. Hāshim Rasūlī Maḥlātī, (Tehran: Dār al-Kutub al-Islāmīyah, 1404/1983), Vol. 8, P. 205.

perspective. After you do this, try to find some compassion in your heart and change your emotional mindset.

When you point out faults based on love and compassion, people are able to sense it and will be more receptive. As such, trying to delay your censure rather than rushing into it may bring about more positive outcomes by lessening tensions and resentment.

Post-Conflict Thoughts

Being Right the Wrong Way is Wrong

وَلَا تَزِرُ وَازِرَةٌ وِزْرَ أُخْرَىٰ ۚ وَإِن تَدْعُ مُثْقَلَةٌ إِلَىٰ حِمْلِهَا لَا يُحْمَلْ مِنْهُ
شَيْءٌ وَلَوْ كَانَ ذَا قُرْبَىٰ

"And no bearer of burdens shall bear the burden of another. Even if one weighted down calls for help with its burden, none of it will be lifted, even by a close relative." [30]

An important reality that people often forget is: Being right the wrong way is wrong.

This can happen in multiple ways. Either through insults, belittling, fear, revenge, or what have you. The net result will be spiritual and marital damage to both sides. For example, if your spouse continues to come home very late without a valid reason, they are at fault. But if you insult them for it, it will not make the situation any better, nor will it bring about a solution. Instead it will cause more resentment, and may even make matters worse in the relationship.

First, it will not allow spouses to process their mistakes when they were the ones who were wrong, instead it will breed resentment and make them forget the actual wrong that they did.

Second, expressing one's correctness the wrong way [with bad manners or inappropriate etiquettes (*akhlāq*)] is a very dangerous habit that can easily be formed as feelings of righteous offense, and

[30] Noble Qur'ān, Sūrah al-Fāṭir (35), Verse 18.

this can feed into one's pride and delude people into thinking that their reactions are justified. Bad manners are bad manners, and they will have negative consequences on one's soul and spiritual development no matter the reason.

Marital happiness should be to the benefit of both spouses. Proving oneself to be right the wrong way will only harm the marriage and both of the spouses.

There are two conclusions which we can derive from this. First of all, a big mistake that we make is in believing that when we are hurt, the ends justify the means. Second, if our message is conveyed wrongfully, then our spouse may, out of anger, deflect the blame on us and past mistakes. As such, being right the right way is productive, but being right the wrong way is counterproductive.

Criticize the Action, Not the Person

لا تنظر إلى من قال وانظر إلى ما قال.

Imām ʿAlī ﷺ said: *"Do not look at <u>who</u> is saying it, but look at <u>what</u> is being said."*[31]

When points of tension are being addressed in a relationship, **facts** should be discussed, **not the person**. There is no need to call the other person names, or associate their faults with their personality, families, looks, or anything beyond the direct issues at hand.

A big mistake that some married couples make is name calling, or attacking the partner personally. For example, if your spouse forgets to do something, do not start insulting them and calling them names. This also means that you should not be sarcastic, nor roll your eyes because even that is insulting.

So what should a person do? Instead of insulting your spouse's intelligence, or attacking their character, talk about the problem itself and explain how it bothers or hurts you. For example, if your spouse leaves the house messy, do not insult them by saying "You

[31] *ʿUyūn al-Ḥikam wa al-Mawāʿiẓ*, P. 241.

always ...," or "Why are you so ..." - but talk about how they left the house messy, and the fact that it really bothers you. Speak about your own feelings, not their personality.

Now, does this mean that the problem will be solved? Not necessarily, but it is more likely to get the change that you want than if you were to shout insults. Degrading them will only lead to resentment, and resentment may cause your spouse to act out and make matters even worse. Be patient and keep repeating the criticism of the action, NOT the actual person.

Even if you are not able to fix the problem completely, you are more likely to have some improvement rather than nothing happening, or God forbid, making things worse.

Being Right vs. Having a Relationship

قَالَ أَنَا خَيْرٌ مِنْهُ ۖ خَلَقْتَنِي مِنْ نَارٍ وَخَلَقْتَهُ مِنْ طِينٍ

"He (Satan) said: 'I am better than him (Ādam), You created me from fire, but You created him from clay.'" [32]

Perhaps one of the reasons why Prophet Ādam (Adam) ﷺ became God's representative on earth and not Satan was because Prophet Ādam ﷺ acknowledged his own mistake, and was not proud.

None of us are perfect. We are not immune to making mistakes. Mistakes can happen to anyone at any time. If people think that they are perfect and better than others, then there will be no reason for them to improve themselves. This is dangerous because they will always see the problems in others, but will never see or acknowledge their own faults.

The subjects and topics that most marital arguments revolve around are petty and inconsequential compared to your long-term happiness in life. Yet arrogantly persisting on being right may have long term negative consequences, especially in matters that are not

[32] Noble Qur'ān, Sūrah Ṣād (38), Verse 76.

so clear cut - in terms of who is right or wrong - which for a lot of people is most of the time. So, think deeply about it, do you just want to be right, or do you want to have a good relationship?

Learn to pick your battles. Many things are not worth insisting on being right about. The cost of being right over trivial matters can sometimes cause long lasting resentment.

Kindness vs. Shaming and Blaming

There is a Persian maxim which says:

ز محبت خارها گل می شود.

Through love, thorns become roses.

By nature, we are created as emotional beings, and our emotions are manifestations of the primordial love that God instilled within us. The only way to truly connect with someone's deep self is through love. If you start with blaming and shaming, you will only drive the person away; but if you begin with kindness and love, you will drive them closer.

The Prophetic way (*sunnah*) of dealing with mistakes was always with kindness, instead of shaming or blaming. When it is appropriate, try to use questions to help your spouse or another family member understand the consequences of their choices.

For example, if your spouse made a mistake or did something hurtful to you, it will be counterproductive if you begin to attack them. Chances are that they will become defensive and perhaps even do more of those things that were hurtful to you.

Instead, if you ask your spouse a question like: "How do you think that makes me feel?" you are more likely to get them to empathize with you and realize the mistakes that were done.

Putting people in the defense will usually shut them down, or make them more aggressive. Empathy on the other hand will have the opposite effect.

Understanding Criticisms as Unmet Needs

قَوْلٌ مَعْرُوفٌ وَمَغْفِرَةٌ خَيْرٌ مِنْ صَدَقَةٍ يَتْبَعُهَا أَذًى ۗ وَاللَّهُ غَنِيٌّ حَلِيمٌ

"Kind words and forgiveness (of faults) are better than charity followed by injury; and God is Self-Sufficient, All-Forbearing."[33]

Criticisms are often taken as **intentional** personal attacks. But it is quite common that the underlying motive behind personal criticisms are not intentional personal attacks, but a way of expressing frustration at an unmet series of needs.

If your spouse criticizes you, then observe and reflect on your spouse deeply, and try to see what unmet need is trying to be expressed between the negative comments or hurtful words.

Here are two examples:

Criticism: "You are the most self-centered person I have met!"
Feeling: Hurt.
Need: Consideration.

Criticism: "You never listen to me when I'm talking!"
Feeling: Upset, feels unimportant.
Need: Undivided attention, quality time.

Sometimes the unmet needs are not too obvious so you may want to ask questions for clarification. Over time, you will get better and better at detecting the unmet need which is being expressed.

Why is this important? When you can see beyond the criticism and understand the need one requires, you are less likely to get angry and say something hurtful or become defensive, all of which will just make the conflict even worse. Hurtful words always end in regret. Not only will it be more likely that you will stay tranquil and calm the situation down, but the real problems of your marriage will more likely be addressed, thus improving the quality of your overall relationship.

[33] Noble Qur'ān, Sūrah al-Baqarah (2), Verse 263.

The Importance of Honesty

إلزموا الصدق فإنه منجاة.

Imām ʿAlī said: *"Be honest, because surely (through) it (there) will be salvation."* [34]

Oftentimes, core conflicts remain unresolved because there is a lack of honesty. Honesty and respect is where conflict resolution begins.

Honesty is the foundation of a relationship. It is the basis of trust. If trust is destroyed, then so is peace. Honesty is therefore the foundational pillar of good relationships.

If honesty is weakened or broken, then communication and love will be tainted, weakened, and start to deteriorate.

Do Not Deny Your Mistakes

كل بني آدم خطاء, وخير الخطّائين التوابون.

Prophet Muḥammad said: *"Every son of Ādam makes mistakes (sins), and the best of the sinners are those who repent."* [35]

When you make a mistake, acknowledge it and apologize. Denying it will only make your spouse angrier. If your spouse is angry and resentful, then they will be less likely to see your humanity and fallibility in your mistake, and more likely to see you as an oppressor.

Apologizing does not always have to come in the form of a verbal "I'm sorry." It can come through other means such as cooking, buying a nice meal, or buying a gift for the person that you transgressed against.

---

[34] *Tuḥaf al-ʿUqūl*, P. 104.
[35] *Nahj al-Faṣāḥah*, P. 609.

General Advice on Conflict Resolution

Be Aware of the False Wisdom of Your Anger

الغضب مفتاح كل شر.

Imām aṣ-Ṣādiq ﷺ said: *"Anger is the key to all evil."*[36]

Our expressions, our words, and reasoning are the result of our internal emotional states. If we are angry inside, then our expressions, our words, and reasoning will be full of anger even if we suppose that they are wise. We cannot be wise if we are not calm.

One of the most dangerous parts of anger is that in that moment, the solutions, answers, and ideas which we think about seem to be the most rational options and reactions possible. Little are we aware that our common sense is almost completely shut down, and we are basically under delusion.

So beware of the false and deceptive wisdom that comes to your mind during a state of anger. If you wish to say something or act while in a state of rage, then make sure to give yourself at least two days before you do anything harsh that you may regret later on.

If after two days you still want to say or do the same thing, then just to be on the safe side give yourself another day or two again before acting out on the options for yourself. Anger is one of the few things that gets better with delay, and it is almost certain that after some time you will realize how foolish your initial wisdom was.

There is always the option to say or do things you have not yet done, but you can never take back your words or actions once they are done.

We should take this into consideration when we feel angry toward our spouses and want to say something "logical" but it could really damage our relationship later on.

---

[36] *Al-Kāfī*, Vol. 3, P. 740.

Five Quick Rules for Marital Conflict

من تزوج فقد أحرز شطر دينه فليتق الله في الباقي.

Prophet Muḥammad ﷺ said: *"When a person gets married, they have fortified half of their religion, so let them fear God (have God-consciousness) in regards to the other half."* [37]

Having a strong marriage is part of our faith. Religion is not only prayer, fasting, or going to *Ḥajj*. Saving and nurturing our marriages is also a very important part of Islam.

There are many different pieces of marital advice that can be given. Perhaps the following are some of the most helpful ones:

1) Be fair in your fights, avoid overkill, and avoid low blows;

2) Be responsive to your partner, acknowledge their needs and try to do something about them, even if it is very small (it is better than doing nothing and ignoring them);

3) Give your spouse the benefit of the doubt, do not assume the worst (this is a very hard one, and it will require you to battle your own self and mind);

4) Lower your expectations of your spouse, and what they should do for you (most divorces are the result of expectations that are set too high);

5) Set aside some private quality time for just each other, not everything has to always involve your kids or work (find a babysitter, even if it is only for 1-2 hours a week).

[37] *Al-Amālī*, P. 518.

7

Dealing with a Difficult Spouse

People are not robots. They are not disembodied minds. We live in our bodies; we have emotions, and these emotions can sometimes be life-fulfilling, or they can get in the way of positive growth. Therefore it is of utmost importance to settle down and try to understand human emotions.

Even if we believe that we are emotionally mature and generally a stable person, marriage is often when we get tested. Especially because we are in a union with someone who is of a different educational, cultural, and familial background to us. This union is more than just a living arrangement, or a project that you are working on together. Marriage has a big role in our lives, and the Qur᾽ān shows us this reality.

The Qur᾽ān mentions how God created Ādam (ʿa) and Ḥawwā᾽ (Adam and Eve) - the first married human couple - from the same soul:

هُوَ الَّذِي خَلَقَكُم مِّن نَّفْسٍ وَاحِدَةٍ وَجَعَلَ مِنْهَا زَوْجَهَا لِيَسْكُنَ

"It is He who created you from a single soul, and made from it its mate, that he might find comfort with her."[1]

[1] Noble Qur᾽ān, Sūrah al-Aʿrāf (7), Verse 189.

In the continual process of marriage over the generations since the creation of humanity, God has described a husband and wife as protective garments for each other:

هُنَّ لِبَاسٌ لَكُمْ وَأَنْتُمْ لِبَاسٌ لَهُنَّ

"They (your wives) are an apparel for you, and you are an apparel for them."[2]

Āyatullāh Nāṣir Makārim Shīrāzī explains that the garment metaphor fulfills three major functions in marriage.[3] First off, it is protective. Just like clothing is meant to protect us from the heat, the sun, or cold weather; similarly our spouse and marriage is supposed to protect people from sins and vices. Second, garments hide our bodily private parts, and any defects we may have in our bodies; likewise our spouses are tasked to hide our faults, defects, and keep our secrets. Third, garments make us beautiful; and on a similar note, our spouses are there to beautify us by helping us develop our character and increase our spirituality and get closer to God.

The Qur'ān sets a correct paradigm in approaching marriage, however our subjective perceptions and difficulties in understanding and managing our emotions inhibit us from approaching ourselves, our spouses, and our overall relationships with an objective approach.

Our expectations, misunderstandings, and misconceptions sometimes make us biased against our spouses. Instead of truly understanding our spouses, we preconceive and imagine them in our minds in ways that are not in accordance with reality. It is often the case that our spouses in real life, and our perceptions of them in our imagination are completely different beings.

Part of the reason why this happens is because we have a lack

---

[2] Noble Qur'ān, Sūrah al-Baqarah (2), Verse 187.

[3] Shīrāzī, Nāṣir Makārim, *Tafsīre Nemūnah*, 27 Vols., (Tehran: Dār al-Kutub al-Islāmīyah, 1374/1995-1996), Vol. 1, P. 650.

of data. For example, most couples live separate lives most of the day. One is working, and the other is at home with the children, or perhaps both are working various jobs in different places. In our experience, couples often overestimate the amount of work that they themselves do, and they underestimate the amount of work and stress that their spouse goes through during the day. This is often a recipe for disaster.

Other examples are more subtle, but perhaps a lot more destructive. We often misjudge our spouse's intentions based on preconceived notions and experiences in the past, either with them or with other people. We label people, compare and judge, jump into absolutes, and black-and-white characterizations; for example: *my in-laws are bad, he's so selfish, she's so lazy, he never loved me, she just wants to use me*, or what have you.

We often forget that there are no absolutes. People's personalities and moral lives are a spectrum. Our spouses are not black and white; they are complex beings with a whole lot of good mixed in with some bad. Intentions change over time, people learn, and they either grow or they regress. The human condition is a constant flux.

ཀྵ

No matter how good your marriage may be, at some point in time your spouse is going to be difficult to deal with. Many couples, be they Muslim or not, will have to deal with difficult spouses in their marriages for years and perhaps even decades to come. But this does not need to be a dire situation. In this chapter we will look at the positive side of having a difficult spouse. We will look at how difficult spouses can be integral keys in the process of self-transformation and attaining the ultimate goal of our creation, namely union with (meeting) God (*Liqāʾ Allāh*).

Before we begin this chapter, there are three key elements that the reader should keep in mind before they try to implement the advice given in this chapter:

Do Not Try to 'Fix' Your Spouse's Emotions

يَا أَيُّهَا الَّذِينَ آمَنُوا لَا يَسْخَرْ قَوْمٌ مِّن قَوْمٍ عَسَىٰ أَن يَكُونُوا خَيْرًا

"O you who have faith! Let not any people ridicule other people: it may be that they are better than them."[4]

A common mistake that spouses, parents, friends, and teachers make when dealing with an emotional person is that they see their emotions as a problem that needs to be fixed and solved. This can either be through punishment or "talking sense to a person" by belittling their emotions. In the latter case for example, it is common to hear hostile questions like "Why don't you appreciate all of the good things that you have in life?" Naturally such an approach will only make things worse.

We feel that these emotions can be taken care of easily and quickly, and when they are not, then we get frustrated and either quit or double-down, and leave the significant other in a worse emotional state than what they started off with.

The issue with trying to 'fix' people's emotions and bring solutions is that we frame the problem as a moral problem, and hence become too judgmental. We think that their emotions are a moral failing, and allow ourselves to reprimand and judge them.

People do not like to be judged or reprimanded. When they are treated as such, they simply go on the defensive which usually means that they will stop listening and will not do what you want them to do. If they do, they will do it with resentment and it will backfire some time in the near future.

The other way of handling your spouse's moods is not to see it as a problem to be fixed, but as a **mystery to be understood**.

When we try to **understand** a mystery rather than **solve** it, we are less likely to become judgemental and depreciate our spouse. Instead, we are more likely to:

[4] Noble Qur'ān, Sūrah al-Ḥujurāt (49), Verse 11.

1. Listen attentively (instead of listening so that we can come up with a comeback or refutation);
2. Validate their feelings (instead of dismissing or belittling them);
3. Understand the situation (this does not mean justifying it);
4. Be more empathetic (instead of being judgmental).

If you want to undertake the understanding rather than the problem-solving approach, then it is important to introspect your own thoughts. You can do this by looking at what kind of questions you ask yourself when your spouse is upset?

The following are a few examples of judgmental and problem-fixing thoughts:

1. Why are they so ungrateful?
2. Why can't they see all of the good that I do?
3. Wow, this isn't such a big deal, why do they have to make such a big deal out of this?
4. They don't need to worry about this, things will get better. If only they could realize this!
5. Why are they so attached to worldly things (*dunyā*)? Don't they know that this world is temporary and the next life is more important?

The following are a few examples of the **mystery-to-be-understood** type of thoughts; and a few examples of questions that one can ask to be in this kind of a frame of mind:

1. What's happening in their mind that is leading to these difficult feelings?
2. What outside circumstances triggered them to act and feel this way?
3. Last time I snapped or was in a bad mood, what set of situations built up in me to feel in such a similar painful way?

No approach is ever perfect and will always have weaknesses of its own. But in an intensely emotional situation, my experience as the īmām of a large center and counseling countless people who come to our office has shown that the mystery understanding approach has been far more effective than the problem fixing one.

When Your Spouse is Angry, Speak through Kindness

نكلم الناس على قدر عقولهم.

Prophet Muḥammad ﷺ said: *"We speak to people in accordance with the level of their intellect."*[5]

When I used to be upset, my wife would call one of my parents and ask them to call me. She would never even hint at them that we had fought. She would just say that the whole family missed them, and would like them to call. They would do so immediately after, and she would make sure to give the phone to me. When I would speak to them, I would get happy and lose all my stress. That was my wife's way of helping me without even saying a word directly to me!

There are some spouses who become very irritable if they are talked to while they are angry or emotional. If this is the case in your situation, then try holding back on your advice, comments, and even compliments for a short while.

Keep your words only to the minimum that is necessary, and show your love through actions (taking care of the kids, cleaning the house, buying gifts, etc). If hurtful things are said to you, do not get defensive. Let your spouse have their space and when things calm down, then you can open up a calm and non-judgmental discussion.

Do Not Withhold Praise

لَئِنْ شَكَرْتُمْ لَأَزِيدَنَّكُمْ

"If you are grateful, then I will surely increase you [in blessings]."[6]

---

[5] *Al-Kāfī*, Vol. 1, P. 51.

[6] Noble Qur'ān, Sūrah Ibrāhīm (14), Verse 7.

Some people think that by withholding encouragement and praise, or worse, by criticizing, they are pushing their spouses to better themselves. This rarely ever works. Most of the time it has the opposite result. The spouse will become even worse than before. They will become bitter, and the marriage will eventually go downhill and this will inevitably hurt the children.

Do not be shy in encouraging your spouse and praising them. More often than not, positive feedback can push your spouse to become a better person. When people feel appreciated, even for the smallest things, they will become more hopeful of the future, have a positive outlook, and be more motivated to do even greater things.

The Blessings of Having a Difficult Spouse

Origins of Some Forms of Negativity

الناس أعداء ما جهلوا.

Imām ʿAlī ﷺ said: *"People are enemies of what they are ignorant of."* [7]

One particular factor that seems to be at the root of the problem of many couples who have reached their limit when it comes to the negativity of their spouse is that those spouses who are at the receiving end of the negativity think that they are entirely at fault.

Although everyone plays a role in making relationships difficult, the negativity of one spouse is not always the fault of the other spouse. Sometimes hopelessness is the result of an inner emptiness, a trouble within the soul. Although negativity comes with blame, its true origin comes from inner misery. It is a further sign that the couple have yet to know each other at a deeper and more meaningful level.

In order to counter this negativity, try to see the inner emptiness and pain of your spouse. Do not make it about yourself, rather look

[7] *Ghurar al-Ḥikam*, P. 28.

beyond and see their pain and sorrow. This will create compassion in you and calm you down. The shift in your attitude may help heal some of your spouse's pain as well.

When this happens, you will realize that often enough, what you think of as negative is not actually negativity, it is your perception of your spouse that is negative. At this moment of realization, often the negativity will end up becoming sweet.

Do Not Force Your Will on Your Spouse

لَا إِكْرَاهَ فِي الدِّيْنِ

"There is no compulsion in religion."[8]

Connect before you correct someone.

We often want to force something upon others that we believe to be good, but forcing rarely brings about any good results in the long run. However, if we put in the time and effort to **honestly and kindly** express what is truly in our minds, and if our spouses accept our ideas, then we will have a better chance of our spouses cooperating with us.

In other words, when you say something to someone and they do not listen, it is generally not a good idea to force them to do that as it will not bring about the results that you wanted. When possible (and reasonable), reap the rewards of this difficulty by being patient. You will derive much more benefit from patience than compulsion.

Compulsion will bring about resentment, and resentment will make it less likely that your spouse will listen to you. Patience calms emotions down, and people are more likely to listen when they are in a calm state, that is, if the demand is reasonable.

Be kind, connect, but do not force. Force will often end up in regret.

[8] Noble Qur'ān, Sūrah al-Baqarah (2), Verse 256.

How You Talk to Your Spouse is How You Talk to God

من لم يشكر المخلوق لم يشكر الخالق.

Imām ar-Riḍā said: *"Whoever is not grateful to the created ones is not grateful to the Creator."* [9]

Your relationship with any single individual is not an isolated event, but it will permeate across the intricacies of all of your relationships. Try spending the day with a person who frustrates you and you will see how it affects your relationships with other people at home, and even the quality and concentration of your prayers (*ṣalāh*).

Your mind is not something which you can simply leave behind, it goes with you wherever you go, including in your prayers and your relationship with God. Dealing with difficult people by exercising patience (*ṣabr*) and compassion (*raḥmah*) will have ripple effects on the entire web and matrix of relationships that you belong to - whether human or Divine. This approach will foster positive growth in your mind and heart which happen to be at the center of your being.

In some sense, it may be said that the way you relate to people will be a reflection of the way you relate to God. In marriage, the way you relate and talk to your spouse will directly affect how you relate and talk to God.

Be Thankful for a Difficult Spouse

الانصاف يرفع الخلاف و يوجب الائتلاف.

Imām ʿAlī said: *"Fairness resolves differences and leads to harmony."* [10]

When we have a difficult spouse, we only see the negative aspect of their difficulty, not the positive side. The positive aspect is that

---

[9] *ʿUyūn Akhbār ar-Riḍā*, Vol. 2, P. 288.

[10] *Ghurar al-Ḥikam*, P. 88.

difficult spouses have lots of great qualities that we tend to overlook or underappreciate. For example, maybe they are tough, but this toughness may help in challenging times!

More importantly though, difficult and challenging spouses can help us learn and grow in our lives.

Think about it, if everyone was nice and kind to us, it is possible that it would lead us to complacency, and we would have little room to practice patience or forgiveness. It is through dealing with difficult and obnoxious people that we practice spiritual virtues like forbearance and compassion. In this sense, your best spiritual friends are those who give you a hard time.

From this vantage point, it would be a good idea to be grateful when difficult people are in our lives, especially our spouses whom we have to deal with on a regular basis.

This does not mean that we should tolerate abuse or violence in our lives;[11] rather it means that we should use every difficult moment as an opportunity for spiritual growth and self reform. We should pray to God for assistance and patience, and thank Him for these difficult people, and when we are grateful as such we will see that their presence will not bother us as much as before, and we will learn to deal with the situation to the best of our ability - seeking help from God Almighty.

Whenever you feel that you are blinded by your negative thinking of your spouse, try to actively look for their good qualities. Also, never forget that sometimes those negative qualities which you dislike so much at the present moment can sometimes become a life saver at other moments in your life! For example, some people used to complain that their spouses did not work, while they were

[11] There are multiple kinds of abuse and various roots for abuse. We have physical, mental, emotional, and spiritual abuse. Each one has a different extent, some may be at the beginning stage, while some are long term and unbearable. Some forms of abuse come from trauma, psychological problems, how one was raised, or even fits of anger. There is no simple solution for the different types of abuse which is why consulting with the right kind of counselor is very important in this regard.

working full time. Yet when the Covid-19 pandemic took place, the fact that their spouse did not work became a lifesaver because the spouse was at home with the young kids while they were doing online schooling.

Hidden Blessing when Your Spouse is Unjust

After Yazīd ibn Muʿāwiyah (may God remove His mercy from him) slaughtered the family of Imām Zaynul ʿĀbidīn ﷺ, the Imām ﷺ took the following approach:

When he was in shackles after the massacre of Karbalā', he uttered the following supplication:

وَ أَجْرِ لِلنَّاسِ عَلَى يَدِيَ الخَيرَ وَ لَا تَمحَقهُ بِالمَنِّ، وَ هَبْ لِي مَعَالِيَ الأَخلَاقِ، وَ اعصِمنِي مِنَ الفَخرِ.

"Let good flow out of my hands upon the people, and dissolve it not by having them feel indebted. Give me the highest of moral dispositions and protect me from haughtiness." [12]

The pain that a person feels from the injustice and insensitivity of people is immense. This is especially true when it comes from one's loved ones. Yet even this injustice presents us with an opportunity of infinite proportions.

One may ask: How? The Lord dwells in the hearts of the broken-hearted and humble people. When injustice is done to you, you have a choice between revenge and resentment, or alternatively, forgiveness and actively wanting the greatest good for that person. The latter can be done through prayers, or genuinely serving the person. You also have a choice of feeling arrogantly righteous on one hand, or on the alternative, introspecting into your own faults, sins, injustices, and insensitivities that you committed in the past and recalling how God showed you mercy despite clearly being in the wrong.

[12] *Aṣ-Ṣaḥīfah as-Sajjādiyyah*, Supplication #20, Part 3.

Humility of the heart (*khushū*) in the midst of injustice and insensitivity is the dual ability to have compassion (*raḥmah*) for your enemy (wanting good for them), and having awareness of your own sins. Compassion and self-awareness are two important tools in self-transformation, and in influencing the transformation of others. They are also critical in proportioning and moderating our responses to a level that is pleasing to God.

Humility of the heart does not finish here, one must be careful that in this, a person does not feel proud or think that they are better than the person doing the injustice.

Furthermore, in the good that you do, you must not make the other person feel that they are indebted to you.

وَلَا تَمْنُنْ تَسْتَكْثِرُ

"And do not give with the expectation to get (more)."[13]

When true humility is in a person's heart, one will empty it of the lower self and make room for the Lord to descend into it. It is in this that one will find true bliss in this world, and eternal bliss in the next.

A fantastic bargain, is it not?

Connect and then Correct

If Your Spouse is Upset, Listen

إنّ الغضب من الشّيطان وإنّ الشّيطان خلق من النّار و إنّما تطفأ النّار بالماء فإذا غضب أحدكم فليتوضّأ.

Prophet Muḥammad ﷺ said: *"Indeed, anger comes from Satan, and Satan was created from fire. Fire is extinguished with water, so when you become angry, then perform ablution (with water)."*[14]

[13] Noble Qur'ān, Sūrah al-Muddaththir (74), Verse 6.

[14] *Nahj al-Faṣāḥah*, P. 686.

When people are upset, they usually speak out of anger and emotions. Most of the time they do not truly mean the things which they say. That is why it is important to calm the other party down, and not take the hurtful things they say to heart.

If your spouse is upset about something, then just sit down and listen to them. Do not interrupt them, or begin giving any advice even if you are just trying to help. In your spouse's eyes, it may be seen as if you are patronizing them, and seem like you are not listening.

If you need to say something, then ask questions and let your spouse find their answers. Give advice when you are asked to give it. You will find that in the act of listening and making your spouse feel heard, you will make your spouse feel much better; and in all likelihood, your spouse will appreciate this tremendously.

Your Spouse is Not Responsible for Your Reaction

كلكم راع وكلكم مسئول عن رعيته.

Prophet Muḥammad ﷺ said: *"All of you are shepherds, and you are all responsible for raising) your own flock."* [15]

We tend to rush to judgment of others before understanding ourselves.

Problematic individuals will provide you with the conditions to react negatively, but ultimately, they cannot make you react in a particular way - that is mostly in your own control.

We often try to blame others, including our spouses, for 'forcing' us to react in a certain way. Our spouses may be able to influence some kind of reaction in us, or be a stimulus to how we react, but the reaction is ultimately in our hands. You cannot control what others do, you are only responsible for how you react. How you react in turn though will influence your spouse, and be a stimulus to their behavior.

[15] *Nahj al-Faṣāḥah,* P. 611.

In Islam, reacting appropriately in any situation that you are put in is being a good shepherd.

Trying to Fix Your Marriage can Backfire

إذا بلغك عن أخيك ما تكره، فاطلب له العذر إلى سبعين عذرا، فإن لم تجد له عذرا، فقل لنفسك: لعلّ له عذرا لا نعرفه (لا اعرفه).

Imām aṣ-Ṣādiq ﷺ said: *"If you hear something from your brother (or sister) that you dislike, then make an excuse for them - up to 70 excuses [i.e. an infinite amount of excuses]. If you cannot make an excuse for them, then say (to yourself): 'Perhaps they have an excuse that we (I) do not know about.'"*[16]

There is a risk involved when you try to save your marriage through fixing and addressing problems. When you attempt to fix problems, you often end up amplifying them. Fixing and addressing problems are very important, but there is something more important than this.

Your spouse and you need to be in a better psychological and emotional state before any genuine fixing is possible.

Instead, it may be helpful to take those efforts and focus them on creating better memories and experiences. They do not have to be large things, they can even be very small things. This direction toward positivity will help reduce the resentment between spouses and replenish a positive mindset when looking back at the marriage.

Once enough positivity is set, and your marriage is on a more solid emotional ground, then you both will notice that so much of your resentment is forgotten, or not considered important anymore. As for the rest, some of it you will be able to address and solve

[16] Al-Iṣfahānī, ʿAbdullāh ibn Nūrullāh al-Baḥrānī, *ʿAwālim al-ʿUlūm wa al-Maʿārif al-Aḥwāl min Ayāt wa al-Akhbār wa al-Aqwāl, (Mustanad Sayyidah an-Nisāʾ ilā al-Imām al-Jawād)*, 10 Vols., Ed. Muḥammad Bāqir Muwaḥḥid Abṭaḥī Iṣfahānī, (Qum: Muʾwassasah al-Imām al-Mahdī, 1413/1992-3), Vol. 2, P. 706.

amicably, while others you will learn to compromise on respectfully, not resentfully.

While you are building these positive and creative experiences, do not forget to make excuses for your spouse when they make a mistake in big or small things. This will help keep resentments in check while you heal your marriage.

Criticism Should be Followed with Three Positive Actions

فَإِنَّ مَعَ الْعُسْرِ يُسْرًا

"Indeed, with hardship (there is) ease." [17]

Negative experiences cause more activity in the brain than positive ones. This is why we remember negative experiences more than positive ones.

It is also why with every negative experience in a relationship (such as a criticism, let-downs, etc.) one must perform multiple positive actions in return (such as praising, acts of service, gifts, etc.) in order to try and counter the effects. Some experts say that for every negative reaction to someone, one must make up for it with three positive ones.

This applies to both your spouse and children equally. For every action or word of criticism or disapproval, it is a good idea to follow it up with three acts of love.

[17] Noble Qur'ān, Sūrah ash-Sharḥ (94), Verse 5.

How to Enjoy Life with a Difficult Spouse

Respond to Your Spouse's Bad Mood with Empathy

وَلَوْ كُنتَ فَظًّا غَلِيظَ الْقَلْبِ لَانفَضُّوا مِنْ حَوْلِكَ فَاعْفُ عَنْهُمْ وَاسْتَغْفِرْ لَهُمْ وَشَاوِرْهُمْ فِي الْأَمْرِ فَإِذَا عَزَمْتَ فَتَوَكَّلْ عَلَى اللَّهِ إِنَّ اللَّهَ يُحِبُّ الْمُتَوَكِّلِينَ

"And had you been harsh and hard-hearted, they would have surely scattered from around you. So excuse them and plead for their forgiveness, and consult them in their affairs. And when you make a decision, then put your trust in God; indeed God loves those who put their trust (in Him)." [18]

The kryptonite of marriage includes being judgmental, defensive, and inattentive, among other things. Some marriage therapists warn that the worst thing a person can do is to stonewall one's spouse, and doing it enough times is almost a sure path to divorce. Stonewalling is usually rooted in anger, resentment, egoism, and other spiritual vices that damage relationships.

These marriage kryptonite do not always come up, but when they do, they often come as a response to our spouse's bad moods. A good way to avoid these vices, especially when they are in response to someone's bad mood is to try empathy. Although this solution may sound like a truism, many people do not really know how to actually be empathetic.

Empathy is different from sympathy. Sympathy is generally defined as 'trying to **understand the suffering** of another person,' whereas empathy is 'trying to **experience the feelings** of another person.' Empathy usually works by trying to recall similar personal experiences, not just acknowledging the person's emotions.

[18] Noble Qur'ān, Sūrah Āl 'Imrān (3), Verse 159.

When your spouse is in a bad mood, try thinking of a similar situation where you felt angry like that, and then ask yourself the following questions:

1. What kind of thoughts and emotions were going through my mind?
2. Did I say or do things that I did not really mean?
3. Did I misinterpret or react negatively to people's kind gestures and words while I was angry?
4. Did I give the impression that I do not care or value those around me when I was feeling those emotions?
5. What was it that I needed the most at that time?
6. How did I wish people would react when I was going through those difficult emotions?

These are just a series of questions that can trigger important empathetic responses in you.

Once you remember these feelings, you may notice yourself becoming less judgmental, a little less defensive, and a little less resentful of your spouse. You will see that your own demeanor and aura will change, and that will definitely have an impact in calming your spouse down.

Remember our previous points; your spouse will not change because you ask them to, they will change in reaction to changes within yourself. If you maintain tranquility and serenity in your reaction to others, then you can be rest assured that your spouse will be positively affected by it even if they do not immediately show it.

Therefore, empathy will be the tool to avoid the feelings of being disgraced or insulted by your spouse, feelings that otherwise often trigger emotions that only make things worse.

Being Calm when Your Spouse is Moody

وَإِذَا خَاطَبَهُمُ الْجَاهِلُونَ قَالُوا سَلَامًا

"And when the ignorant address them (harshly), they respond [with words of] peace." [19]

It is inevitable that your spouse's bad mood at some point in time is going to get to you. You may become angry, frustrated, or annoyed. Sometimes you will be sad; and other times you will feel hopeless and full of despair.

It is important to take a step back and observe your emotions. Being aware of such strong emotions is often a great way to put things into perspective. Do not push them away; make sure to validate them, and remind yourself that it is totally normal to feel that way. This simple awareness often helps reground our rational thinking, and helps us make better choices when we have to deal with difficult moments.

Do Not Speak Ill of Your Spouse to Others

إذا حدّث الرّجل بحديث ثمّ التفت فهي أمانة.

Prophet Muḥammad ﷺ said: *"If a person says a word to someone, then turns away, those words become a trust."* [20]

Do not tell your marriage secrets to your family, friends, or people who are influential figures in your community. Do not tell your colleagues at work, or mention anything on social media. If you speak ill about your spouse, then this is violating their trust and God is not pleased at all with you disclosing their defects. If your spouse finds out, then they will take it as an attack to their dignity and pride, and the wound will be very difficult to heal.

[19] Noble Qur'ān, Sūrah al-Furqān (25), Verse 63.

[20] *Nahj al-Faṣāḥah,* P. 192.

Sometimes words can be even harder to heal from than physical hurts.

Avoid speaking ill about your spouse to anyone else. Yes, advice from wise people is important, and sometimes consulting with certain individuals may be needed in order to help your marriage. However, there are some people who simply speak ill of their spouses out of habit, or in order to get "something off of their chest" without the intention of wanting to actually fix their marriages or make things better.

If you happen to be a person who does the latter, then be mindful that you are training and rewiring your mind to think negatively about your spouse. The more you speak unfavorably about them, the more you will make your own negativity worse, and the harder it will be to reverse this. Do you think that this will help your marriage or break it? How will your children survive in this kind of an environment?

On the other hand, if you get into the habit of saying positive things about your spouse (even when it is hard), then you will rewire your mind to think more positively about them as well. Do you think you will be more or less happy in life when you do this? How about your children? Do you think your changed attitude and perspective will help your spouse become better or worse? Our experience of counseling thousands of couples confirms that things will only become better!

8

Reality of Marriage and Divorce

أَفَحَسِبْتُمْ أَنَّمَا خَلَقْنَاكُمْ عَبَثًا وَأَنَّكُمْ إِلَيْنَا لَا تُرْجَعُونَ

"Do you think that We created you aimlessly and that you will not be brought back to Us?"[1]

What to Expect When You Get Married

Marriage is not temporary, nor is it between two people only, there are other individuals involved like other family members, and then children who come about from this sacred union. Marriage is not limited to only one aspect of your life; it takes over your whole being.

It is very rare that your spouse will remain the same person over the course of your marriage as they were when you first married them. Your spouse's personality and interests will change as time goes by, and they will become a different person over time.

This is why marrying someone based on mutual interest (e.g. hobbies) - that is, other than a shared dedication to your religion - is not always the best choice in choosing a partner because those mutual interests will most likely change as the years progress.

[1] Noble Qur'ān, Sūrah al-Mu'minūn (23), Verse 115.

People often change after getting a new job, having kids, suffering from deteriorating health, or having to deal with some difficulty or trauma in life.

Experience shows that what matters the most is the **character** of the person you marry. You can find thousands, perhaps millions of people who share your taste in movies, the food you enjoy to eat, or what have you. You can even find evil people who share your political views. However, sharing these things in common does not mean that you will have a successful marriage. What is important is to possess good manners and valuable moral traits such as commitment, respect, good family relationships (with one's siblings, parents, etc.), and most of all a healthy relationship with God.

Do not choose a person because you share the same hobby, or because you find them attractive, or they have a lot of wealth; rather look at other higher things such as how they treat waiters in a restaurant, how they deal with difficult people in their lives, or how respectful they are with their parents and siblings. Also look at how they are able to control their emotions and desires - not just when they are angry, but also when they are excited. Do they lose all composure when they are happy? If so, then that is not a good sign! Therefore, remember that these are the kinds of things that will really make a difference in the success or failure of your marriage.

Infatuation has a nasty way of fooling your mind especially when it comes to someone of the opposite gender, so it is best not to rely on your own judgment. Talk to a wise person in your community whom you trust; someone who will be honest with you, and is looking out for your best interest, and has more experience than you.

What to Expect after Marriage

It may be perceived that after marriage, people will come to their senses about expectations and the reality of love. However, unfortunately it is often the case that even after marriage, people are still confused and hold on to false and damaging beliefs that exacerbate their problems which risk pushing some marriages to the brink of divorce.

Just like a person should check one's expectations **before** entering into marriage, these expectations and our understanding of how love works need regular revision and objective assessment.

Below are three major issues that we have observed in our years as religious marriage counselors regarding how expectations and love are misunderstood:

1. Your Spouse will not Stay the Same Over the Years

لا تأسف عليهم ولا تغضب ولا تنتقم لنفسك.

Imām ʿAlī ﷺ said: *"Do not have regrets over them (those who hurt you), and do not get angry such that you want to take revenge for yourself."* [2]

One of the biggest misconceptions which we have in life is that we believe our spouses should not change, even though it is perfectly okay for us to change.

Oftentimes couples will say: "This is not the same person that I married ten years ago, they have completely changed." With this kind of an approach, know that this is not a marriage, but a science experiment in cryogenic preservation.

People will change throughout the years. Everyone will age, mature, and gain new experiences through various events which are bound to take place that will change a person's outlook on life.

You are not the same person that you were ten, or even five years ago. So how can you expect that your spouse will remain the exact same? Imagining that your spouse should never change in personality is betting against the reality of nature.

[2] Al-Qummī, ʿAlī ibn Ibrāhīm, *Tafsīr al-Qummī*, 2 Vols., Ed. Tayyib al-Mūsawī al-Jazāʾirī, (Qum: Dār al-Kitāb, 1404/1983-1984), Vol. 1, P. 36.

2. Understanding Selfless Love vs. Demanding Love

لا يؤمن أحدكم حتى يحب لأخيه ما يحب لنفسه.

Prophet Muḥammad ﷺ said: *"None of you will truly believe until one loves for their brother what they love for themself."*[3]

You will not get love, actually more precisely, you will not be genuinely loved if you "demand" it. If anything, **demanding** love will often have the opposite effect in that it will push people away. Attracting love comes from selflessly serving others without expecting anything in return. This is where you take joy in making others happy for its own sake, not for the sake of being acknowledged, praised, or gaining some worldly benefit.

In this sense, your love will come off as real and genuine. People, especially spouses, will appreciate that even if they do not show or express it. It was this selfless love which made even the enemies of Prophet Muḥammad ﷺ love him.

3. The Quality of Your Relationship with Your Spouse is More Important than the Quality of Your Relationship with Your Kids

وَيَا آدَمُ اسْكُنْ أَنتَ وَزَوْجُكَ الْجَنَّةَ

"O Ādam, dwell you and your wife in paradise."[4]

The nucleus of a family is the husband and wife. Ādam and Ḥawwāʾ were the first nucleus of a family. If husbands and wives do not make their relationship strong, then very little good will come out of this relationship.

The quality of your marriage, and your relationship with your spouse has a greater impact on the psychological, spiritual, and emotional health of your children than your direct relationship with your children. This seems counterintuitive for many, and often

[3] *Nahj al-Faṣāḥah,* P. 678.

[4] Noble Qurʾān, Sūrah al-Aʿrāf (7), Verse 19.

people dismiss this out of hand, but then their marriage and children suffer severely as a result.

The primary source of emotional and psychological stability for children is seeing stability in the marriage of their parents. Children derive a sense of security and belonging from this, and as a result, they will have proper emotional and psychological development.

Therefore, as mentioned, the quality of the relationship between parents is more important for children than the quality of their relationship with the children themselves. Although the latter is very important, the former is even more important.

ꕥꕥ

When we lose the reality of marriage, the path sometimes leads to divorce. In this chapter, we will look at several marriage issues from three pertinent lenses:

1. The Causes and Consequences of Divorce;
2. Dreams vs. Reality in a Marriage;
3. Letting Go of Destructive False Hopes.

The Causes and Consequences of Divorce

Your Spouse is Not Responsible for Your Happiness

وَمَا أَصَابَكُم مِّن مُّصِيبَةٍ فَبِمَا كَسَبَتْ أَيْدِيكُمْ وَيَعْفُو عَن كَثِيرٍ

"And whatever affliction befalls you is because of what your (own) hands have earned, yet He excuses many [of them]."[5]

A sure way to a difficult life is if you hold people responsible for your happiness.

Happiness is not a choice that we make in life, if it was, then everyone would be happy. Rather, happiness is the byproduct of the

[5] Noble Qur'ān, Sūrah ash-Shūrā (42), Verse 30.

choices which we make in life. These choices are how we train our minds to react to external events.

Our spouses can be catalysts to the strong emotions we feel (whether they are positive or negative), but the kinds of mental training that we give ourselves, and the reactions which we have are ultimately in our own hands.

Making our spouses responsible for our happiness is an act of pride. It delegates all responsibility and blame for our misery to someone else, and ignores the root of the problem - namely the self.

Ultimately speaking, we cannot control what happens to us externally, but we can discipline ourselves - with a lot of practice and forbearance - in **how we react** to those events. If we rely on anyone to make us happy or miserable, then this will distract us from the real source of our satisfaction in life which is ourselves.

Reminder: There are Two People in a Relationship

كما تدين تدان.

Imām aṣ-Ṣādiq said: *"You reap what you sow."* [6]

Remember that one of the primary reasons for failure in marriages is forgetting that there are **two** people in the relationship.

Selfishness is one of the greatest causes for divorce in our community. Some people only think about themselves. When they think of their spouses, they only think of them to the extent that they are useful in serving their interests and desires. They forget that their spouses have wills, wishes, and desires of their own that need to be respected.

Compassion, and setting aside one's own pride are critical elements for success in marriage. But compassion can only happen when we acknowledge that there is more than one person (ourselves) in the relationship.

---

[6] Al-Barqī, Aḥmad ibn Muḥammad ibn Khālid, *Kitāb al-Maḥāsin*, 2 Vols., Ed. Jalāl ad-Dīn Muḥaddith, (Qum: Dār al-Kutub al-Islāmīyah, 1371/1953), Vol. 1, P. 107.

Put that Smartphone or Gadget Away

قول الرجل للمرأة: إني أحبك لا يذهب من قلبها أبدا.

Prophet Muḥammad ﷺ said: *"When a husband says to his wife 'I love you' it will never leave her heart."* [7]

Having a deep and effective communication with love will bring peace and joy in your life, more than your smartphones or any other gadgets.

Just because you may be sitting beside your spouse it does not mean that you are present with them. When you are together, put away any smartphones, tablets, laptops, etc. - even if it is for just 30 minutes. Use that half an hour for even idle chat, it will do wonders for your happiness in life, and the overall quality of your marriage.

Of course, this means speaking with your spouse without checking your phone every few minutes. Put it on silent and store it far away from your vision.

Unfortunately, device addiction has become so deeply ingrained among us that it is almost impossible for some people to stay away from their gadgets for more than a few minutes even, yet people do not realize how it is destroying the quality of their family and social relationships, and the overall quality of life.

Your Spouse Cannot Read Your Mind

أفلا شققت عن قلبه حتى تعلم أقالها أم لا؟!

Prophet Muḥammad ﷺ said to Khālid ibn Walīd: *"Did you open his heart to find out if he said it (sincerely) or not?!"* [8]

Khālid ibn Walīd had entered into a battle with a member of the Ḥuraqah tribe who happened to be at war with the Muslims.

---

[7] *Al-Kāfī,* Vol. 11, P. 316.

[8] Al-Qurṭubī, Muḥammad ibn Aḥmad, *Al-Jāmiʿ al-Aḥkām al-Qurʾān*, 20 Vols, (Tehran: Intishārāt-i Nāṣir-i Khusruw, 1364/1985), Vol. 5, P. 324.

One member of the tribe surrendered to Khālid and professed the testimony to the Islamic faith, meaning that he had converted to Islam. In this kind of a situation, Islam considers the individual to be a new person and allows them to start life anew as a Muslim.

However, Khālid believed it to be a ploy to save himself and still went ahead and killed him, regardless of him having become a Muslim. When Prophet Muḥammad ﷺ heard about this incident, he was very upset and uttered the words above regarding the sincerity of the person who had been killed by Khālid. He was essentially telling Khālid that only God can see into the hearts of human beings, and he had no right to make any judgment for he could not open the heart of the other person and read his true intentions. The Prophet ﷺ kept repeating this phrase to him, and was very upset at him over this incident until the end of his days.

One of the most destructive things which often leads a couple to divorce is the belief that your spouse can read your mind. What is also destructive is the belief that appearances are always truthful. What do we mean by this?

A large number of divorces that often happen are usually met with disbelief by one of the partners because they were not aware of the built-up dissatisfaction and resentment of the other spouse. In these cases, the disappointed partner does not show their built up resentment for a very long time. The issue at hand here is the following fact: Even happily married couples cannot really hear what the other person is NOT saying.

Not communicating properly and frequently enough can often lead to a breakup. Why does this happen?

Most individuals are usually concerned about other people's reactions. They are not sure how they themselves will be critiqued, or how the situation might get more tense. But in the case of couples, one problem is that fear and denials are not strategies to improve a marriage. At some point in time, all of your resentments will come out whether you like it or not. A lot of divorces which happen are not the result of big mistakes, rather they are an accumulation of years of built up anger.

Here is a good example from my life: when I come home and I lay my head back with my hand on my forehead, my wife knows that I have a headache and she will bring me water and tylenol.

Others may see this and expect their wives to do the same without direct verbal communication. They may expect their wives to read their minds based on what they saw from my own relationship with my wife.

But this is a mistake. Over our decades of marriage, my wife and I have learned to interpret our subtle expressions at home. This line of subtle understanding was built up over the years through direct communication.

Remember that your spouse is not a magician or a fortune teller. Important matters and feelings need to be communicated between couples in order to build up a good relationship.

Winning an Argument at the Cost of Your Marriage

وَعَاشِرُوهُنَّ بِالْمَعْرُوفِ ۚ فَإِنْ كَرِهْتُمُوهُنَّ فَعَسَىٰ أَنْ تَكْرَهُوا شَيْئًا وَيَجْعَلَ اللَّهُ فِيهِ خَيْرًا كَثِيرًا

"And live with them in an honorable manner; and should you dislike them, maybe you dislike something while God has placed much good in it."[9]

Oftentimes, we feel a lot of satisfaction and pride when we win an argument, but this may not be healthy in the long term for your relationship or marriage. Look at what your goal is in marriage: Do you want to improve your marriage, or just create opportunities where you practice feeling good by proving that you are right?

When one of you "loses" an argument, the real loser is your

[9] Noble Qur'ān, Sūrah an-Nisā' (4), Verse 19.

marriage. Remember that there are no winners or losers in marriage arguments. When you insult or put your spouse down, it is likely that it will create resentment and further deteriorate your relationship.

When there are issues between the two of you, you win and lose together. For this reason, try working cooperatively, make compromises, and do not keep score with your loved one. In this very difficult world, you need to be alongside one another. You either grow together, or you both break down together.

Rights vs. Responsibilities in Marriage, Which Comes First?

وأما حق الزوجة فأن تعلم أن الله عز وجل جعلها لك سكنا وأنسا فتعلم أن ذلك نعمة من الله عليك فتكرمها وترفق بها

It has been narrated from Imām as-Sajjād ﷺ that he said: *"The right of your wife is that you should know that God has made her a repose and a comfort for you; you should know that she is God's favor toward you, so you should honor her and treat her kindly and gently."* [10]

Marital life however, is not only about rights. They are primary mostly in the cases of disputes, but in everyday life abiding by and only living according to one's rights is not sustainable and will lead to chaos.

Our main focus should be on security, and protecting the sacred institution of marriage which is through the primacy of responsibilities, passion, love, and sacrifice. As such, we need to have a paradigm shift in our thinking when it comes to our spouses.

Understanding the meaning of life begins with grasping the significance of responsibility. Our responsibility first begins with God, then spreads toward His creations. In some ways, this may

[10] Note that these kinds of traditions and spousal rights usually go both ways. In the case of this *ḥadīth*, the rights outlined also apply to the wife's approach to her husband as well. *Jāmiʿ al-Aḥadīth ash-Shīʿah*, Vol. 25, P. 536.

contradict certain selfish understandings or interpretations of the modern notion of the primacy of rights (which some people espouse) where rights as a principle must always supersede responsibilities and duties.

It is interesting to note that the word for 'right' in Arabic is *ḥaqq* which also means 'responsibility' in its classical form. It is therefore crucial to always see rights and responsibilities/duties as mutually inclusive and important in our lives. If this were to truly become visceral in people's minds, then a lot of dysfunctional marriages could be saved and would probably even thrive.

The Opposite of Love is Not Always Hatred, But Fear

إِذَا مَسَّهُ الشَّرُّ جَزُوعًا

"When evil touches them (people), they are anxious."[11]

People often become selfish, not because they are necessarily evil, but because sometimes they are fearful and anxious.

Perhaps the worst aspect of living a life of fear and anxiety is that it denies us the possibility of experiencing life. A state of anxiety makes people coil into their cocoons. They deny themselves the opportunities for establishing and nurturing their ambitions in life, and more importantly their social relationships. Many people become moody, angry, and distant with their spouses and children because they live under perpetual anxiety. This feeling of uneasiness makes it almost impossible for them to think about others.

Their sense of fear gives them justification for their aloofness. Not only is this justification wrong, but the continued persistence on this withdrawal from life will only make things worse. It will continually damage the already existing relationships, and thereby bring about actions of betrayal that will make matters even more depressing, and it will also bring about **extreme** regret in old age.

[11] Noble Qur'ān, Sūrah al-Ma'ārij (70), Verse 20.

Think about it...when you are old and dying, and you have very few joyous memories to remember, and you realize how many opportunities you lost with your spouse, your children, parents, and even friends; and perhaps worse, how much of what you worried about was for nothing, or simply not worth all of the positive moments that you lost while you were worrying about insignificant things. Wake up while you can, and seize the opportunity to be present and joyful with your loved ones. Do not be of those countless people who fall into depressive regret in old age. Time is very short, make the most use of it before it is gone forever.

Financial Success can Sometimes Lead to Divorce

قَالَ نُوحٌ رَبِّ إِنَّهُمْ عَصَوْنِي وَاتَّبَعُوا مَنْ لَمْ يَزِدْهُ مَالُهُ وَوَلَدُهُ إِلَّا خَسَارًا

"(Prophet) Nūḥ (Noah) said: 'My Lord! Indeed they have disobeyed me, (and are) following those whose wealth and children will only add to their loss.'" [12]

People often see financial constraints as a cause for divorce. However, financial success can often be a greater reason for divorce. With financial success comes a lot of responsibilities such as: more accounting matters, increased staff, bureaucracy, higher taxes, more debt, etc.; and as a result, one's mind is saturated with more intrusive thoughts and stress. This is not to mention how busy one becomes during financial success because making money can be very time consuming.

When minds are too busy and loaded with different tensions, many people become disconnected because they have little time for their marriage and children, and as a result, divorce becomes more probable.

Of course there are some people who do not primarily see

[12] Noble Qur'ān, Sūrah Nūḥ (71), Verse 21.

success in life just by having a surplus of money. These people put effort into strengthening their families and giving them the due attention, even when they become wealthier.

Therefore, if you pray for financial success, make sure you know what you are getting yourself into as it may not bear the outcome which you want. All worldly gains come at a high price in this world and the next.

Be Consistent in Your Acts of Goodness, Avoid Randomness

وَلِكُلٍّ وِجْهَةٌ هُوَ مُوَلِّيهَا ۖ فَاسْتَبِقُوا الْخَيْرَاتِ ۚ أَيْنَ مَا تَكُونُوا يَأْتِ بِكُمُ اللَّهُ جَمِيعًا ۚ إِنَّ اللَّهَ عَلَىٰ كُلِّ شَيْءٍ قَدِيرٌ

"Everyone has a direction to which one turns; so take the lead in all good works. Wherever you may be, God will bring you all together. Indeed, God has power over all things." [13]

We often show our appreciation to strangers, but when it comes to our own spouses - the people who deserve our praise the most - we become stingy in giving it because we think that what they do is simply their duty. This paradigm needs to change. Instead of competing over who can point out each other's duties the most, we should compete on who can show appreciation the most.

If you want to fix your marriage and family life, then be **consistent** in your acts of goodness, and try to avoid randomness. Random acts of good may be counterproductive, and could even lead to resentment because your spouse will begin to expect erratic behavior after brief moments of kindness and consideration.

In other words, these acts will not be interpreted as well intentioned expressions of love, but as erratic emotions which will then be followed by bad behavior. In this sense, good acts could become triggers for worry, anxiety, and unpredictability.

[13] Noble Qur'ān, Sūrah al-Baqarah (2), Verse 148.

If you want to instill relational and emotional stability in your marriage, then your kindness and good acts need to be consistent. Consistency brings about a feeling of security and predictability - two key factors for a happy marriage.

Throwing Money at Marriage Problems

أَلْهَاكُمُ التَّكَاثُرُ

"Vying for (worldly) increase distracts you." [14]

There are people who think that all problems can be solved by money. For these people, money can lead to the destruction of a marriage. One may ask: How? Whether you are rich or poor, you will have marital problems. Sometimes it is tempting to throw money to try and cover up a problem instead of going through the struggle of resolving their roots and learning to transform in the process.

A spouse may be pacified with gifts or vacations temporarily, and you may have a semblance of happiness. But every time you reach a tense moment, you will probably end up spending even more money to resolve an issue until you will reach a point in your life where money will no longer solve any of your problems.

That is when the stark reality will set in, and you will realize that during all of this time, the tools which were necessary to manage human difficulties were not developed at all, and problems cannot be resolved with finances and bribes. So, what is the conclusion here? There are certain issues in life that only a committed and humble will for transformation can solve; and money - although very important in many aspects of one's life and relationships - can sometimes have the opposite effect of what is desired.

[14] Noble Qur'ān, Sūrah at-Takāthur (102), Verse 1.

Dreams vs. Reality in a Marriage

A Good Marriage is Something You Struggle to Make

وَأَن لَّيْسَ لِلإِنْسَانِ إِلاَّ مَا سَعَى

"And nothing belongs to human beings except what they strive for." [15]

A good marriage is not something that you will find; it is something that you have to struggle to make. We have an erroneous understanding in our culture that love is found, or that somehow we have a soul mate waiting for us.

We are complex and difficult beings. We may seem to be nice to each other initially, but end up being difficult after marriage.

It is very rare to find people who are perfectly compatible with each other. The most successful couples that I have seen in my years as a religious counselor are ones who have struggled the most in their marriages. They have found ways to develop patience, compromise with each other, forgive one another, and fix their expectations and behaviors in their marriage. These are not easy to obtain, they require humility and a strong will to establish, and one needs to fight off despair in the process.

Beautiful and large buildings do not pop out of nothing, they are built with care and patience. The same principles apply to marriages.

Many people expect that everything should be handed to us without any effort, or we think that everyone gets everything with ease. However, this is definitely not the case. The mentality of entitlement is a dream and is not compatible with the reality of this world.

[15] Noble Qur'ān, Sūrah an-Najm (53), Verse 39.

Dating Standards are Not for Marriage

و إذا خطـب إليـك رجـل رضيـت دينـه وخلقـه وأمانتـه فزوّجـه،
فـانّ اللّـه يقـول: إِن يَكُونُـوا فُقَـرَاءَ يُغنِهِـمُ اللَّـهُ مِـن فَضلِـه.

Imām aṣ-Ṣādiq ﷺ said: *"If a man comes to you as a suitor, and you are satisfied with his religion, his character, and his trustworthiness, then marry him, for God says (in the Qur'ān): 'If they are poor, God will enrich them from His bounty.'* [16] *"* [17]

When looking for a marriage partner, some people look for a person as if they are simply going to date them. The problem of the "dating standard" for marriage is that the potential partner's qualities are vastly different from the standards one would seek if one were TRULY thinking in the long term. Sometimes we fool ourselves into believing that we are thinking long term, but we are not. This is where the advice of wiser and more experienced people can come in handy.

Perhaps a good analogy is that of buying a new car. Imagine that you were going to a car dealership to buy your first car. However, the catch is that the car you buy is going to be the only car you will ever have. In other words, you will still be driving that car when you are in your 60s and 70s (assuming, of course, that cars last that long). Now with this new perspective in mind, you are more likely to get a car that will suit your needs for decades to come. A roofless sports car, or a small beetle car will not do. They may be fun for now, but what about when you have kids? What about when you go on trips with your family? What about when you are old and sick?

When we are considering a life partner we need to look ahead to the future, and see what kind of a person will be a good match for us holistically. Someone who will be a righteous parent for our

[16] Noble Qur'ān, Sūrah an-Nūr (24), Verse 32.

[17] Shaykh Ṣadūq, *Al-Muqni'*, (Qum: Mu'assasat al-Imām al-Mahdī, 1415/1995), P. 306.

children, and someone whom we can grow with together in the servitude of God.

We cannot replace spouses like cars and nor do we want to. Cars can be replaced, changed and upgraded based on needs but you cannot upgrade a human being this way. No one is perfect, but you can look for who matches you holistically better in terms of circumstances and personality.

In Islamic law, there is a concept of *kufw* or "multi-level compatibility" which has been highly stressed upon, and under certain circumstances can also be a condition for the validity of marriage. *Kufw*, depending on the Muslim jurist you follow, can range from religious and spiritual compatibility to more mundane but life altering points of marital harmony. Basically when it comes to compatibility you don't want to look at just one part of the person. All parts of them such as their career, education status, religiosity, age, looks, and more should be considered. It may be that the person is highly compatible in their religiosity and career but their age and education are not as compatible. As a person looking for a spouse, your responsibility is to look at the holistic person not just one or two parts of them and understand your requirements and the minimum level of acceptability before making your decision. This is different from dating where the standards may just be an enjoyment or appearance.

When considering a marriage partner, beware of the dating standard syndrome. What may be unimportant/important, appealing, fun, and exciting to you now can end up being a disaster and a reason for divorce in the future. Dating standards are not marriage standards.

Loving Someone Does Not Mean You will Love Life Together

وَعَسَىٰٓ أَن تُحِبُّوا۟ شَيْـًٔا وَهُوَ شَرٌّ لَّكُمْ وَٱللَّهُ يَعْلَمُ وَأَنتُمْ لَا تَعْلَمُونَ

"And it may be that you love something but it is bad for you; and God knows while you do not know." [18]

Compatibility is critical for the success of a marriage.

You may be infatuated with someone. They may be charming, attractive, or simply make you feel good to the point that you feel you have fallen in love with them. However, just because you may love someone, it does not mean that you are compatible with that person and suited to live and love life together.

Infatuations and emotions are fleeting, but compatibility in family, culture, personal values, and religious directions are often long-term factors that do not change so easily.

Someone may be outgoing, adventurous and fun, but this may clash with your future plans of having a quiet and settled family life.

Therefore, consulting with wiser elders and scholars in your community can sometimes give you a better perspective on choices in life, rather than following the emotionally charged ones that you may incline toward.

What True Commitment in Marriage Really Is

فَٱصْبِرْ صَبْرًا جَمِيلًا

"So be patient - with a patience that is beautiful." [19]

There is a general misunderstanding as to what commitment really is in a marriage.

Oftentimes we are confronted with issues regarding our spouses,

---

[18] Noble Qur'ān, Sūrah al-Baqarah (2), Verse 216.

[19] Noble Qur'ān, Sūrah al-Maʿārij (70), Verse 5.

and try to make quick and rash decisions. But decisions as such are usually not good because they are based on momentary thoughts, whereas marriage is a long term and extended commitment and reality which cannot be objectively judged as a whole through small experiential fragments of feelings and thoughts.

In other words, you should not assess the value of your marriage based on certain thoughts and feelings that you may be having at a particular moment, rather you should be patient and have a wider outlook at the entire situation. You will often find that small prices are worth paying for the more permanent results of your marriage.

Real commitment is not about staying in a marriage when things are going well, or even when things are not going so well; real commitment in a marriage is when you stay committed to your spouse even if you have every right to leave the marriage. It is this kind of an attitude which will give your marriage the possibility of real success. Of course, this adherence must be within the limits of Islamic morality, and one must be cautious of the red zones.

Your Wife's Work at Home is Priceless

كتب الله الجهاد على الرجال والنساء في جهاد الرجل بذل ماله ونفسه حتى يقتل في سبيل الله وجهاد المرأة أن تصبر على ما ترى من أذى زوجها وغيرته.

Imām 'Alī said: *"God prescribed a long-life spiritual struggle (jihād) for both men and women. The struggle (jihād) of a man is that he sacrifices his money and life [for his family], even as far as being killed for the sake of God; and a woman's struggle (jihād) is (for her) to have patience from the hurt she experiences from her husband and his fervor."* [20]

---

[20] *Al-Kāfī*, Vol. 5, P. 507.

جهاد المرأة حسن التبعل.

Imām ʿAlī ﷺ also said: *"The struggle (jīhād) of a woman is to be good natured (with her family)."*[21]

There are many men who have good careers and make a lot of money, however they do not see the value of their wife's work at home. What often happens is that even though some of the women do not need to, they end up working outside of the home, and they think that this is a good thing. They do not realize how detrimental this can be for peace and tranquility of home. Household duties and children are often focused on less, or sometimes even neglected altogether. The wife becomes more stressed as she has to deal with unruly coworkers and bosses, and becomes too tired to tend to her primary duty in Islam which is her family at home.

Some wives feel forced to do this - either because society teaches them that making a salary is more valuable than the blessings one gets from serving her family, or because the husband looks down on her because she is not bringing home a paycheck.

Husbands must realize that in Islam it is their duty to bring home the paycheck and provide for the family, not the wife's responsibility. If he makes enough money and the family is able to live off of a single income, then there is no reason why he should directly or indirectly pressure his wife to work outside of the home. Her work at home is infinitely more valuable in the eyes of God. A husband must always make sure to praise his wife and her invaluable work at home which is usually harder than working an outside-the-home career.

It is important to understand that sometimes a wife may want to work outside, or that sometimes her job may not affect her family or children. At other times, women may have to work as two incomes are necessary for survival; or husbands are not able to work due to some health issues, or they are single moms who have no choice but to work and provide for their families. These cases are different from

[21] *Al-Kāfī*, Vol. 5, P. 507.

what we have outlined above.

The aim is to have a peaceful environment at home, and if this can be achieved then the goal has been met.

Falling In and Out of Love Many Times During Marriage

وَاعْلَمُوٓا أَنَّمَآ أَمْوَالُكُمْ وَأَوْلَادُكُمْ فِتْنَةٌ وَأَنَّ اللَّهَ عِنْدَهُۥٓ أَجْرٌ عَظِيمٌ

"And know that your possessions and children are only a test, and that God has with Him a great reward."[22]

People fall in and out of love (and back in again) during marriage regularly. Unfortunately, people make a bigger deal out of it than it reallyis.

If there is a silent saboteur of marriages and other close relationships, then it would be a misunderstanding of what love is. The most popular conception of love sees it as some form of intense or deep emotion of liking someone. But it is more than self-evident that emotions are rarely stable, we have our highs and lows, and no one is immune to this.

Our general disappointments in life, health, mental well-being, loss of a job or loved one, or even the opening up of new opportunities and careers, birth of children, the upbringing of children (even as teenagers and young adults), the irregularity of our sleep, poor diet, or you name it - all of these things directly impact our emotions, and as such they will inevitably impact our behavior and how we feel toward our spouses and families.

It is often common to hear that one spouse has "fallen out of love" in regards to the other spouse. Many people react dramatically to this and even consider or pursue divorce.

But here is the secret: falling "out of love" is not a big deal, and sometimes can be expected.

Love is an intense and deep emotion which is highly unstable,

[22] Noble Qur'ān, Sūrah al-Anfāl (8), Verse 28.

and is impacted by a myriad of controllable and uncontrollable factors in your life. If you feel that you do not "love" your spouse anymore, then it usually means that you do not like them at that moment, but not that this feeling will necessarily last forever.

Oftentimes, people will leave their spouse for someone else because they "fell out of love" with them, and "fell in love" with a new person - only to find that they soon fall out of love with their new spouse, and sometimes even fall back in love with their previous spouse. Therefore, these emotions can be quite fluctuating, unreliable, and disastrous; and taking them too seriously can often lead to drastic consequences. They do not just impact you, but they impact your children and extended families as well.

Some spouses even "fall out of love" for ten, fifteen, or more years - only to "fall back in love" after their children grow up, and they have a chance to look back at their lives, relax, and catch up on things once again. Believe it or not, the best couples and relationships in marriage usually manifest themselves around 35 years after their wedding!

So, the question here is: Then what is real love in Islam? The word used in the Qur'ān for love is *mawaddah* which can literally be translated 'as compassion and caring.' In technical Qur'ānic language, the word refers to 'a sacrificial commitment to the good of the other,' but it is not necessarily an emotional desire. In fact, you can be committed to a person for their good, but not really love them at the particular moment!

This does not mean that this kind of love precludes passion and deep emotion, but it means that it is by definition an active commitment for the good of the other person. In other words, although passion and duty are not opposites of one another, duty does not always include or entail passion and deep desire or emotion.

So what should you do if you do not feel a deep emotion of love toward your spouse? We would suggest the following:

1. Your emotions are important and need to be considered,

but they can also be unreliable and lead you to make poor decisions.

2. A love relationship cannot be found; it must be made, and that too over time. Thus, this will entail a lot of struggle and patience to develop. It varies from couple to couple, but it can take many years before you see the real fruits of it.

3. Just like you fell out of love, you can fall back into love with your spouse. Think of all the times you stopped liking your spouse just to start liking them again - no matter how short it was.

4. Qur'ānic love (*mawaddah*) is about being humble. Humility in Islam is not thinking less of yourself, but thinking less "about" yourself. Doing so will increase your blessings in life, and lead you to being more grateful, happy, and satisfied with your life and marriage in general.

Letting Go of Destructive False Hopes

Unfaithfulness Can be Symptom of a Troubled Marriage

اَلرِّجَالُ قَوَّامُوْنَ عَلَى النِّسَاءِ

"Men are the maintainers (caretakers) of women." [23]

Once I was in the presence of one of my teachers, and a man came and complained to him about his wife. He was upset that his wife was having a conversation with an unrelated man, and he believed that she was being unfaithful to him.

My teacher responded: "Do you satisfy her at home, meaning, do you give her emotional support and companionship, and do you give her proper attention?" The man was speechless which indicated that he did not do this. My teacher then responded that he should

[23] Noble Qur'ān, Sūrah an-Nisā' (4), Verse 34.

blame himself and not his wife for her actions, and instructed him to fulfill his duty as a pillar of emotional support at home for her. He then recited the above verse of the Qur'ān to him: "Men are the maintainers of women."

Being a caretaker means that you are the pillar of your family, specifically your wife. Just like a table has four pillars, a man's responsibility is also a fourfold pillar at home with his wife. He is supposed to be a caretaker in terms of giving hope to the family, he needs to maintain financial stability, he should provide emotional fulfillment and kindness at home, and he must show expressions of intimacy.

Many people often express that the two main reasons for divorce are unfaithfulness (cheating), and destructive money decisions. However, it has often been the case that these are not "reasons" for divorce, but rather symptoms of a problematic marriage.

This usually includes a lack of meaningful and deep relationships, and lack of proper attention and affection which usually pile up into destructive decisions and habits that end up making an already bad marriage even worse. Sometimes they may be the result of prior unresolved traumas in life. Of course, this is not a be-all and end-all explanation of marriage problems, but it is one observation that may be relevant to many people.

The Purpose of Marriage is Not Only Happiness

هُنَّ لِبَاسٌ لَكُمْ وَأَنْتُمْ لِبَاسٌ لَهُنَّ

"Your wives are a garment (apparel) for you, and you are a garment (apparel) for your wives." [24]

We misunderstand the purpose of marriage, and think of it as just a happy-go-around where there is no place for disagreements, and that everything should be perfect.

[24] Noble Qur'ān, Sūrah al-Baqarah (2), Verse 187.

In other words, a lot of people are under the assumption that the point of marriage is just joy and happiness. Unfortunately, this understanding of marriage leads to a whole host of problems and disappointments. The primary purpose of marriage is about character development and self reformation. In other words, it is supposed to teach you patience, compassion, altruism, learning to see beyond just yourself, anger management, responsibility, and so on.

Many of these positive traits that we regard so highly are not developed through smiles, joys, and romanticism - rather they are developed through hardships, tears, disagreements, regrets, and failures. When things get tense in your marriage, do not despair. Try to see them as pains which can help you build a better version of yourself. The beautiful fruit of this endeavor will be happiness.

More precisely, the purpose of marriage in Islam is multifold; and some of its purposes are the following:

1. Creation of lineage (founding of future generations);
2. To find peace, blessings, and love in one's life;
3. Purification of the soul from temptations;
4. Completing half of one's faith;
5. To establish focus, vision, and purpose in one's life;
6. To have stability and enjoyment;
7. To be blessed with God's grace in this life and the next.

Therefore, in order to truly benefit from these blessings, and become a better human being, we need to work hard in our marriages and attain the pleasure of God in this world and the eternal hereafter.

Your Real Full-Time Job is Your Family

هُوَ الَّذِي خَلَقَكُم مِّن نَّفْسٍ وَاحِدَةٍ وَجَعَلَ مِنْهَا زَوْجَهَا لِيَسْكُنَ
إِلَيْهَا ۖ فَلَمَّا تَغَشَّاهَا حَمَلَتْ حَمْلًا خَفِيفًا فَمَرَّتْ بِهِ ۖ فَلَمَّا أَثْقَلَت
دَّعَوَا اللَّهَ رَبَّهُمَا لَئِنْ آتَيْتَنَا صَالِحًا لَّنَكُونَنَّ مِنَ الشَّاكِرِينَ

"It is He who created you from a single soul, and made from it its mate, so that he might find comfort with her. So, when he was intimate with her, she bore a light burden and passed [some time] with it. When she had grown heavy, they both invoked God, their Lord (saying): 'If You give us a healthy [child], we will surely be among the grateful.'" [25]

A person's real full-time job is not outside of the house, rather it should be at home. Outside work is just a means of living. Many people do not become aware of this reality until it is too late, and then they are full of regrets. Unfortunately though, our regrets do not change the past. Too many people end up realizing that they could have settled with less money and/or property, and instead nurtured their relationship with their children and spouses, however it is usually too late when they come to understand this.

Money comes and goes, but the psychological damage that is done to your spouse and kids by your absence can be permanent. Even if recovery is possible (and it can be possible), the time lost can never ever be recovered. As the saying goes: "God forgives, but time does not."

Treat Your Marriage Better than Your Career

رَبَّنَا هَبْ لَنَا مِنْ أَزْوَاجِنَا وَذُرِّيَّاتِنَا قُرَّةَ أَعْيُنٍ وَاجْعَلْنَا لِلْمُتَّقِينَ إِمَامًا

"O our Lord! Grant us from among our spouses and offspring comfort to our eyes, and make us a leader for the God-conscious ones." [26]

[25] Noble Qur'ān, Sūrah al-Aʿrāf (7), Verse 189.

[26] Noble Qur'ān, Sūrah al-Furqān (25), Verse 74.

At work and in the world outside, we will come across situations and people that we do not like. But because we value our careers and jobs, we will control our behavior, be respectful, and look for help when needed in order to improve. We may not have discipline in our work ethic and behavior for the sake of the people there necessarily, but for something greater, meaning our sense of fulfillment in our jobs and wanting to maintain them, we will put up with things that may be very difficult to tolerate otherwise.

When it comes to our marriages, we should see it the same way. The grand purpose of our marriage is to please God through the process of self transformation, and bettering ourselves to become true human beings, and marriage is one of the best ways to do this, even though it may be very difficult. We need to look at the grander scheme of things and not let our emotions and frustrations get in the way of our principal goal, namely serving God through respecting the institution of marriage and family, and being patient with the good and difficult people that we will come across.

Going Over the Pros and Cons of Staying Together

إنّ إبليس يضع عرشه على الماء، ثمّ يبعث سراياه فأدناهم منه منزلة أعظمهم فتنة يجيء أحدهم فيقول فعلت كذا و فعلت كذا فيقول ما صنعت شيئا و يجيء أحدهم فيقول ما تركته حتّى فرّقت بينه و بين أهله فيدنيه منه و يقول نعم أنت

Prophet Muḥammad ﷺ said: *"Verily, Iblīs (Satan) places his throne over water*[27] *and he sends out his squadrons. The closest to him in rank are those who are greatest at causing disorder. One of them says: 'I have done such and such a thing,' and Iblīs responds: 'You have done nothing!' Another one says: 'I*

[27] Water is likely used symbolically here where Satan tries to imitate God and His Knowledge, because water is often symbolic of God's Knowledge, and His Throne can be symbolic of His Power.

> *did not leave this man alone until I separated him from his wife.' Iblīs embraces him and says: 'You have done well!'"* [28]

Success lies in dedication, perseverance, and fighting against areas of despair. Most marriages do not end because of abuse or adultery, they end because the couples fall apart from each other, and one or both of the spouses give up. In times like these, some people adopt the strategy of going over the pros and cons of staying together in marriage, as if their relationship is some form of business calculation. They do so innocently thinking that it may be a way of trying to convince themselves to stay in the marriage. More often than not, going over the pros and cons of marriage will often open up one's mind to doubts and even nefarious influences. Experience shows that this approach usually ends up in divorce.

There is a reason for this. Going over the pros and cons of one's marriage places a person's mind against commitment. It expands the opportunities for doubt, takes away meaningful action and effort, and weakens one's trust in God, in oneself, and in one's marriage. In situations like these, take out all of the other options, except commitment to one's marriage. See how to make the best of it, but do not depend on feelings because positive and negative feelings will come and go, and sometimes they may even last for a long time. When the pros and cons approach is taken and marriages end, good opportunities rarely come about, and more bad choices are made over time. This is sometimes not realized in the short term, and regrets come in the long run, but by then it is way too late.

The ultimate outcome of your relationship is in the hands of God. Put in a sincere effort and do your best, but stay committed and leave it to God's decision, not your own. Things have a way of turning out better than you expect, even though it may take years. Your primary goal in marriage is not just to be happy, but more importantly it is to grow spiritually and become closer to God. This process involves struggle, patience, and perseverance.

[28] *Nahj al-Faṣāḥah*, P. 268.

9

Changing Your Spouse

Alignment of Heart, Mind, and the Reality of Marital Life

The Heart Takes Longer to Change than the Mind

The mind is the commanding power of human thinking, but the heart is the container of the human spirit. When we discuss the mind and heart, we are not referring to them in their physical senses, but in the spiritual one.

The mind is the nobility of human beings. It has a million uses and helps us navigate our complex world. It allows us to invent wondrous things. Yet the mind has its limits. It can lead us to confusion and deception. Even though Satan ultimately knew better, he still refused to prostrate to Prophet Ādam ﷺ because his ego-veiled heart prevented him from doing so.

أقرب ما يكون العبد من الله عز وجل وهو ساجد، وذلك قوله عز وجل واسجد واقترب.

From al-Washshā' who said: "I heard (Imām) ar-Riḍā ﷺ say: *"The closest a servant is to God, Exalted and Glorious is He, is when one is prostrating, and it is for this reason that He, Exalted and Glorious, says [in the Qur'ān]: 'Prostrate and draw near [to Him].'* [1]" [2]

During prostration, the heart is raised above the mind. It is through the heart that we know the Lord because it is the heart which is the instrument of knowledge, and in particular, Divine knowledge. The heart is the vehicle for compassion and empathy with others.

God says in the Qur'ān:

فَإِنَّهُ نَزَّلَهُ عَلَىٰ قَلْبِكَ

"Then indeed he (Angel Jibrā'īl - Gabriel) brought it (the Qur'ān) down upon your heart." [3]

Notice here that the ultimate form of knowledge, namely the revelation (*wahī*), was not revealed to the mind, but rather to the heart.

As such, the heart is the seat of knowledge and understanding according to Islam, but it is an instrument which takes time to unveil and develop.

Our minds and thoughts are volatile. They can be changed relatively easily under the right circumstances. The heart is different though. It is much harder to change the heart because it is the center of our being and knowledge. Its transformation is at the core level of one's being, therefore it naturally takes longer to change it.

You will find that you may be able to change your spouse's thoughts, but not their heart. You can realize this through their emotions. Spouses often complain that they are able to convince their spouses about something, but in their attitudes they can still see that deep down inside they are not persuaded. For example, in their thoughts they may be assured that they can trust again, but

[1] Noble Qur'ān, Sūrah al-'Alaq (96), Verse 19.

[2] *Al-Kāfī*, Vol. 6, P. 9.

[3] Noble Qur'ān, Sūrah al-Baqarah (2), Verse 97.

their heart says otherwise.

This can often lead to discouragement, but it should not. One needs to be patient and give some time as the heart is careful and has a drag time. It can take days, weeks, or even several months for the mind and heart to align together.

The key is to be consistent and persistent, do not give reason for the heart to stop changing. It may not be apparent at first, but it will eventually become visible. Therefore, look at the bigger picture and the consequences of your decisions; have patience, control your desires and anger, and rely truly on God, and you will see positive results and a change of heart over time.

Love cannot be imposed - it can only be nurtured, polished, and discovered over time.

Change takes time and patience; and the heart needs this the most.

Be a Comedian in Your Home

ان احب الاعمال الى الله ادخال السرور على المؤمنين.

Prophet Muḥammad ﷺ said: *"The most beloved of actions to God is bringing joy to the believers."* [4]

Laughter is the best medicine. It brings people together, and cheers up the hearts. It strengthens the immune system, boosts up one's mood, reduces stress, and alleviates physical pain. There is perhaps nothing which has as immediate an effect on changing one's negative mood into a positive one as laughter does.

The world is not always an easy place to live in. Stress comes from many different places and various avenues in life. Laughter helps to relax your body and heart. It will help increase communication and cooperation at home. It strengthens marriages, and helps spouses become more intimate with each other. It makes couples more willing to spend time together.

[4] *Al-Kāfī*, Vol. 3, P. 383.

Here are a few tips on how to be humorous at home:

1. Make healthy jokes which are funny to the other person, not just yourself. Jokes should never lead to anger.
2. Learn to laugh at yourself. When you do something embarrassing, learn to see the funny side of it and show it.
3. Instead of complaining about a certain situation, try to find the funny element in it and learn to laugh.
4. Always keep the joking appropriate and permissible. Never make fun of your spouse, or bring up a past flaw in the form of a joke. That is counterproductive. Make jokes about innocent matters, but never at the expense of someone else's dignity, otherwise this will remove the blessings of God upon us.
5. Always joke at the right time and a suitable place. There are certain tense situations where even a nice joke can backfire.

Perhaps this may be difficult at first, but you will get better at it over time. Comedians do not become comedians overnight - they develop their talents over time, and eventually become pros at it!

Give Advice with Love, and Avoid Criticism

اذْهَبَا إِلَىٰ فِرْعَوْنَ إِنَّهُ طَغَىٰ فَقُولَا لَهُ قَوْلًا لَّيِّنًا لَّعَلَّهُ يَتَذَكَّرُ أَوْ يَخْشَىٰ

God says in the Qur'ān addressing Prophet Mūsā (Moses) ﷺ and Prophet Hārūn (Aaron) ﷺ: *"Go, both of you, to Pharaoh, for he has indeed rebelled. Then speak to him in a gentle manner, perhaps he will take admonition or fear (God)."*[5]

If you are going to give some advice to your spouse, then make sure you first begin your talk by expressing how much you love them. Generally, your words will have more of an effect on your spouse

[5] Noble Qur'ān, Sūrah Ṭahā (20), Verses 43-44.

when they feel that they are coming from sincere affection.

We often try to give advice to our spouses, but in reality, what we see as "advice" is sometimes criticism and judgment. In order to avoid this, we should keep two things in mind:

1. As we mentioned in another chapter, precede and follow up your advice with words of praise. This is called the "sandwich" method where you start with a compliment, give your advice, and then finish it up with another compliment.
2. Do not talk about your spouse's character or personality. Give advice on specific behaviors only. For example, you can advise your spouse about the importance of taking out the trash, but do not scold them for being "absent-minded." Furthermore, do not make generalizations. You can point out that they forgot to do something, but do not say that they "always" forget, or that they are forgetful by nature.

When advice is given in a soft and loving manner, then your spouse will be more receptive to that advice, and make more of an effort to try and change.

Have Good Akhlāq for God, Not for Worldly Fear

قُلْ إِنَّمَآ أَعِظُكُم بِوَٰحِدَةٍ ۖ أَن تَقُومُوا۟ لِلَّهِ مَثْنَىٰ وَفُرَٰدَىٰ ثُمَّ تَتَفَكَّرُوا۟

"Say: 'I give you only a single advice - that you rise up for God's sake, in pairs or individually - and then reflect.'" [6]

When you show good manners and patience to someone because you fear them, it can lead to serious problems. The anger, resentment, and all other internal problems get bottled up, and the person who publicly shows good manners or patience may snap once they are in a position of power. For example, some people may show great patience and manners in front of a boss, but they will totally lose

[6] Noble Qur'ān, Sūrah Saba (34), Verse 46.

their cool with their children and spouses. Since they are no longer in a position of fear, all of those bottled-up negative emotions will have free rein to come out and wreak havoc.

One may ask then: What is the solution? When dealing with a boss, or someone else who is in a position of power (or in a position to hurt you), change your intention (*niyyah*). Instead of being good, patient, and showing good manners for the sake of fearing that person in authority, do these things for the sake of God because He wants you to keep equanimity and respect in the face of stress.

When you do this, you will find that your negative feelings will get bottled up less, and you will be more likely to show the same attitude with people who you fear less, such as your spouse and children, and remain more calm with them as well.

This is what true spiritual character (*akhlāq*) is all about in Islam. Good manners and patience done for the sake of something or someone other than God is not proper moral etiquette *(akhlāq)*, rather it is servitude to illusion and this ephemeral world (*dunyā*), and it will break down sooner or later.

When your good morals and behavior are more regular than irregular, then your spouse will generally pick up on this, and your spiritual aura will also change toward the right direction. Of course, it is normal to sometimes slip back into non-optimal character, but the important part is to keep on trying and getting better at it over time.

A Person Cannot Connect with One's Spouse in Fear

من خاف الله عز وجل خاف منه كل شئ، ومن لم يخف الله
أخافه الله من كل شيء

Prophet Muḥammad ﷺ said: *"Whoever fears God, the Exalted and Mighty, all things will fear them; and whoever does not fear God, God will make them fear everything else."*[7]

When a person is in a state of self-preservation, it is often hard to connect with others. Fear has multiple sources, and many of them are completely understandable. The specific kind of fear and self-preservation that we are speaking about here is one of the most common forms of anxiety - fear of shame or fear of abandonment. A person cannot have a meaningful relationship if all one thinks about is their own worth, or if they catastrophize about the future that will follow thereafter.

In these kinds of fears and worries, people often become defensive and insist on being right at all times. They do not grow, and they lose the precious tools that keep people connected with others, those being humility and love. This is how fear ruins relationships.

Why does this happen? Many of our attempts at self-preservation come from a sense of shame that we carry.[8] Shame can sometimes be good, but it can become toxic when we do not root our self-worth in God's unconditional love, and hence give birth to toxic shame. When our self-worth and dignity is grounded in something other than God, then that sense of self-worth and love can never truly be unconditional.

When our sense of worth does not come from God's unconditional love, mistakes can often lead to shame because our sense of 'goodness' is grounded in our own image and other people's image of being 'good.' So, we often refuse to accept mistakes and do not grow as a result of this. We suffer because we cannot experience life to its fullest, nor can we be humble enough to truly love ourselves and others because our false pride keeps us isolated and alone.

Think about it, can an arrogant person who thinks that they are superior to others truly connect with people? Pride is an illusion,

---

[7] Al-Shuʿayrī, Muḥammad ibn Muḥammad, *Jāmiʿ al-Akhbār* (Najaf: Maṭbaʿat Ḥaydarīyah, n.d), P. 98.

[8] Note that we are not referring to moments of actual danger in which self-preservation is rational. We are referring to the everyday worries and anxieties that many people suffer from in this modern day and age.

and its source is in toxic shame. Finding our self-worth in God necessitates that we also see the same worth in others as well, thus laying the grounds for humility and connection.

Change Yourself to See Changes in the Future

Find the Truth in What Your Spouse is Saying

وَأَطِيْعُوا اللّٰهَ وَرَسُوْلَهُ وَلَا تَنَازَعُوْا فَتَفْشَلُوْا وَتَذْهَبَ رِيْحُكُمْ وَاصْبِرُوْا ۚ إِنَّ اللّٰهَ مَعَ الصَّابِرِيْنَ

"And obey God and His Messenger, and do not dispute, or you will lose heart, and your strength will be gone. And be patient; indeed Allah is with the patient ones." [9]

When there is tension between you and your spouse, your children, or even a friend, then it is sometimes better to try to find truth in what the other person is saying, rather than trying to just defend yourself. Sometimes when we hold resentment against someone else, we get defensive and reject everything they say even if it is the truth and to our own benefit. We may even do the exact opposite of what they are telling us because of this resentment. This is a sign that you need to take a step back and analyze the deeper problem of what is going on.

Defensiveness is when we attack a person in order to distract them from our own faults and insecurities. Thus, even when what is being said is true, we do this because we do not want to feel hurt and humiliated. But this tactic will only make things worse in the long run, and we too will not accomplish our goal in life of self transformation and pleasing God.

Defensiveness comes in many forms. Sometimes it is through attacking directly, at other times it is stonewalling or ignoring one's spouse. Other times it could be bringing up the past, or trying to

---
[9] Noble Qur'ān, Sūrah al-Anfāl (8), Verse 46.

convince your spouse that they are crazy.

So how can we take steps to address our own defensiveness? Here are a few tips:

1. Defensiveness is a phenomenon that makes you look outside of yourself. It makes you look at others rather than yourself. The first step is to develop an awareness that you are being defensive, and redirect your attention to yourself. You cannot address a problem without noticing it first.
2. Part of the process of self-awareness is to validate your emotions and needs that are prompting you to be defensive. This does not mean **justifying** them, it means acknowledging your inner triggers, such as your fears and insecurities which are leading you to behave this way.
3. Develop compassion for yourself. Acknowledge that defensiveness is a normal human reaction, but that you do not need to act upon it. Develop the awareness that the short-term pleasure of defensiveness will simply hurt you and your marriage more in the long run.
4. After your spouse says something that triggers your defensiveness, do not respond immediately. Try anticipating that at some point in your conversation or reaction you may say something defensive. **Be mindfully present with the defensiveness.** Organize your thoughts, and make sure to filter out defensive remarks as best as you can. Remember this rule: The quicker and more spontaneously you respond to your spouse after a criticism, the more easily trapped you will be in defensiveness. Always pause, think, and evaluate your emotions before you respond to them.

By following some of the above points, we will be able to reanalyze our reactions and try to take in what is being told to us to better ourselves, rather than become defensive and not acknowledge the problem at hand.

Healthy Self-Esteem and Defensiveness in Marriage

Defensiveness is often the result of a habit that has developed over time. It is usually a reaction to our fears, anxieties, and insecurities. Once you have developed an awareness of your defensiveness and have learned to manage your reactions, it is important to address the root of the problem of defensiveness, namely your fears and insecurities.

The clearest way to do this is to address the problem of self-esteem. The higher your self-esteem is, the less likely it is that you will become defensive.

Remember that in Islam, self-esteem is different from pride. You can have self-esteem and be humble at the same time. In one tradition from the eighth Imām, Imām ar-Riḍā ﷺ, he explains what humility really means:

ما حد التواضع الذي إذا فعله العبد كان متواضعا؟ فقال: التواضع درجات منها أن يعرف المرء قدر نفسه فينزلها منزلتها بقلب سليم، لا يحب أن يأتي إلى أحد إلا مثل ما يؤتى إليه، إن رأى سيئة درأها بالحسنة، كاظم الغيظ عاف عن الناس، والله يحب المحسنين.

A narrator asked: "What is the definition of humility for a servant of God through which one may be considered humble?" Imām ar-Riḍā ﷺ responded: *"There are several levels of humility. Among them is to know the value of one's self, and to place it where it deserves with a peaceful heart; and one should not like to behave toward others in a way different from what one loves others to behave toward them. If a person finds an evil behavior (in oneself), then they should change it to a virtuous one. Those who suppress their anger are safe from people; [then the Imām quoted the Qur'ān as follows]: 'And*

God loves the virtuous ones.' [10] " [11]

Pride, on the other hand, is believing that you are better than others, or that you are higher than what you really are. It is not wanting for others what you want for yourself. It is also being hostile toward the truth. In one tradition, Imām aṣ-Ṣādiq ﷺ says the following about pride (*kibr*):

وما سفه الحق قال يجهل الحق ويطعن على أهله.

"It is a person disregarding and ignoring the truth,
and attacking the people of truth." [12]

Healthy self-esteem is valuing yourself and your talents as God has designed for you. It is acknowledging that everything we have is from God, and being content with His decree. It is accepting the truth and honoring other people.

In order to develop self-esteem and reduce defensiveness, it is therefore important that we become aware of our value and talents, and develop them in the service of God, but never at the expense of seeing ourselves above the rest of His creations.

For example, you can pick areas in your life that you do not feel too great about in which you think you can improve yourself, and do much better. Take action and create healthy habits to strengthen those areas in your life (e.g., exercise and physical appearance, intellectual depth, etc).

In the end, remember that the ultimate source of security is with God. The word for "faith" in Arabic is *īmān* and its root meaning is "security." Defensiveness is ultimately a symptom of weakness in faith. Put in an adequate amount of care and effort to develop your faith by avoiding sins, doing good charitable practices such as reciting prayers, and helping others. As your faith strengthens, your

---

[10] Noble Qur'ān, Sūrah Āl 'Imrān (3), Verse 134.

[11] *Al-Kāfī*, Vol. 3, P. 321.

[12] Ibid., P. 758.

need for defensiveness will weaken.

As genuine faith increases, your defensiveness will decrease, and your spouse will most likely lower their defensiveness and be more receptive to change then as well.

Experiential Gifts vs. Physical Gifts

تهادوا تحابوا، تهادوا فإنها تذهب بالضغائن.

Prophet Muḥammad ﷺ said: *"Give each other gifts and affection will grow. Give each other gifts for they will remove resentments."* [13]

Physical gifts are very good to give to your spouse. They have a way of reducing resentment and creating affection. Giving physical gifts regularly is a great way to help your marriage and your spouse's demeanor toward you.

However, the problem with physical gifts is that they are often forgotten over time. If you want to give your spouse a memorable gift, then as an example, try giving an experiential gift such as going to a place you have never been to. It does not have to be big and expensive - it can be a trip to another town or national park that is not too far away.

Dr. Thomas Gilovich, a psychology professor at Cornell University who has been studying the relationship between money and happiness for over 20 years, argues that upon initial receipt, material and experiential purchases produce the same amount of satisfaction. However, over time, the satisfaction with material things goes down, but the satisfaction with experiences go up.[14]

Although this may seem bizarre, it makes total sense. Physical gifts are objects and will remain outside of ourselves, whereas

[13] *Al-Kāfī,* Vol. 9, P. 746.

[14] Cassano, Jay, *The Sciences of Why You Spend Your Money on Experiences, Not Things,* Fast Company, March 30th 2015, https://www.fastcompany.com/3043858/the-science-of-why-you-should-spend-your-money-on-experiences-not-thing.

experiences become part of our identity and thus become part of us. We are, as Gilovich says: "The sum total of our experiences."[15] As such, the growth of who we are, and how we relate to ourselves is immensely more important and satisfying in life than the objects that we acquire.

Experience-based gifts also help enhance relationships. You are more likely to connect with someone whom you took a vacation with than someone who bought you an expensive computer. Spending time with people directly to develop relationships undoubtedly causes more satisfaction in life and helps us bond with them more than physical gifts. Physical gifts, although important, are just temporary icebreakers.

You will find that as affection grows and resentment recedes during these experiences, your spouse and marriage will change for the better. It is a slow but almost inevitable process if done right.

Solving Marriage Problems is Not Always the Solution

فَاعْفُوا۟ وَاصْفَحُوا۟ حَتَّىٰ يَأْتِىَ ٱللَّهُ بِأَمْرِهِۦٓ ۗ إِنَّ ٱللَّهَ عَلَىٰ كُلِّ شَىْءٍ قَدِيرٌ

"So excuse [them] and overlook (their actions) until God issues His command. Indeed, God is All-Powerful over everything."[16]

Whenever you try to solve a problem in your marriage, another one is bound to come up. Instead of focusing too much on just solving problems, focus on creating more positive experiences with your spouse. You will be surprised how over time, the problems will occur less and less.

Part of human conditions is that problems are universal, and there is nothing we can do to avoid them. If we spend our lives just trying to fix problems, then we will find ourselves depleted,

[15] *The Sciences of Why You Spend Your Money on Experiences, Not Things.*

[16] Noble Qur'ān, Sūrah al-Baqarah (2), Verse 109.

discouraged, and demoralized.

Problems are a normal part of life and they can be beneficial for us sometimes, especially in our marriages. We do not always have to try to solve them. Our energy is limited and a precious resource in this world. Sometimes we can just set them aside, and channel our energies in being creative in our relationships, such as coming up with new and fun experiences which will help us make better memories and establish new energy together.

You will find that when you are creative in your relationship, many of your problems, and ultimately even your marriage troubles will automatically be resolved. This is because most of our problems are a result of our emotional perceptions of phenomena as problems.

Therefore, remember this: Sometimes creating meaningful change in your marriage means to stop trying to solve problems (as this often ends up in more quarreling), and constant firefighting is not a long-term solution for your marriage, in fact it will only make things worse.

Let Go and Let God Deal with It

من صبر على سوء خلق امرأته أعطاه الله من الأجر ما أعطى أيوب (عليه السلام) على بلائه. ومن صبرت على سوء خلق زوجها أعطاها الله مثل ثواب آسية بنت مزاحم

Prophet Muḥammad ﷺ said: *"A man who is patient with the bad behavior of his wife, God will grant him the rewards that He gave Prophet Ayyūb when he was afflicted with tragedy (he will get this reward each time he shows patience when his wife pains him). And a wife who is patient with the bad behavior of her husband, God will grant her the rewards of Āsiyah bint Muzāḥim (wife of the Pharaoh during the time of Prophet Mūsā who was patient with the tribulations that her husband put her through)."* [17]

There are plenty of people who try everything possible to 'fix' their spouses and their relationships. They attempt different techniques and act in the most perfect way they can think of - even in the tensest moments of their relationships. But sometimes, no matter what a person does, their spouse will not relent. They may improve their behavior in the best possible way, but their spouse stays the same or even gets worse, and when this happens they tend to snap and react negatively.

Know that sometimes we just need to let go. We have a hard enough time controlling ourselves, let alone others, or that which is outside of us! We should also know that we can influence events and people in our lives, but we cannot control their ultimate outcomes. Results and outcomes are only in the hands of God. Sometimes our obsessing over the ultimate outcomes of things that we cannot control can be us unconsciously trying to take over God's role as the ultimate Lord and manager of this world.

Obsessing over results can also be counterproductive in other ways. When we try to control people, we become tense. When we become tense, we become angry. When we become angry, we become depleted; and when we become depleted, we become depressed. It is not a nice cycle to be in, and we fall into the danger of undoing all of the progress that we may have made, as well as losing our spouse's trust along the way.

Learn to work through the **process,** and make God's pleasure your **primary** aim. Be attached to the **process**, not the **results**. Leave the ultimate results to God, and you will find that you will reap better results than what you could have imagined - all the while keeping your emotional health intact.

Oftentimes, things do not work out to our benefit no matter

---

[17] Āsiyah is known as Bithiah in the Jewish tradition. For the tradition itself, see Aṭ-Ṭabrisī, Ḥasan ibn Faḍl, *Makārim al-Akhlāq* (Qum: ash-Sharīf ar-Rāḍī, 1412/[1991-1992]), P. 473.

how hard we try because we do not allow space for God to act in our lives. God is respectful of our spaces, and will come into our lives when we allow Him to. True faith is to realize and accept that God knows what results are in our best interests. If we let Him make the ultimate decisions, then they will come in our favor. We will also work through the process much better since tensions and anxieties will also ease, allowing us more room to work with a clear mind. Success with people will come through peace, not tension and control.

A word of caution: Letting go does not mean that one does not try. Do the best you can and try to get the finest results, but do not be attached only to the results. Remember that the **ultimate and final** results are with God. Also note that sometimes you may get results and outcomes that you do not like, but they may be in your favor later on in the future, although that may not be apparent to you right now, but sometimes years or even decades afterward you will realize the reality of this.

High Price of Emotional Decisions

Never Use Your Spouse's Past Flaws Against Them

إذا اسىء اليكم فاعفوا واصفحوا كما تحبون أن يعفى عنكم.

Imām ʿAlī said: *"If someone hurts and saddens you, then pardon and forgive them just as you would like people to forgive you."* [18]

There are very few things in marriages which are as destructive for relationships as using a spouse's past sins or mistakes against them. Many couples are often on the verge of divorce because they cannot let go of past shortcomings. For example, a wife will be upset that

---

[18] *Tuḥaf al-ʿUqūl*, P. 151.

she caught her husband watching pornography many years ago. Even though he has not looked at it for over 15 years, she still brings it up during conflicts or in the form of jokes.

Similarly, there are situations where a wife had a relationship with another man in her younger years before she was married to her current husband. Even after a decade, the husband still brings up the topic and blames his wife for her past sins. Alternatively, he may have caught her at some point in time speaking to someone whom she had a relationship with sometime in the past, yet he accuses her of being emotionally unfaithful to him now, even though that aspect of it stopped a long time ago.

There are numerous different sins that a husband or wife may have committed in the past, some which were way before they even got married to each other. However, one thing is common in that constantly bringing up past sins will almost always end in resentment against the accuser; and this can sometimes even end up in divorce.

So here is an important question: If your spouse is growing in resentment against you because you keep bringing up past sins which they cannot go back in time to change, how likely do you think they will be willing to change for the better? How much do you think your spouse will be willing to commit to making your marriage more successful? Perhaps they will feel guilty at first, and have lots of good will to try and change; but if the past is constantly brought up even though they have repented and stopped their evil doings, then it will lead to nothing but hatred, discouragement, and hopelessness.

Despite **all** of our continuous flaws and sins, God **still** forgives us. Therefore, it is our task as Muslims to also learn to forgive. Forgiving does not mean forgetting, but it means letting the past stay in the past without bringing up anything related to it - either directly, or indirectly such as in the form of a joke or taunting the other person. A joke may seem innocent to you, but it will remind the individual about their previous actions, and this can lead to resentment. Therefore avoid anything that can bring up past sins in a negative way.

You need to let go and trust your spouse again, and stop judging them for their past actions. Once they begin to feel comfortable and secure with you again, then that is when and where real change will begin to take place.

Deep Down Inside, Your Spouse Knows Their Flaws

حسن الظن من أفضل السجايا وأجزل العطايا.

Imām ʿAlī ﷺ said: *"Optimism (and having a good opinion about others) is one of the best qualities that a human being can have, and one of the most fruitful of God's blessings [which can be bestowed upon a person]."* [19]

If your spouse has deep flaws, then it is most likely that they are aware of them, even if they justify them or pretend that they do not exist.

If your spouse is ungrateful, angry, messy, overweight, unhealthy, forgetful, lazy, or struggling and suffering because of any other character flaw or habit, then it is most likely that deep down inside, they are well aware of these shortcomings.

Your job as a spouse is not to scold them or even remind them about something that they most likely already know deep within. This will most likely lead them to bitterness and resentment against you, and ruin your marriage, as well as their chances of reforming themselves.

Your job is to encourage their positive traits, and love them despite their flaws. It means that you acknowledge yourself as being responsible for what God has allotted to you in this world.

---

[19] *Ghurar al-Ḥikam*, P. 345.

This kind of an approach with your spouse does not mean that you approve of their misdeeds, but rather it is a way of giving your spouse the power to reform themselves for the better which primarily comes from positive encouragement and non-judgmental and non-critical affection.

Of course there are certain cases where direct and explicit intervention is necessary, but in most cases, they are counterproductive.

You will always get more out of someone through positive encouragement, rather than negative criticism. The 'seemingly positive effects' of criticisms are short-term, and they will create long-term problems; whereas positive encouragement will give people the hope and motivation they need to change for the better.

Do Not Compete on Who had the Worst Day

خياركم الينكم مناكبة و اكرمكم لنسائهم.

Sayyidah Fāṭimah az-Zahrā' ﷺ said: *"The best of you are those who are kind and gentle to people, and honor their wives even more."*[20]

ما اصطحب اثنان إلا كان أعظمهما أجرا و أحبهما إلى الله عزوجل أرفقهما بصاحبه.

Prophet Muḥammad ﷺ said: *"Surely, when two people are companions to one another [such as in marriage] one of those two receives more Divine rewards and is more beloved to God, [namely] the one who is friendlier and kinder to one's companion, and is more lenient and tolerant [of the other one's flaws]."*[21]

---

[20] Al-Iṣfahānī, ʿAbdullāh al-Baḥrānī, *ʿAwālim al-ʿUlūm wa al-Maʿārif wa al-ʾAḥwāl min al-Āyāt wa al-Akhbār wa al-ʾAqwāl*, Ed. by Muḥammad Bāqir Muwaḥid Abṭaḥī (Qum: Mu'assasat al-Imām al-Mahdī, 1413/1993), P. 909.

[21] *Al-Kāfī*, Vol. 3, P. 312.

If your spouse had a stressful day, do not argue with them about how your day was worse than theirs. If you do so, then you are indirectly telling them that their feelings do not matter as much as yours. Rather, be humble and listen compassionately, and give them all of the support that they need at that moment.

Chances are that by doing so, you will help your spouse feel better, and in turn your bad day will probably turn around as well. That will be much better than both of you making your day even worse than it already is by trying to compete or argue who had the more stressful day.

Just remember that whatever you do, do it for the pleasure of God, and avoid keeping scores. Instead of competing on who had the worst day, try to compete on who can be the most compassionate listener.

Avoid Suspecting Your Spouse

لا يغلبن عليك سوء الظن فإنه لا يدع بينك وبين خليلك صلحا.

Imām ʿAlī said: *"Do not keep doubting others for doubt will not leave any space for reconciliation between you and your friend."* [22]

Living in such an interconnected and technology-based world has created countless opportunities for secret communications and various types of relationships. This reality, unfortunately, has made suspicion and mutual distrust more prevalent among married couples.

One of the most destructive elements affecting marriages today is suspicion; however most of these suspicions are usually false, yet no less damaging. The roots of false suspicions often lie in fear and insecurity of the accuser.

The net result is that it erodes marriages, alienates one of the

---

[22] *Tuḥaf al-ʿUqūl*, P. 79.

partners, and makes it more likely that one of the spouses will end the marriage and marry someone else! Equally as bad, the accusing partner often ends up demeaning oneself, and eroding their own dignity by doubting, suspecting, spying, and questioning the other spouse. Not to mention that spying on someone is a sin from the Qur᾿ānic perspective:

يَا أَيُّهَا الَّذِينَ آمَنُوا ... وَلَا تَجَسَّسُوا ...

"O you who believe...and do not spy on one another."[23]

The more negatively you think about your spouse, the more they will become distant from you, and the less likely it is that they will change for the better. Change the way that you think about your spouse, and chances are that they will change as well. People change when they are trusted, not when they are judged and condemned, especially when they are innocent of what they are being accused of.

[23] Noble Qur᾿ān, Sūrah al-Ḥujurāt (49), Verse 12.

Conclusion

Where the Problem Truly Comes From

A fundamental reality of the condition of human beings is that they suffer and face challenges. In response to challenges, many people look for miracles and quick fixes to get away from the discomfort of their problems in life. However, chasing after quick fixes often ends up making us pay a higher price, and we end up using up more energy to fix those initial problems.

Marriage and relationship challenges are visceral and require time, effort, and patience to deal with effectively. Deep rooted reform and transformation takes a lot of time - not weeks or months, but often **years**.

Perhaps the greatest challenge for martial reform is despair at how long and difficult of a process it can sometimes be. But there is no need for despair. The greatest rewards and blessings in life often take years of struggle to acquire, and in the process, we come out transformed as better human beings.

Our task is not to see the thousands of steps which are ahead of us, but to see the step that is immediately in front. It is good to plan for the future, but never at the expense of what is needed and necessary at the present time. We must take one step at a time. We cannot take our thousandth step without even having taken the first one.

One of the most important steps is to change the paradigm of our challenges from negative to positive, then from positivity to hope, from hope to action, and finally from action to passion, and believing that we have the qualities and potential necessary for changing ourselves. Then, if God wills, we will eventually be able to change those around us as a consequence of our own transformation.

One of the quintessential reasons why marriages become dysfunctional is because of the inability of spouses to see their own personal faults. Instead of fundamentally introspecting ourselves, we look to control, change, and blame others. Combined with the tendency to find quick fixes, their marital and family situation does not get much better. In fact, sometimes it just becomes worse.

But the reality is this: there are no immediate or fast miracle fixes. Problems do not come from nowhere, and it is very rare for one spouse to be completely at fault. Many of our problems come from our own actions, mishandling of our spouse's failures and mistakes, and not seeing that there are better ways to go about our relationships.

Running away from our problems will not only make the problems bigger, but it will lead to greater confusion and further loss of grounding and purpose in life. Eventually, the problem will catch up with us, and corner us in such a way where we will have to pay an even bigger price than we would have if we initially addressed it in a healthy and wise manner.

Facing the consequences of not taking responsibility for a problem does not always have to manifest itself in a divorce. Sometimes it can manifest itself as a bodily sickness because of denial or depression, and at other times it can manifest itself in a dysfunctional child in the form of low self-esteem, low self-efficacy, anxiety, academic problems, low emotional intelligence, and sometimes even addiction or involvement in violent crimes. It is a known fact for example, that the majority of people in prison convicted of violent crimes come from dysfunctional families.

The Paradigm Shift

من كثر إحسانه أحبه إخوانه.

Imām ʿAlī said: *"Whoever does much goodness and kindness, their brethren will love them."*[1]

Part of the paradigm change mentioned above is understanding that ultimately, we do not have control over the world. At most, we only have control over certain aspects of ourselves. Learning this key aspect of life will free us from many of our frustrations. Understanding that we do not have ultimate control is freedom from tension and stress, and it will give us the opportunity to be creative and positive in our lives.

This means that we will **never** have control over our spouse. It does not mean though, that we are helpless and cannot change them. What we can and must do is **influence** them by cultivating compassion and emotional intelligence in our marriage. Much of what we have discussed in our book are tips on better cultivating awareness of our emotions, and that of our family members.

We need to be compassionate not only to ourselves, but also have compassion and empathy for our spouse and families. No matter how moody your spouse or other family members are, try to speak gentle words. Always be with a smile. Maintain a pleasant face. This kindness comes from understanding who your spouse or children truly are, and how vulnerable they may be. This understanding comes from emotional intelligence, and this awareness is what keeps our compassion going. Eventually you will reap the rewards of your kindness.

The essence of transformation is patience, perseverance, compassion, and kindness to all beings. This change for the better can sometimes take a very long time, but in all honesty, genuinely every good thing takes time to materialize. Be understanding and empathetic, and you will not regret it.

---
[1] *ʿUyūn al-Ḥikam wa al-Mawāʿiẓ*, P. 618.

Glossary

Adab (pl. is Ādāb): Manner (manners). Normally used when talking about the morals and manners which are taught by Muslims, however may differ by culture.

Adabiyāt: Literature.

Aḥkām: Islamic rulings which are derived by Muslim Jurists that cover the entire life-cycle of a Muslim–things which they are obligated to perform, and things which they are prohibited from engaging in.

Ahlul Bayt: The 'People of the Household' - refers to specific members of the family of Prophet Muḥammad ﷺ, and is confined to the 14 Immaculate ones *(Maʿṣūmīn).* The first is Prophet Muḥammad ﷺ himself; then his daughter Sayyidah Fāṭimah az-Zahrāʾ; her husband, ʿAlī ibn Abī Ṭālib; their two sons, Ḥasan ibn ʿAlī and Ḥusayn ibn ʿAlī; and the nine Imāms from the progeny of Ḥusayn ibn ʿAlī which include: ʿAlī ibn Ḥusayn as-Sajjād, Muḥammad ibn ʿAlī al-Bāqir, Jaʿfar ibn Muḥammad aṣ-Ṣādiq, Mūsā ibn Jaʿfar al-Kāẓim, ʿAlī ibn Mūsā ar-Riḍā, Muḥammad ibn ʿAlī al-Jawād, ʿAlī ibn Muḥammad al-Hādī, Ḥasan ibn ʿAlī al-ʿAskarī, and Muḥammad ibn al-Ḥasan al-Mahdī.

Ākhirah: Hereafter or the next life.

Akhlāq: Etiquettes.

Al-Fātiḥah: The first sūrah of the Qurʾān, which is 'The Opening Chapter.' It must be recited in every daily prayer *(ṣalāh);* and is commonly recited and sent as a gift of prayer for the deceased.

Alḥamdulillāh: Arabic phrase which means: 'All praise belongs to Allah.'

Allah: The Arabic term for God, a culmination of all His Names and Titles.

Awliyā': Close, intimate friends of Allah ﷻ who have reached a high spiritual status through their own efforts.

Barakāt: Blessings that stem from Allah ﷻ based on the actions of an individual.

Bismillāhir Raḥmānir Raḥīm: (I begin) In the Name of Allah, the All-Kind (or All-Beneficent), the All-Merciful (or All-Compassionate).

Dīn: There are multiple meanings for this, including religion, way of life, or (Day of) Judgment.

Dunyā: This transient world/Worldly or lowly life.

Du'ā': Supplication or prayer; a deep connection and communion between an individual and Allah ﷻ.

Fitnah: Corruption or disorder; also means a test or tribulation in life.

Fiṭrah: Innate-nature which Allah ﷻ has placed in every human being.

Ḥadīth: A tradition or narration from Prophet Muḥammad ﷺ, Sayyidah Fāṭimah az-Zahrā' ؑ, or the 12 Imāms ؑ that include their sayings, actions, or advice.

Ḥajj: A pilgrimage to Mecca that is performed in the 12th Islamic month, Dhul Ḥijjah, which is obligatory upon every Muslim–man or woman–once in a person's lifetime when certain conditions are met.

Ḥalāl: A term used by Muslim Jurists when discussing things that are allowed or permissible for a Muslim to do, eat, etc.

Haybah: Prestige or status.

Ḥikmah: Wisdom.

Imām: A Divinely-appointed leader chosen by Allah ﷻ; can also refer to a community religious spiritual guide, or the leader of the prayers.

Īmān: Deep-faith, conviction in Allah ﷻ, and all things which a person is required to believe in to be considered a true believer.

Inshā'Allāh: Arabic phrase which means: 'God-willing,' or 'if God wishes.'

Itminān al-Qalb: Tranquility in the heart.

Jihād: Struggle; there are two types of jihād–the major one which is known as Jihād al-Akbar means to struggle against one's passions and desires, and to control the wants of the soul; the minor jihād which is known as Jihād al-Aṣghar means the struggle on the battlefield or war front against those who physically attack others in times of war.

Kāfir: Has multiple meanings in the Qur'ān, but its general meaning is 'to cover.' It has been used in the Qur'ān to mean 'a farmer' - as they cover the seed with dirt; and it can also refer to a non-believer in God as they cover the innate-nature of belief that has been given to every human being by Allah ﷻ.

Khaṭā': An arching term which means 'to miss the mark;' can also mean 'a mistake.'

Khushū: Humility of the heart.

Kibr: Means pride, which is a major sin.

Kufw: Multi-level compatibility, this is a term normally used to describe the compatibility between a man and women in terms of marriage.

Liqā' Allah: The goal of our creation, namely, reaching God in a metaphorical/metaphysical sense.

Marḥūmīn: Literally means: 'One who has been shown mercy by Allah,' and is in reference to someone who has passed away.

Masjid: Mosque, the place of worship for Muslims.

Mawaddah: A deep-seeded reciprocal relationship and love for an individual; the Qur'ān obligates Muslims to have this level of love for the specific family of Prophet Muḥammad ﷺ.

Maʿrifah: Deep cognizance or understanding; wisdom; or the proper implementation of awareness.

Maʿṣūm (pl. Maʿṣūmīn): Literally means: 'One who is immaculate, and inerrant (free from all sins, flaws, and impurities) through the Divine protection of Allah ﷻ on one level; but on another level they do not commit sins due to knowing the outcome of them.

Nafs: Soul.

Niyyah: Intention–the reason why a person performs any action in terms of acts of worship directed toward Allah ﷻ; the intention becomes the most important thing as it determines the rewards that a person will receive from the Almighty One.

Qurb: Seeking proximity to Allah ﷻ through acts of worship and good deeds.

Qur'ān: The last of the Divinely-revealed Books that was revealed to Prophet Muḥammad ﷺ by Allah as a guidance for all of humanity; also referred to as the Noble Book of the Muslims.

Raḥmah: Compassion or mercy.

Riḍā': Being content with whatever Allah ﷻ decrees for us, rather than complaining or being quick to make judgments against Him.

Ṣabr: Patience, fortitude, and determination in life; realizing that life is full of challenges, and one must be actively patient and work hard to overcome adversities.

Sajdah: Prostration, where a person puts at least seven parts on the ground–the forehead, the two palms of one's hands, the two knees, and two toes–as a show of humility and humbleness to Allah ﷻ alone.

Ṣalāh: Literally means 'prayer' and in the Islamic terminology, this word refers to the specific method of prayer which has been legislated by Allah ﷻ for Muslims to recite on a daily basis.

Salāmun ʿalaykum: Arabic phrase which means 'Peace be upon you.' This is the customary, Qur'ānic greeting which Muslims use to salute one another.

Ṣalātul Jamāʿah: Congregational Prayers, these are prayers which are recited in a group format in which there is one person–the imām–leading the congregants in prayer.

Shukr: Gratefulness–normally shown to Allah ﷻ for all that He does and provides for us; also used in regards to people when they help us in one way or another, or give us something.

Ṣirāṭ al-Mustaqīm: Literally translated as 'the Straight Path;' refers to the path or way as outlined by Allah ﷻ in the Qur'ān where Muslims actively seek guidance from Allah ﷻ to be directed toward and continuously be kept on.

Subḥanallāh: Arabic phrase which means 'All glory and praise belongs to Allah (God).'

Sunnah: The Prophetic way–the life and customs of Prophet Muḥammad ﷺ which Muslims are encouraged to follow in their daily lives.

Takbīr: Arabic phrase of 'Allāhu Akbar' which means that God (Allah) is Greater than anything which He is compared to.

Tarbiyah: Upbringing–most often it refers to rearing and nurturing children, or the community as a whole.

Tawfīq: Literally means 'the ability or opportunity to achieve success,' and is regarded as being a Divinely-granted gift from Allah ﷻ to individuals that gives them the ability to thrive toward success.

Ziyārah: Visiting the house of Allah ﷻ in Mecca, Arabia; or the graves of Prophet Muḥammad ﷺ in Medina, or the Imāms ؑ; or visiting the burial places of other important personalities.

ʿIlm: Knowledge.

ʿUlamāʾ: Scholars, usually refers to the learned ones among the Muslims.